CW01189589

RARE MALTS

RARE MALTS
FACTS, FIGURES AND TASTE

ULF BUXRUD

Quiller Press

Copyright © 2006 Ulf Buxrud
Copyright of all pictures of Rare Malts bottles belongs to Ulf Buxrud

The Rare Malts Selection series logo is a trade mark of Diageo and is used by permission

First published in the UK in 2006
by Quiller Press, an imprint of Quiller Publishing Ltd

British Library Cataloguing-in-Publication Data
A catalogue record for this book is available from the British Library

ISBN 1 84689 007 1
ISBN 978 1 84689 007 9

The right of Ulf Buxrud to be identified as the author of this work has been asserted in accordance with the Copyright, Design and Patent Act 1988

The information in this book is true and complete to the best of our knowledge. All recommendations are made without any guarantee on the part of the Publisher, who also disclaims any liability incurred in connection with the use of this data or specific details.

All rights reserved. No part of this book may be reproduced or transmitted in any form or by any means, electronic or mechanical including photocopying, recording or by any information storage and retrieval system, without permission from the Publisher in writing.

Printed in Hong Kong

Quiller Press
An imprint of Quiller Publishing Ltd
Wykey House, Wykey, Shrewsbury, SY4 1JA
Tel: 01939 261616 Fax: 01939 261606
E-mail: info@quillerbooks.com
Website: www.countrybooksdirect.com

CREDITS AND PERMISSIONS

All bottle pictures are photographed by Carl Hansson and the author and are published with their permission.

Picture of Aultmore distillery belongs to John Dewar & Sons Ltd, UK and is published with their permission.

Pictures of the distilleries Benromach, Blair Athol, Caol Ila, Clynelish, Craigellachie, Glendullan, Inchgower, Mortlach, Royal Brackla, Royal Lochnagar, St Magdalene, Teaninich belong to Jean-Marie Putz, Whisky Info, The Hague, Holland and are published with his permission. All other illustrations are from the Diageo Archive and are used with their permission.

The RMS map and the Rare Malts Selection Series trade marks belongs to Diageo plc., UK and are published with their permission.

Photo of Charles MacLean en face was taken by Dmitry Plisov and is published with Charles MacLean's permission.

Charles MacLean's Colour bar illustration belongs to the *Whisky Magazine*, UK and is published with their permission. The Flavour Wheel is based on original illustrations in Charles MacLean's *Malt Whisky* (Mitchell Beazley) and also *Whisky Magazine*, UK. David Wishart's profile table is from *Whisky Classified* (Pavilion Books). The 'Pentland Wheel', is an illustration belonging to The Scotch Whisky Research Institute and is published with their permission. The Spider-web diagram is an illustration belonging to Macallan, UK and is published with their permission. The Profile chart is an illustration belonging to Anova Books Company Ltd, UK and is published with their permission. The illustration is from the work *Whisky Classified: Choosing Single Malts by Flavour*, ISBN 1 8620 57168.

The Bar chart is an illustration belonging to Mainstream Publishing, UK and is published with their permission. The illustration is from the work *The Scotch Whisky Directory*, ISBN 1 8401 87506.

Thanks to Dr Nicholas Morgan and Christine Jones at Diageo plc, for assistance.

The author and publisher will be grateful for any information and suggestions that will assist them in keeping future editions up-to-date. Although all reasonable care has been taken in preparation of this book, neither the publisher, editors nor the author can accept any liability for any consequences arising from the use thereof, or the information contained therein. The author's email address is ulf@buxrud.se and may be used for reporting found errors and inconsistencies but also for information and suggestions.

This book, the first ever to portray Diageo's Rare Malts Selection series, is dedicated with love to Birgitta, Petra and Jill.

RARE MALTS
SELECTION

Each individual vintage has been specially selected from Scotland's finest single malt stocks of rare or now silent distilleries. The limited bottlings of these scarce and unique whiskies are at natural cask strength for the enjoyment of the true connoisseur.

NATURAL CASK STRENGTH

PRODUCT OF SCOTLAND RARE MALTS SELECTION
33 ELLERSLY ROAD EDINBURGH SCOTLAND EH12 6JW

Contents

Foreword (by Charles McLean) viii
Introduction 1

Notes about Rare Malts Selection Series 2
The creators and custodians 2
How the Rare Malts are selected 2
Release policy 3
Versions released 3
Bottling practice 3
Numbering systems 7
Age and age calculation 7
Alcohol by volume 7
Bottle sizes 7
Packaging 7
Bottle labels and label variations 7
North American or USA label versions 8
South African (RSA) or B297 code versions 8
Production code 8
Back label 8
Medals and awards 8
International wine and spirit competition awards 8
Misprints and inconsistencies 10
Further information 10

Comments to the Tasting Notes 11
Methods and recordings 11
Tasting conditions 12
Explanation of elements and terms used 14
    Peaty/Phenolic/Smokey
    Sherried/Winey
    Fruity/Estery
    Floral/Aldehydic
    Cereal/Malty
    Feinty

    Medicinal/Maritime
    Woody
    Vanilla/Honey
    Nutty/Creamy
    Spicy
    Sulphury

Nomenclature and Definitions 17
Barley 17
    Saladin box malting
    Drum malting
    Mills and milling
    Yeast and fermentation
    Lauter mash tun and traditional mash tun
    Two-and-a-half distillation
    Shell and tube condensers and traditional worm condensers
    Copper and stills
Casks and the importance of oak 22
Charles Doig and pagoda-roofed kilns 24
Licence laws of 1644, 1784, 1823 24
Pattison crash of 1899 25
The rise of Diageo 25

The Distilleries 27
Distillery map 27
Auchroisk 28
Aultmore 32
Banff 35
Benrinnes 39
Benromach 42
Bladnoch 46
Blair Athol 50
Brora 54

Caol Ila 58
Cardow (formerly Cardhu) 62
Clynelish 66
Coleburn 70
Convalmore 73
Craigellachie 76
Dailuaine 80
Dallas Dhu 84
Dufftown-Glenlivet 88
Glen Albyn 91
Glen Esk (formerly Hillside) 95
Glen Mhor 99
Glen Ord 102
Glendullan 106
Glenlochy 110
Glenury Royal 114
Inchgower 118
Linkwood 122
Mannochmore 126
Millburn 129
Mortlach 133
North Port 137
Port Ellen 141
Rosebank 145
Royal Brackla 149
Royal Lochnagar 153
St. Magdalene 157
Teaninich 160

Special items and releases 164
Bibliography 166
Index 167

FOREWORD

ULF BUXRUD once had an outstanding collection of old Macallan malts – whiskies from the 1940s, rare commemorative bottlings, eighteen-year olds from every year since 1960: fifty three expressions in all. On 20 April 2002, to celebrate his sixtieth birthday, we drank the lot.

Before the tantalising image springs to mind of two large middle-aged men, sitting, perhaps in a sauna at Ulf's home in Malmö, Sweden, drinking for days and days, may I say that this event took place in the Landmark Hotel, London, in the company of forty invited guests – whisky savants from the UK, (Michael Jackson, Marcin Miller, Sukhinder Singh, Jack Milroy, Doug McIvor and Helen Arthur), and from overseas (John Hansell, Norman Shelley, Giuseppe Begnoni and Mamoru Tsuchiya); the men who had made the whisky, Willie Phillips and David Robertson; friends of Ulf's from Sweden and around the globe; and his delightful and long-suffering wife, Birgitta.

For Ulf Buxrud is a generous man and a great lover of whisky, as well as being a connoisseur of global standing, with an encyclopaedic knowledge of the subject. Like other leading collectors of my acquaintance, nothing gives him greater pleasure than sharing a rare and ancient whisky with friends – so long as they appreciate it!

Over the past few years (after he finished off a large portion of his collection of Macallans!) he has sought out the Diageo (formerly United Distillers and Vintners) 'Rare Malts Selection series' – a collection of outstanding examples of the makes of thirty-six distilleries owned, selected and bottled by the largest whisky distiller in the world. The series began in 1995, the casks being selected by Maureen Robinson, Diageo's Master Blender, to offer not only superlative whiskies, but whiskies which reflected the character of each distillery – many of them closed and gone for ever.

Charles MacLean

This book is not only an historical account of a legendary collection of malt whiskies – as such it would be of interest to the collector only – it contains fascinating general information about malt whiskies, about how to evaluate them and about the histories of the individual distilleries. I have written nine books about Scotch, but still learned a lot from Ulf's text!

Diageo's Rare Malts Selection has deservedly won favour among connoisseurs and collectors of fine whisky. In 2005 the range was discontinued, although the company will continue to issue rare malt bottlings under a different label.

Does this mean, Ulf, that you will hold a similar celebration for your seventieth birthday? I hope I am invited!

CHARLES MACLEAN
Edinburgh, February 2006

INTRODUCTION

This book is an endeavour to document (boring for some, fascinating for others) the facts of a formative segment of whisky history. It is also an attempt to mirror the pleasure and joy surrounding the rise of a cottage trade that became an industry. This book neither reflects common technical details, such as the general way of converting barleycorn to bottled nectar, nor is it a textbook for whisky-related chemistry. However, if there is an oddity or a rarely explained link to the facts, figures and other basics of whisky production mentioned among the distillery portraits it is dissected in the chapter 'Nomenclature and Definitions'.

The Rare Malts Selection (RMS) series is liquid history bottled for the whisky enthusiast looking for a time document as well as a pleasant encounter with traditions and artisanship.

The foundation for the series is the remaining minimal stock of antique whisky – whisky that stems from now-demolished or mothballed distilleries, and also from old, venerable casks tucked away on the premises of ongoing operations. A decision made in 1993 lead to a launch of the longest consecutive series of single malt whiskies ever issued. Sadly, the series' sustainability was lost in 2005 due to the speedy depletion of this non-renewable resource.

United Distillers and Vintners Ltd (UDV), the driving force behind the RMS, launched the series in 1995. Initially it was intended for the global tax-free market. A few years later, when Diageo was formed by mergers and acquisitions, the availability of the RMS series was broadened widely, from up-market retail shops to specialist shops nearly everywhere.

The series is an historic illustration performed by a wide selection of very old malt whisky from distilleries that in the past constituted UDV's realm and leadership in the world of malt whiskies. Several distilleries are long gone and lost forever; some are mothballed and others alive and well, still holding an archive of liquid records of past days.

The constituents of the series were selected from a special window of time: the trade's revolutionary period from 1969 to 1981. To reflect the characteristics of this period a diversity of whiskies spanning from eighteen to thirty years old were carefully chosen. Altogether, 121 versions were released – a vast amount of expressions from this glorious era.

The intention of this book is not to serve as an epitaph for a halted series, but rather to document its first half. It is my staunch belief that the curator of a legacy, cleverly manifested in the Rare Malts Selection series, has just taken time out. Hence, I assume Diageo will return to its role as a rightfully proud heir to a heritage, after a well-deserved intermission.

Ulf Buxrud

Ulf Buxrud

Notes about the
RARE MALTS SELECTION SERIES

THE CREATORS AND CUSTODIANS

Mike Collings – the man who invented the classic malts Johnnie Walker's Blue and Green Label, among other brands – was the mastermind behind the Rare Malts Selection (RMS) series. The concept of the series sprung to his mind long before its official launch in 1995 for the duty free markets and later for the domestic markets. His inspiration was the enthusiasm so long recognised for the individual character of very old single malts, bottled from the cask at the original cask strength. Such sought-after bottlings were and still are being made by independent merchants or by respected connoisseur clubs, acquiring odd casks from the trade. Many are very good, but there are also traps for the unwary. Hence, Mike was certain that customers would prefer their malt whiskies, stemming from this realm, to be bottled from the casks under perfect, controlled conditions but would also like to know that these malts had been specially *selected* from the widest remaining stocks of rare old malt whiskies to survive in Scotland. Combined with a binding parameter that not only should the casks be chosen for their rarity, but also because they had reached a consistent and unsurpassed standard of excellence, he had a winning concept. Mike retired from Diageo in 2005. He was the Malts Marketing Director in the UD days and then moved on to run UDV Global Duty Free and then Diageo Global Duty Free, where he ended his career as Marketing Director. Already in 1988, during his UD/UDV days, he devised a malt whisky development strategy for the group that was designed to create premium and super premium brands. Part of this involved the creation of a consumer platform that allowed people to understand easily and enjoy the diversity and depth of flavour that malt whisky offers.

Diageo's Master Blender Maureen Robinson selected the casks being used. Advertising artist Gerry Barney and copywriter Ian Crammond became responsible for formulating the RMS series with stunning graphic design and exquisite linguistic presentation, a work that they began in early 1993.

Mike passed the care of the RMS over to Jonathan Driver and Dr Nicholas Morgan a couple of years after launching the range, when he moved on to UDV Global Duty Free. Jonathan and Nick were hugely important to the further development of the RMS over time, from the late 1990s to the end of its days.

HOW THE RARE MALTS ARE SELECTED

All bottlings are made without chill filtering or colour additives and at natural cask strength. A statement on the label verifies the exact alcohol by volume (ABV) strength at bottling. Any whisky not bottled at natural cask strength is bottled at a lower strength, achieved by adding water. Since the end of the 1970s, the trade introduced a praxis to mature production at a fixed ABV equal to 63.5%. Several of the series were laid down for maturation before this change at much higher strengths; up to 75% ABV was not uncommon. As a rule of thumb, the whisky will lose 3 to 5% ABV during each ten years it spends in a cask. As older whiskies (pre 1980) matured initially at higher % ABV they can be bottled at much higher strengths than younger versions. Each cask develops its individual characteristics during the maturation; hence, older casks are sought after by independent merchants to be bottled for connoisseurs and enthusiasts. They are usually bottled in very limited quantities as a single cask yields rather few bottles. Many are often very good, others may show weakness inherited from the cask. Further, these casks may have changed hands several times and been moved around, disturbing the maturation cycle. The casks selected for the RMS series have all been matured and

Rare Malts Selection series

looked after according to the producer's firm regime and policy. Whisky matured in oak casks reaches sooner or later a peak beyond which no improvement will be achieved. The time for such a peak to occur may vary from cask to cask, but is usually attained within twenty years.

The resources used for RMS are the last remaining stocks of rare old malts in Scotland. When the selection of casks is made at least twice as many casks are rejected than selected. The casks for the RMS series are chosen not only for unsurpassed excellence and rarity, but also for consistency. Only if at least three casks, from a single year, show identical character or consistency and a perfect quality, are they selected as candidates for marrying and bottling.

Release policy

The RMS series was originally streamlined for the tax-free market and not for the usual over-the-counter market in high streets or elsewhere. Releases were limited to three per annum, one spring and two parallel in autumn. The two autumn releases were based not only on different distilleries but also on bottle sizes to meet special requirements for selected export markets. Four or, on a few occasions, five versions were included per release. This system was kept up for the first four years, from 1995 to 1998, after which the releases were reduced to one per annum in the autumn because of the dwindling stock of suitable older malt whiskies. The new regime was in effect from 1999 until the series' very last release, the autumn release of 2005.

Official releases of the series include eighty-two different full-size bottles and ten 200ml bottles, specially packaged. Due to circumstances of a technical nature as well as different legal requirements, twenty-nine other versions were released but were not classified as unique releases. Altogether 121 versions have been available over the lifespan of the series.

Versions released

The core of the RMS series is from thirty-six distilleries. Many of the distilleries are represented by several versions of different ages, % ABV, or year of distillation. Together they constitute a 'flavour range' as each version is unique from its relatives stemming from the same distillery. Of the 121 available versions at least 104 are identified as belonging to the 'flavour range category'.

Then there is the 'exterior versions range', with different bottle sizes, labels and packaging. (Misprints form another category.) At least seventeen versions belong to this group. The fluid content of each version in this category is usually not unique but a duplicate of versions belonging to the 'flavour range'. The 'exterior versions range' comprises eight bottles with 'USA' labels, one with 'RSA' labels, seven 200ml and one 750ml.

These are all highlighted in the table on pages 4–6, which also identifies time and season of releases, and are listed at the end of each distillery portrait as well.

Finally, there was an unofficial re-packaging scheme by an unrelated source where the dark blue paper box was replaced with a wooden box. Nine versions in this category are identified. All nine versions in this category are indentified. All nine versions were selected from the core group of the eighty-two official versions (see the section on 'Packaging').

Bottling practice

The conventional method of normalising (vatting) several casks into one batch is practised. Such a batch may consist of casks from different production occasions during a defined calendar year. As a year of distillation, or vintage, is specified for the RMS series it is not permitted to spice the batch with older casks. That habit is accepted in order to improve non-vintage single malts; however, the age statement still has to show the age of the youngest whisky in the batch. A standard batch consists of twenty to twenty-five casks and usually yields about 5,000 to 6,000 700ml bottles, or earlier 750ml bottles. Over time, the volume and the % ABV changes per cask, hence, the batch reflects the average % ABV and the flavour profile becomes normalised. The upper limit per batch may vary from time to time depending on the number and type of casks that went into the normalising. The highest number of bottles yielded from a batch is about 12,000. During 1995–97, some versions were divided into smaller batches, but issued at the same time as the same seasonal version. A typical example is the

Rare Malts

Listing is per release season

Distillery	Region	Age	Distilled	% ABV	Released/note
Brora	Northern Highlands	20	1974	57.5	1995/1 70cl.
Dallas Dhu	Speyside	24	1970	58.0	1995/1 70cl.
Millburn	Highlands	18	1975	58.5	1995/1 70cl.
St. Magdalene	Lowlands	23	1971	59.0	1995/1 70cl.
Brora	Northern Highlands	22	1972	54.9	1995/2 70cl.
Glendullan	Speyside	22	1972	62.6	1995/2 70cl.
Glenury Royal	Highlands	23	1971	61.3	1995/2 70cl.
Linkwood	Speyside	22	1972	59.3	1995/2 70cl.
Clynelish	Northern Highlands	22	1972	58.95	1995/2 75cl.
Glenlochy	Highlands	25	1969	62.2	1995/2 75cl.
Glen Esk/Hillside	Highlands	25	1969	61.9	1995/2 75cl.
Mortlach	Speyside	22	1972	65.3	1995/2 75cl.
North Port	Highlands	23	1971	54.7	1995/2 75cl.
Clynelish	Northern Highlands	23	1972	57.1	1996/1 75cl.
Glenlochy	Highlands	26	1969	59.0	1996/1 75cl.
Glen Esk/Hillside	Highlands	25	1970	61.1	1996/1 75cl.
Mortlach	Speyside	23	1972	59.4	1996/1 75cl.
Linkwood	Speyside	23	1972	58.4	1996/1 75cl. RSA
Aultmore	Speyside	21	1974	60.9	1996/2 70cl.
Benrinnes	Speyside	21	1974	60.4	1996/2 70cl.
Glen Esk/Hillside	Highlands	25	1970	60.1	1996/2 70cl.
Craigellachie	Speyside	22	1973	60.2	1996/2 70cl.
Brora	Northern Highlands	20	1975	59.10	1996/2 75cl.
Glendullan	Speyside	23	1972	62.43	1996/2 75cl.
Teaninich	Highlands	23	1972	64.95	1996/2 75cl.
Caol Ila	Islay	20	1975	61.12	1996/2 75cl.
Dailuaine	Speyside	22	1973	60.92	1996/2 75cl.
Royal Lochnagar	Highlands	23	1973	59.7	1997/1 70cl.
Dallas Dhu	Speyside	21	1975	61.9	1997/1 70cl.
Teaninich	Highlands	23	1973	57.1	1997/1 70cl.
Caol Ila	Islay	21	1975	61.3	1997/1 70cl.
Dufftown-Glenlivet	Speyside	21	1975	54.8	1997/2 70cl.
Clynelish	Northern Highlands	24	1972	61.3	1997/2 70cl.
Mannochmore	Speyside	22	1974	60.1	1997/2 70cl.
Glen Esk/Hillside	Highlands	25	1971	62.0	1997/2 70cl.
Linkwood	Speyside	22	1974	61.2	1997/2 75cl.
Glen Ord	Northern Highlands	23	1973	59.8	1997/2 75cl.
Glendullan	Speyside	23	1973	58.6	1997/2 75cl.
Inchgower	Speyside	22	1974	55.7	1997/2 75cl.
Royal Lochnagar	Highlands	24	1972	55.7	1997/2 75cl.

Rare Malts Selection series

Distillery	Region	Age	Distilled	% ABV	Released/note
Benromach	Speyside	19	1978	63.8	1998/1 70cl.
Glendullan	Speyside	23	1974	63.1	1998/1 70cl.
Mortlach	Speyside	20	1978	62.2	1998/1 70cl.
Royal Brackla	Highlands	20	1978	59.8	1998/1 70cl.
Clynelish	Northern Highlands	23	1974	59.1	1998/1 70cl
Port Ellen	Islay	20	1978	60.9	1998/2 70cl.
Brora	Northern Highlands	21	1977	56.9	1998/2 70cl.
Glen Ord	Northern Highlands	23	1974	60.8	1998/2 70cl.
St. Magdalene	Lowlands	19	1979	63.8	1998/2 70cl.
North Port	Highlands	19	1979	61.0	1998/2 75cl.
Cardhu	Speyside	25	1973	60.5	1998/2 75cl.
Glenury Royal	Highlands	28	1970	58.4	1998/2 75cl.
Rosebank	Lowlands	19	1979	60.2	1998/2 75cl.
Caol Ila	Islay	20	1977	61.3	1998/2 75cl.
Caol Ila	Islay	21	1977	63.1	1999 70cl.
Glenury Royal	Highlands	29	1970	57.0	1999 70cl.
Rosebank	Lowlands	20	1979	60.3	1999 70cl.
North Port	Highlands	19	1979	61.2	1999 70cl.
Port Ellen	Islay	22	1978	60.5	2000 70cl.
Teaninich	Highlands	27	1972	64.2	2000 70cl.
Cardhu	Speyside	27	1973	60.02	2000 70cl.
Coleburn	Highlands	21	1979	59.40	2000 70cl.
Brora	Highlands	24	1977	56.1	2001 70cl.
Bladnoch	Lowlands	23	1977	53.6	2001 70cl.
Millburn	Highlands	25	1975	61.9	2001 70cl.
Glen Mhor	Highlands	22	1979	61.0	2001 70cl.
Rosebank	Lowlands	20	1981	62.3	2002 70cl.
Caol Ila	Islay	23	1978	61.7	2002 70cl.
Glen Albyn	Highlands	26	1975	54.8	2002 70cl.
Linkwood	Speyside	26	1975	56.1	2002 70cl.
Brora	Highlands	20	1982	58.1	2003 70cl.
Convalmore	Speyside	24	1978	59.4	2003 70cl.
Auchroisk	Speyside	28	1974	56.8	2003 70cl.
Blair Athol	Highlands	27	1975	54.7	2003 70cl.
Royal Lochnagar	Highlands	30	1974	56.2	2004 70cl.
Rosebank	Lowlands	22	1981	61.1	2004 70cl
Inchgower	Speyside	27	1976	55.6	2004 70cl
Banff	Highlands	21	1982	57.1	2004 70cl
Glen Mhor	Northern Highlands	28	1976	51.9	2005 70cl
Linkwood	Speyside	30	1974	54.9	2005 70cl
Glendullan	Speyside	26	1978	56.6	2005 70cl
Millburn	Northern Highlands	35	1969	51.2	2005 70cl

· Rare Malts ·

The following table shows the twenty-nine other versions. Listing is per release season.

Distillery	Region	Age	Distilled	% ABV	Released/note
Brora	Northern Highland	22	1972	58.7	1995/1 70cl.
Brora	Northern Highland	22	1972	59.1	1995/1 70cl.
Brora	Northern Highland	22	1972	60.02	1995/1 70cl.
Brora	Northern Highland	22	1972	61.1	1995/1 70cl.
Brora	Northern Highland	20	1975	54.9	1995/1 70cl.
Dallas Dhu	Speyside	24	1970	60.54	1995/1 70cl.
Dallas Dhu	Speyside	24	1970	60.6	1995/1 70cl.
Dallas Dhu	Speyside	24	1970	59.91	1995/1 70cl.
Millburn	Highland	18	1975	58.9	1995/1 70cl.
St. Magdalene	Lowland	23	1970	58.1	1995/1 70cl.
St. Magdalene	Lowland	23	1970	58.43	1995/1 70cl.
Glenury Royal	Highland	23	1971	61.3	1995/2 75cl. SIZE
Clynelish	Northern Highland	23	1972	57	1995/2 75cl. RSA
Glenlochy	Highland	26	1969	58.8	1995/2 75cl. RSA
Mortlach	Speyside	23	1972	59.4	1995/2 75cl. RSA
Brora	Northern Highland	20	1975	59.1	1995/2 75cl. USA
Caol Ila	Islay	20	1975	61.12	1995/2 75cl. USA
Clynelish	Northern Highland	22	1972	58.64	1995/2 75cl. USA
Glenlochy	Highland	25	1969	62.8	1995/2 75cl. USA
Glen Esk/Hillside	Highland	25	1969	61.9	1995/2 75cl. USA
Mortlach	Speyside	22	1972	65.3	1995/2 75cl. USA
North Port	Highland	23	1971	54.7	1995/2 75cl. USA
Teaninich	Highland	23	1972	64.95	1996/1 75cl. USA
Caol Ila	Islay	20	1975	61.18	1996/2 75cl.
Glen Ord	Northern Highland	23	1972	62.43	1996/2 75cl.
Dailuaine	Speyside	22	1973	60.92	1996/2 75cl. USA
Glendullan	Speyside	23	1972	62.43	1996/2 75cl. USA
Linkwood	Speyside	23	1974	61.2	1997/1 75cl.
Caol Ila	Islay	21	1977	61.3	1999/1 70cl.

For details concerning the special releases of the ten 200ml bottles see section entitled 'Special items and releases' page 164.

Brora 1972/22 years old. This version was released in five different % ABV (one official and four others).

Numbering systems

Each bottle carries a sequence number, with the exception of earlier versions, released from 1995 to 1997, which may lack such sequence numbers. Assigned sequence numbers usually end at 5,000–6,000 bottles. However, in some cases they stretch up to 12,000. When this occurs, the main tranche of the release carries traditional labels and the remaining portion usually carries labels reflecting local regulations such as a B297-number for bottles earmarked for the South African market.

Age and age calculation

The age statements shown for the RMS series express the age in numbers of full calendar years. However, the content of the bottle may in some cases be a fraction of a calendar year older. This is forthcoming when the result of the computation 'Year of bottling' minus 'Year of distillation' show a value larger than the given age statement. Earlier bottlings lack information concerning bottling year and month.

Alcohol by volume

The % ABV noted on the front label is the average cask strength of a normalised (vatted) batch. The % ABV is usually printed as the standard European % ABV, but sometimes with the US proof notation added between brackets. Both label versions may occur for the same release.

Bottle sizes

Not all bottle sizes are unique; meaning a given release with a given % ABV may be divided and bottled in different bottle sizes. Several bottle sizes have been used. The 200ml is used for the popular, mixed five-pack sample (5 x 200ml). One such pack was issued in 1995 and another in 1996. The 700ml, which is the most frequently used size, is usually present on all non-North American markets. Finally, the 750ml is the size used in the Americas. Several 750ml versions have, at various occasions, been re-exported to various European markets. One version, the Glenury Royal 1971/23 years old is bottled in a 700ml as well as in a 750ml version.

Packaging

The standard bottle is usually delivered in a dark blue paper box. However, some versions come 'naked', i.e. no traditional dark blue paper box at all. This is true for special editions earmarked for markets such as North America and South Africa. There are also the two mixed five-packs (5 x 200ml), each of which come in a handy, easy-to-carry cardboard box.

From the 2002 release, the % ABV is printed within a yellow field on the dark blue box. Previously, this information was given on a sticker or not given at all on the box. Older paper boxes and bottles are marked 'Produce of Scotland' and newer ones are marked 'Produced and bottled in Scotland'.

Some versions are 're-packed' wooden boxes. These are not special versions; the dark blue paper box has simply been replaced with a wooden one. The source for the wooden boxes is the large Dutch retail chain Gall & Gall. This firm bought regularly issued RMS versions from Diageo and then re-packaged the bottles in exclusive wooden boxes. Hence, these bottles are 'package' versions and not content versions. They were made between 1998 and 1999 and earmarked for the Dutch market. It seems that this was a one-time action that probably will not be repeated. At least nine versions have been re-packaged by Gall & Gall and the original boxes have been lost.

Bottle labels and label variations

Since 1997, a note has been added to the bottle's main label. It displays the month and year of when the actual bottling occurred. This information does not necessarily coincide with the official release month and year. For example, all versions of the 2004 release, which was officially in October 2004 in the UK, are marked April 2004.

A major difference is found on bottles from the very first release in 1995. These early versions lack sequence numbers. Further, the main label's red bottom line says 'Limited bottling' on these versions. All others carry the text 'Limited edition'. Another inconsistency is the way that the volume figures are printed on the paper boxes compared to the bottles' main labels. Box volume information is printed either as '0.75L/75cl/750ml' or '75cl/750ml' or '70cl/700ml'. Bottle labels are usually printed as '70cl' or '75cl', with a few exceptions: the Mortlach 1972/23 years old, North Port 1971/23 years old (USA label) and Teaninich 1972/23 years old (B297 label), among others.

Identical fillings, meaning bottles from the same release, may have one standard and one secondary label version. The secondary label type is used for special regions where label information must follow local requirements.

North American or USA label versions

These labels display the USA Proof value besides the regular % ABV note. There are ten of these versions.

South African (RSA) or B297 code versions

These labels carry an additional symbol consisting of a rectangle with the code B297 inscribed. This is a 'code of origin' demanded by South African authorities. There are four of these versions.

Production code

A production code is printed on the glass on the back of the bottles. It is sometimes covered by the back label but is visible through the glass. This code does not appear on bottlings before 1998.

Back label

A symbol describing 'UK Units' inscribed in a bottle symbol was recently added to the back label. The reason for this is an attempt to raise the awareness of how much alcohol people are actually drinking. Hence, the UK drink industry has standardised the concept of 'units' of alcohol. A UK unit is the legal definition of one standard drink, defined as any amount of liquid containing 10 grams of alcohol. Eight grams is approximately equivalent to 10ml.

To calculate the number of units/standard drinks in a bottle multiply its ABV% by the size of the bottle in litres (typically 0.7). Example: a 0.7 litre bottle of 60% ABV yields 60 x 0.7 or 42 units/standard drinks.

Medals and awards

Quality attracts praise, and the Rare Malts Selection did so from the beginning. Over the years Cardhu, Brora (Trophy for Best Cask Strength Single Malt, 2004), and most memorably Glenury Royal (1996 winner of the overall Trophy for Best Single Malt Whisky over twelve years old and of the Ian Mitchell Memorial Trophy for most outstanding Single Malt Scotch Whisky) won Gold Medals at the International Wine and Spirit Competition.

In no less than three out of five recent years – 1999, 2001 and 2003 – all four Rare Malts won IWSC medals. So high was the standard that every Rare Malt released was expected to deserve at least a commendation, usually a medal. At the Monde Selection in Brussels, Grand Gold Medals were received in 1996 for Brora, Glenury Royal, and Linkwood.

Were these award winners truly the best of the best? With a selection of such exceptional quality, it's very hard to say. Every Rare Malt has been prized by those who drink it.

International wine and spirit competition awards

In 1996, the Glenury Royal 1971/23 years old 61.3% ABV received the Gold medal at the International Wine and Spirit Competition and the Ian Mitchell Memory Trophy as the most outstanding/best single malt over twelve years old. This version is bottled in a 700ml as well as a 750ml version. Both versions are delivered without the regular dark blue paper box and they carry a 'neck hanging' award brochure.

International wine and spirit competition awards

Distillery	Age	Year	% Abv	2004	2003	2002	2001	2000	1999	1998	1997	1996
Glenury Royal	23	1971	61.3									Gold +Trophy
Linkwood	22	1972	59.3									Bronze
Brora	20	1975	59.1								Silver	Silver
Clynelish	24	1972	61.3							Silver		
Glen Esk/Hillside	25	1971	62.0							Bronze		
Brora	21	1977	56.9						Silver			
Caol Ila	20	1977	61.3						Bronze			
Glen Ord	23	1974	60.8						Bronze			
Port Ellen	20	1978	60.9						Silver			
Caol Ila	21	1977	63.1					Silver				
Glenury Royal	29	1970	57.0					Bronze				
Rosebank	20	1979	60.3					Comm.				
Cardhu	27	1973	60.2				Gold					
Coleburn	21	1979	59.4				Bronze					
Port Ellen	22	1978	60.5				Gold					
Teaninich	27	1972	64.2				Silver					
Brora	24	1977	56.1			Gold						
Bladnoch	23	1977	53.6			Silver						
Port Ellen	22	1978	60.5			Bronze						
Rosebank	20	1981	62.3		Silver							
Caol Ila	23	1978	61.7		Silver							
Linkwood	26	1975	56.1		Silver							
Glen Albyn	26	1975	54.8		Bronze							
Brora	20	1982	58.1	Gold + Trophy								

Misprints and inconsistencies

The Royal Lochnagar 1972/24 year old version is a victim of a misprint. The bottle's main label indicates that the year of distillation is (correctly) 1972; however, the dark blue paper box claims 1974.

On Diageo's earlier issues of 'A guide to every Rare Malts bottling' the Glendullan 1974/23 year old 63.1% ABV, bottle size 700ml was wrongly listed as 24 years old. The correct age, as printed on the bottle's main label, is 23 years.

On some labels for the St. Magdalene, the 'T' in the 'St.' on the front label is printed in a normal fashion (t). On others it is printed in a two-character fashion, where a smaller 't' is placed on the top of a dot.

Millburn 1975/18 year old 58.5% ABV; Millburn 1975/18 year old 58.9% ABV; St. Magdalene 1970/23 year old 58.1% ABV; and St. Magdalene 1970/23 year old 58.43% ABV were are all bottled at least twelve months before the RMS series was officially launched in spring 1995.

Further information

Further information regarding the RMS series may be obtained from Diageo via (letters only, no telephone, fax or email enquiries):

The Secretary,
Diageo PLC,
The Rare Malts Selection series,
Edinburgh Park,
5 Lochside Way,
Edinburgh EH12 9DT,
Scotland UK

or at the web site www.buxrud.se/raremalt.htm

Comments to the Tasting Notes

Methods and recordings

Tasting whisky seriously, or rather a sensory evaluation of whisky is a two-step function. First there is the structure analysis phase and then the descriptive phase. Both are important in that they present a picture not only of the whisky *per se*, but also of the taster and his perceptive consistency now and over time. The lack of a structure analysis makes a verbal description flawed, as there is no mechanism to understand the taster's interpretation of absence and presence of elements and their interplay. Failing to provide a systematic structure analysis chart simply prevents the enjoyer from comparing the taster's perception horizon relative to his or her own.

The structure analysis phase deals with dissecting the whisky according to the presence or non-presence of a set of standardised elements. The first step is to assign each element a value according to its degree of intensity. Usually, a scale from 1 to 5 is used where 1 expresses a trace and 5 expresses a dominant presence. Zero stands obviously for not present. Having taken advantage of the use of profile tables for structure analysis in wine-tasting circles, I have found it practical to continue along this route. For a lengthy period I have applied this technique to whisky tasting in a form that may be labelled as a modified 'Wishart Profile Table'. This model is used throughout the book.

The descriptive phase is the real communication phase. It is the art of associating and describing experiences of complex sensations in a subjective way. This is the arena where the whisky tasting world's wordsmiths and jugglers of adjectives and adverbs meet in order to share similar perceptions, or perhaps question and debate our differing ones. It is my staunch belief that without the support of an underlying perception and structure analysis it is nearly impossible, as a beholder, to develop an understanding of the motive and foundation for the associations and conclusions at which a taster arrives. My verbal observations are in table form, adjacent to the structure analysis tables.

Feature	Profile
●●●●	Body
●	Sweetness
●●●●	Smoky
●●●●	Medicinal
	Tobacco
	Honey
●●	Spicy
	Winey
●	Nutty
●●	Malty
●	Fruity
	Floral

0		Not present
1	●	Low hints
2	●●	Medium notes
3	●●●	Definite notes
4	●●●●	Pronounced

David Wishart's profile table (Whisky Classified, *Pavilion Books*)

One model – not used here – mixes the standardised elements with rigid verbal descriptors and presents them in a wheel graph. During the late 1970s a group of sensory scientists (Dr Jim Swan and Dr Jennifer Newton, et al.) at the Scotch Whisky Research Institute in Edinburgh suggested such a descriptive language and a presentation graph for whisky tasting and evaluation. Named 'The Pentland Wheel', it became the accepted tool of classifying

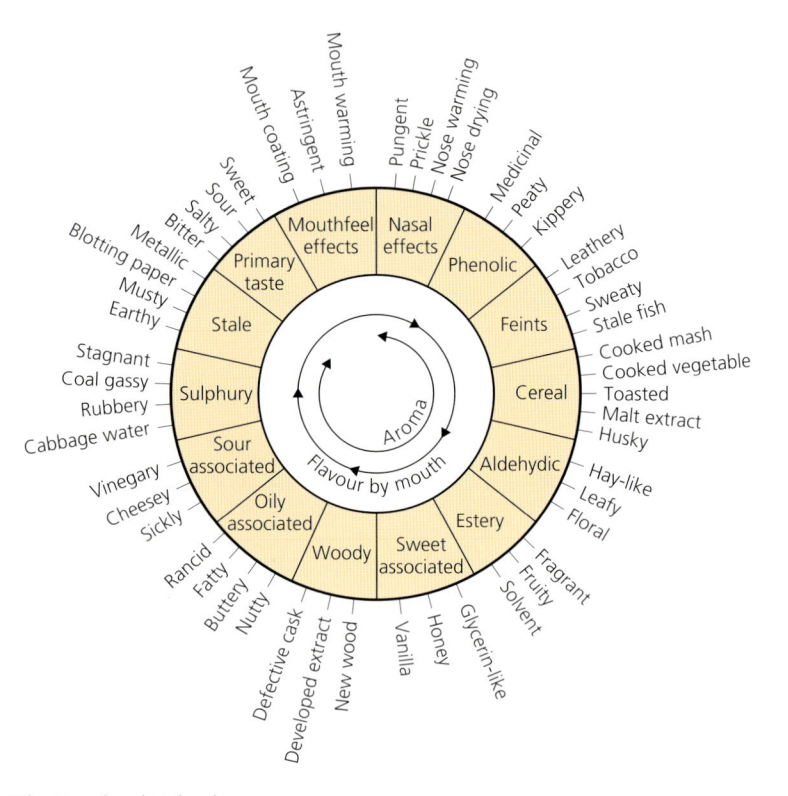

The Pentland Wheel

whisky aromas and flavours. The Pentland Wheel has been modified by Charles MacLean to be more useful for the consumer as well as the pro. His wheel reflects the elements that comprise a whisky in an improved and pedagogic way. With its eight segments and three tiers, the wheel identifies the aromatics that stem from input and process as well as the maturation phase. In popular terms these eight segments are grouped as cereal, fruity, floral, peaty, feinty, sulphury, woody and winey. The tiers are used to move from vague to more precise descriptors within a segment. Also, a colour scheme was developed, classifying the colours of whisky from 0 to 20, where 0 is clear as water and 20 is dark as molasses. The spectrum includes shades of light yellow to dark brown. This colour scheme model is used throughout this book.

Other tools to support and facilitate the documentation of the structure analysis phase have been proposed by several professional tasters and nosers. Commonly, they all rest on the foundation initially suggested by the Scotch Whisky Research Institute and its Pentland Wheel. The predominant ones are the spider-web diagram by David Robertson, the bar chart by Philip Hills and David Wishart's profile table. All are well functioning attempts to describe graphically the structure of flavour profiles in a condensed way. The pros and cons with these graphic methods are that they provide a rather clear picture of the taster's perception, distortion and blind spots, relative to one's own perceptiveness, but also his weakness. One strength of these methods is their ability to expose possible inconsistencies when studying how a taster is forming an opinion of similar subjects, now and over time. On the negative side is the rigid and retarded means of communication – the lack of 'filling in the blanks'.

Saying that, and to demonstrate my view on this topic, I have included a structure analysis as well as a verbal flavour description according to my own, absolutely subjective, organoleptic perception and ability. I have refrained from assessing 'quality' in terms of points or other scales, simply because I abstain from acting as judge of taste in this context.

Tasting conditions

The tasting for this publication occurred in the late spring of 2005. Geographically, southern Sweden became the area of preference for the exercise, simply because my RMS bottles rested there, waiting to be fully enjoyed.

Colour bar

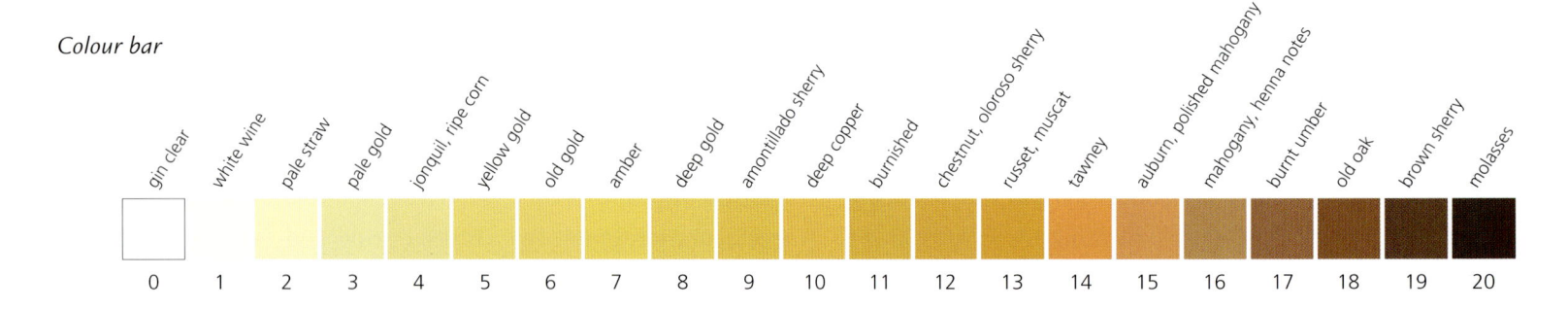

0	1	2	3	4	5	6	7	8	9	10	11	12	13	14	15	16	17	18	19	20
gin clear	white wine	pale straw	pale gold	jonquil, ripe corn	yellow gold	old gold	amber	deep gold	amontillado sherry	deep copper	burnished	chestnut, oloroso sherry	russet, muscat	tawney	auburn, polished mahogany	mahogany, henna notes	burnt umber	old oak	brown sherry	molasses

Comments to the Tasting Notes

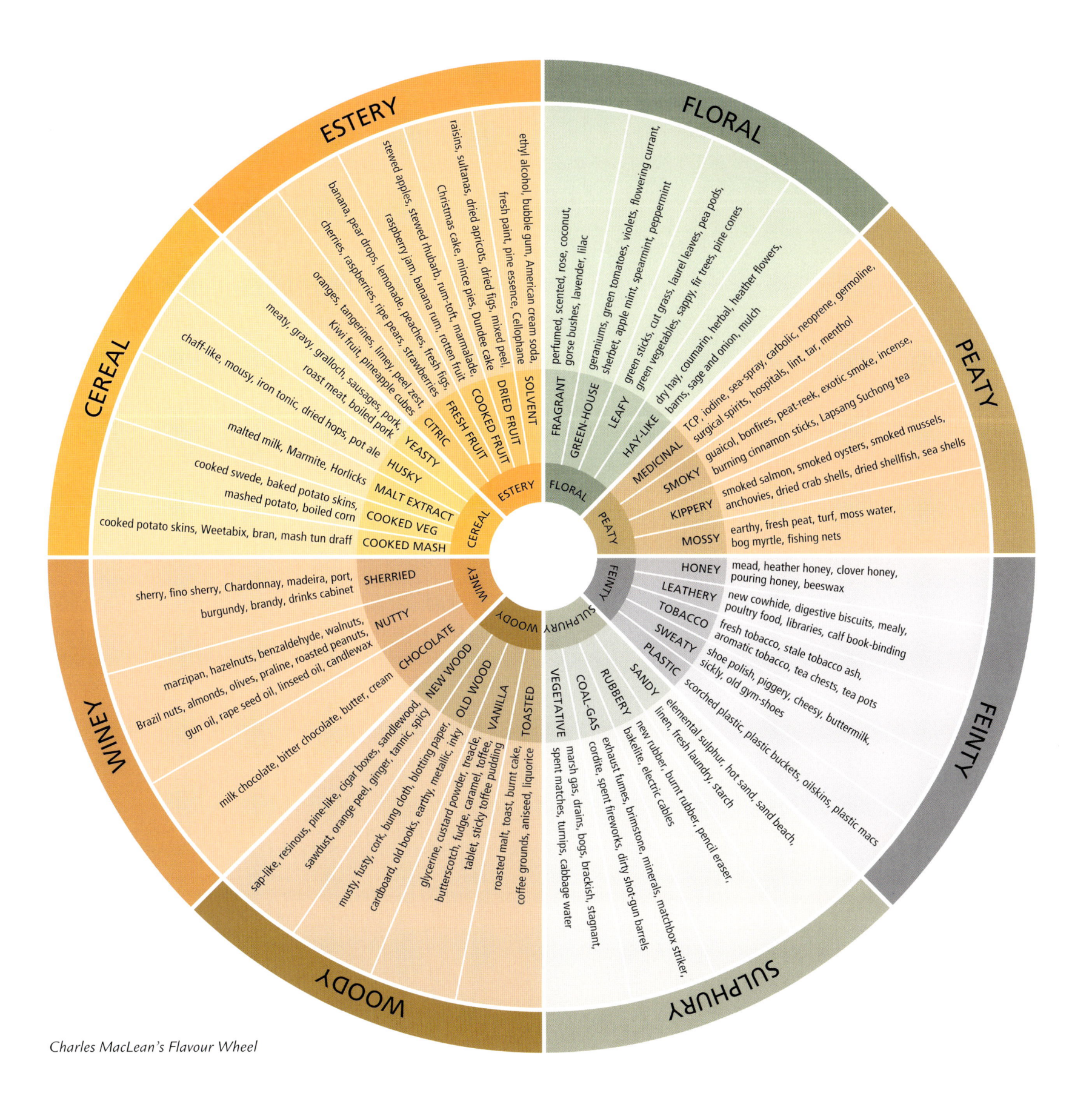

Charles MacLean's Flavour Wheel

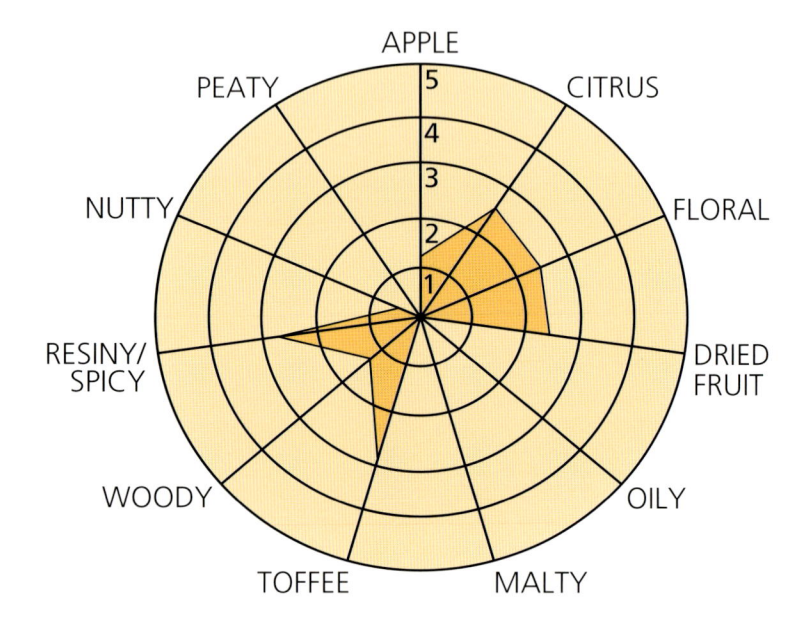

Spider-web diagram by David Robertson

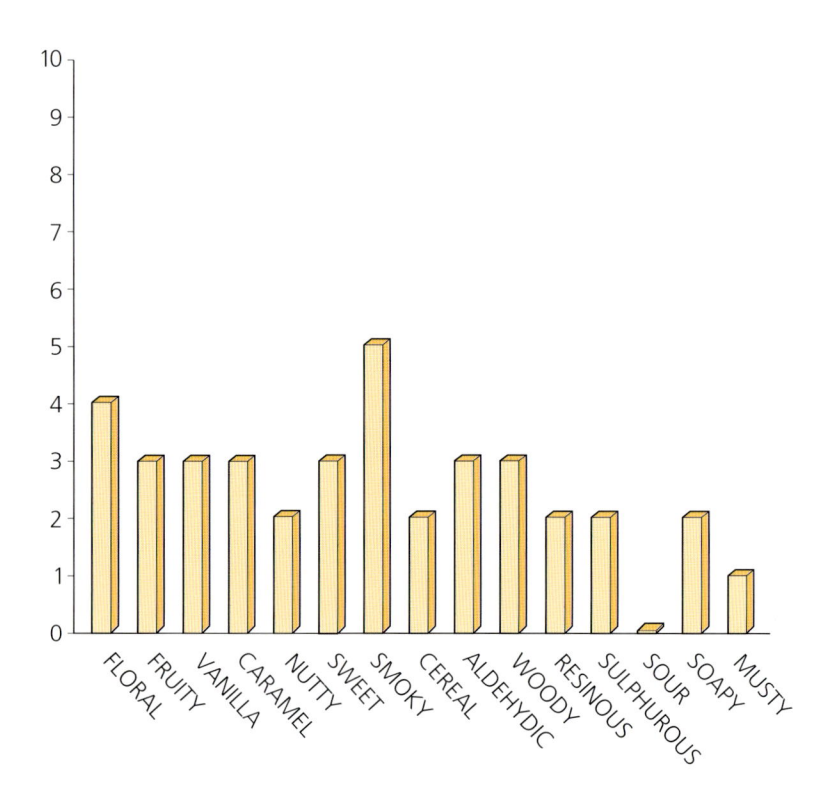

Philip Hills's bar chart

The close encounter with each and every RMS version selected lasted for a period of eighteen consecutive days. The daily workload was limited to two versions and allocated to the early hours. Not an unpleasant way to start a gloomy Scandinavian day or to welcome a sunny one.

The vessels used were classic sherry copitas, the tool of the trade. Two glasses of the two RMS versions to be sampled were provided at each session. The two samples were selected from the stock in random order. Presentation was half-blind, which means that the origin of the samples was known but not the order of serving. The amount poured was four centilitres per glass. The second glass of each of the two samples was diluted with four centilitres' demineralised water. All samples were of cask strength, varying between 53.6% ABV (Bladnoch) and 65.3% ABV (Mortlach). They were served at room temperature, including the water. The watered-down samples ranged from 27 to 32% ABV.

Explanation of elements and terms used

Each chart element except for the colour is assigned a weight ranging from 0 to 5. The weights represent 0 for not present, 1 for a trace, 2 for low, 3 for medium, 4 for pronounced and 5 for dominating notes. For the colour, the range is from 0 to 20, where 0 is clear as water and 20 is dark as molasses. The spectrum includes shades of light yellow to dark brown. The values assessed are not intended to be averaged and serve as a score for the whiskies.

The scope of each descriptive element, except the colour element, is to determine absence or presence including its frequency. These elements are standardised in the following manner.

Peaty/Phenolic/Smokey

These are flavours that originate not only from water that flows through peat bogs, but also from when peat and coke are used in the kilning process. Flavour range is from light to pungent and from mossy, earthy, peaty, phenolic notes to bonfires, burnt heather and arson.

Comments to the Tasting Notes

Sherried/Winey

These are flavours from a cask's previous content. It may have contained fortified wines like sherry, port and Madeira, or table wines of different grape varieties. Madeira often contributes a light oxidized note. Also, casks with a previous content of distilled alcohols like cognac, rum and calvados sometimes come into play.

Fruity/Estery

Estery flavours of *fruity* types are formed by acidic reactions during the fermentation and maturation. Others are formed through catalysis during the distillation. Flavours range from pear drops to fresh citrus and tropical fruits; strawberry and other red berries to peach and melon. Dried fruit, sultanas and raisins, Christmas pudding and fruitcake are frequently used descriptors for this category, as well as nail polish, varnish and acetone.

Floral/Aldehydic

Estery flavours of *floral* types are often formed by acidic reactions during the fermentation and maturation, but they can also be caused by aldehydes, formed when alcohol is exposed to air during distillation in pot stills. Flavours are aromatic and fragrant, ranging from leafy, sappy, newly cut grass, hay, heather and herbal to greenhouse and summer meadows. Mint, violets and honeysuckle are other descriptors.

Cereal/Malty

Characteristics of the malted barley are carried over from fermentation. Usually it disappears during maturation. Flavour range is from simple grain and cereal to distinct barley, but also from mealy, husky, mashy to malt-extract and biscuits. Yeasty notes and cooked veggies are other descriptors.

Feinty

The final spirit from the spirit still at the end of distillation, feints are also known as tails or after-shots. The feints are low in alcohol, and the majority is returned for re-distillation. Feints are formed during the distillation as well as the maturation phase. In a small proportion they are the essential elements in the flavour of a whisky. If present above a moderate level it makes the whisky undesirable. Flavours range from hessian cloth and ageing books to leather and leather goods like car seats and saddles. Tobacco and mustiness like naphtha are other descriptors.

Medicinal/Maritime

The maritime, or 'salty', notes are often said to be the result of maturing whisky in appropriate microclimate conditions. Perhaps this may be a contributing factor, but these notes, medicinal and maritime, are in general developed by the fermentation and distillation process. The salt level found in whisky is not sensorially detectable; however, it is not inappropriate to describe a sensory sensation as 'salty' even in the absence of such substance. Flavour range is from brine, sea foam, seaweed to salt, iodine and also turpentine and carbolic acid.

Woody

Oaky aromas, bitter tannins and astringent mouthfeel are all derived from the oak container. The tannins, which are related to the age and the number of times the container has been used, contribute in a moderate amount to the balance. Longer maturation extracts more tannins, but contrary to wine the tannins are not markers of quality. Excess tannins may show that the whisky acquired age, but overshadows its attributes. Tannic bitterness is different from the bitterness that occurs from excess use of the only permitted additive, the spirit caramel (E150a). Spirit caramel is not sweet.

Vanilla/Honey

Vanilla and honey flavours stem from the oak species used for the maturing vessels. The vanilla-like and other aromas are mainly caused when the oak lignin undergoes oxidation during its contact with alcohol and oxygen. Contrary to popular belief, *Quercus alba*, or American white oak, the wood that bourbon casks are made of, yields a lower concentration of vanillin than their European genus. So, where does the strong scent of vanilla found in bourbons come from? The answer lies in the practice of charring or toasting the cask's inner surface. The honey notes may be released by catalysis of aldehydes during the distillation process but are usually extracted by maturation in oak casks of Quercus alba, especially new ones. The flavour range includes heather-honey, butterscotch, fudge, toffee, caramel and vanilla.

Nutty/Creamy

The nutty flavours are built up in well-matured whiskies and generally relate to whisky of higher quality. These aromas are lactones extracted from the oak vessel during the maturation phase. European species of oak such as *Quercus robur* and *Quercus petraea* are rich in lactones. The lactone also contributes to a buttery, creamy, or slightly oily structure. Flavours range from coconut, walnut, hazelnut, almonds to chocolate.

Spicy

Spicy flavours are extracted from the oak vessel, especially new ones, during the maturation phase. Pine-resin notes are occasionally found as a flavour from new oak. Flavours range from ginger, nutmeg, cloves to cinnamon and pepper, but can also include cedar, sandalwood and pine.

Sulphury

The different copper parts of a pot still participate as a catalytic element during the various distillation steps. For instance, this property removes natural sulphur formed during the fermentation process and contributes to chemical reactions during the distillation phase. Hence, experiments where vital parts have been replaced with stainless steel failed to produce adequate whisky. Undesirable sulphur notes can be caused by new pot stills or careless operating of the still. They can also occur if the casks aren't rinsed carefully enough after they have been sterilised inside by burning sulphur.

Nomenclature and Definitions

The portraits of the thirty-six distilleries that constitute the RMS series share some common technical data that might need an extended explanation. Such joint information is compiled under this heading in order to avoid repetition. Events of historical nature that are common for several distilleries are also summarised here.

Barley

Barley varieties are not a static matter; they come and go. New varieties promising enhanced yields in the fields and higher starch and lower protein contents, leading to increased volume of alcohol in the distillery, are the key factors that draw interest. Ask the distillers if a specific barley variety contributes to a whisky's flavour and aroma, beyond the basic range of cereal and biscuity notes, and if such character plays a primary role when selecting a barley, and the answer to both questions is usually no. What the distiller is looking for is barley with a low level of nitrogen and high starch content. Does the 'terroir' of the barley play a role? No. Currently, Scottish whisky distillers import barley from nearly all barley growing countries around the globe.

During the last four to five decades several new varieties of barley have emerged, ever improving the yield parameters mentioned. A typical lifespan for a new variety, which in general takes up to ten years to develop, is three to ten years. At the time of writing, the Optic variety is the preferred choice among the maltsters and distillers. Long before the much-acclaimed Golden Promise (GP) became available in 1965, Lothian and Borders were the dominant varieties. GP promised no particular soil preference and early harvest, a factor important in an area with unstable autumn weather. Furthermore, GP was of a dual type: good for feeding purposes but also a good balance of nitrogen and starch, perfect for malting. No wonder it became a favourite. From the early seventies until the early eighties, GP accounted for 95% of malted barley grown on Scottish soil. Sadly, GP was found to be susceptible to mildew and many growers replaced GP with the next generation of barley. GP is still around, but plays a minor role in whisky production, less than 2%. The next major variety to arrive was Triumph, with an increased yield in harvest and better resistance to diseases. Triumph became available in the early eighties, but its triumph over GP did not last long. The next one to enter the scene was Chariot (1992), promising an increased yield in pure alcohol. Chariot quickly rose to a top position as the most preferred barley within the malt whisky distilling trade. Since the mid nineties, Chariot has supplied 45% of the market. The Optic, the Chalice and the Decanter varieties, all developed during the nineties, later became the main players in the field. Since 2000 Optic replaced Chariot as one of the leading varieties. Optic and Chalice are now (2005) responsible for 45% each, and the remaining 10% of the market is mainly provided by GP and Decanter.

Optic and its contemporary siblings, including Chariot, yield around three metric tonnes per acre, compared with GP's unpredictable yield of two to two and a half metric tonnes per acre. The yield of pure alcohol has risen from approximately 390 to 415 litres per metric tonne, with Optic, Chalice and Decanter as the top performers.

Troon, introduced by Nickerson in 2005, showed very good nitrogen levels and became the major variety for the Diageo group in 2006, replacing Decanter. Nickerson is the largest plant breeding and seed development company in the European Union and also the breeder of Decanter. The majority of Troon is sourced from growers in north-eastern Scotland.

Saladin box malting

The Saladin Box, a 19th century French invention, is a process able to rationalise the production of malt. Charles Saladin's invention made it possible to substitute the traditional labour-intensive malting floor practice with a mechanised solution. The system consists of a long concrete trough, or box, with a perforated floor (around 50m long and 1.5m deep and wide). The steeped barley to be malted is poured into it and air is blown through the perforations to control the temperature. The modern versions have mechanical turners, like giant Archimedes screws, turning the germinating barley and moving it slowly along the bin. The older ones were fitted with forklike turners that automatically travelled backwards and forwards along the length of the box and stirred its content. The corkscrew effect ensured that the barley at the bottom was moved to the top. A similar technique was used by the German Wanderhaufen malting whose equipment was once used at Inverhouse Distillery. When the malted barley was ready for the drying kiln, it was pumped out through hoses. A problem associated with these boxes was the weakness of the mechanical turners. Hence, the next evolutionary step was the development of a more efficient and durable construction, known as the compartment system or drum maltings. The first Saladin plant in the UK was built in 1891. The largest one in use had a capacity of 100 tonnes. Tamdhu distillery is the last one to use such a system.

Drum malting

Drum malting, also known as the compartment system, is a rather modern integrated and fully automated construction and differs from the older Saladin box system. The steeped barley is deposited on perforated floors in a single bed through which moist cool air is drawn by fans to control temperatures. Large turning machines periodically agitate and redistribute the malt. When germination is completed, the malt is scooped onto conveyors by mechanical shovels. The conveyors deposit the germinated malt in the kiln house on its perforated metal floors. Through this floor, hot air enriched with a desired level of phenols is drawn by fans. These phenols are generated by combusting peat, primarily locally harvested, with or without coke added. The level of phenols is specified in part per million (ppm) per metric tonne. Most of the phenols do not survive the distillation process. If and when a phenolic ppm is specified it is a value for the malted barley, not the final bottled whisky. The kiln floors are sectional so that they can be opened. After drying the malt is dropped directly through into hoppers. These hoppers feed the conveyors, which, in turn, transport the finished malt to storing containers.

Mills and milling

The purpose of milling is to grind the barley to a fitting mix of flour, grist and husks. A traditional distribution is 10% flour, 20% husks and 70% grist. This will create a mash, not too dense and not too watery, which will effectively drain the water through it.

There are several types of mill equipment in use across the trade. The predominant one is the archaic Porteus mill. Another one is the four-roller Boby Mill, manufactured by Robert Boby of Bury St Edmunds. His company was later taken over by Vickers Ltd. Vickers launched a modified version of the mill, named Vickers' Mill in the 1960s. Teaninich uses an odd piece of equipment, an Asnong Hammer Mill, which grinds the malt by using revolving hammers to pound it against a perforated grate. Auchroisk have put a German six-roller Buhler Miag Mill to work – one of the few, perhaps the only one, in use among malt distilleries.

Yeast and fermentation

None of the distilleries described in the following pages have in modern times maintained yeast cultivations by themselves. They all rely on commercial yeast producers. The two major types of yeast strains mentioned throughout the book are Distiller's and Brewer's. A major disparity is that Brewer's yeast is recovered from an anaerobic fermentation while Distiller's yeast is grown aerobically, which makes Distiller's yeast more vital and rapid and less contaminated by other micro-organisms or unwanted types of yeast. Brewer's yeast is supposed to contribute to a more estery character while Distiller's yeast gives better alcohol yields. A combination of the two types will give a good ethanol yield as well as an estery character, as shown by J D Hay et al. in *Enhancement of Estery Character in Scotch Malt Distillates*.

Further, the major types of Distiller's yeast used today are divided into the following categories: *Distiller's M* or *Mauri Strain Yeast* – developed by DCL and Maclays brewery of Alloa; *Distiller's*

Turbo Yeast – developed in Sweden, gives a faster fermentation and higher ABV (18%) yield; *Other Distiller's Yeast versions* such as Quest, Quest MX Blend, MX, and WMM have gained popularity. Other categories of yeast such as *Dry Yeast*, developed from the Mauri Strain yeast to improve handling and storage life, and *Fresh Yeast*, mainly used in the US for bourbon, are rarely used in Scotland; one of the few exceptions is Glenburgie.

The fermentation time, the minimum time needed for the yeast to convert most of the wort's sugar into alcohol, usually varies between forty-four to sixty hours. However, the time may be extended up to five days. This is often practiced over weekends. The length of the conversion time affects the character of the spirit and its complexity. A 'short' fermentation time of forty-four to forty-eight hours yields a spicy and nutty spirit with low wash acidity. Residual bacterial action is kept at a minimum level. A 'long' fermentation time, also known as malolactic fermentation, increases the ABV level to a point where all the yeast cells die. This allows some bacterial actions which will increase the complexity by adding several new flavour components, congeners, and raise the acidity level of the spirit. This allows for a broader, fruitier, spectrum of congeners. Both methods are usually practised by a distillery.

The fermentation occurs in wash backs, traditionally made from Scottish larch or Oregon pine. Since the early 1960s stainless steel vessels, with optional temperature control, have been gradually introduced. The hygienic and control aspects often outweigh tradition: stainless steel vessels are easier to clean and the risk of bacteria colonies, left in un-cleaned cracks and knot holes, tainting successive batches is eliminated.

Lauter mash tun and traditional mash tun

The mash tun has the function of being a combined conversion and wort separation vessel. After mashing, when the starch has been broken down, it is necessary to separate the liquid extract (the wort) from the solids (spent grain particles and adjuncts). Wort separation is important because the solids contain large amounts of protein, poorly modified starch, fatty material, silicates, and polyphenols (tannins). The method of separating the wort from the mash solids, and the equipment used, is mainly a matter of choice on the part of the individual producer and sometimes a matter of tradition. Wort separation may be carried out by any of a number of different methods such as the traditional mash tun, the semi-Lauter and the full Lauter mash tun.

The top of a tun is usually spherical or conical and fitted with wood or copper lids with vents for releasing the vapours of the hot mash. Previously made of cast iron, the bottom of the tun has been made of stainless steel since the 1960s. It may be flat or sloped or it may be constructed with several concentric valleys with intervening ridges. Suspended above the true bottom of the tun is a false bottom of milled, slotted, or welded wedge wire steel plates that act as the filtering system. The Lauter tun, unlike the traditional mash tun, is equipped with rakes to assist mash transfer and for levelling the bed and facilitating filtration of the liquid from the mash. Rakes are more important when the mash is stirred and mixed, such as with temperature-controlled infusion or decoction mashing. Unlike single-temperature infusion mashing, the mash loses its entrained air and sinks onto the false bottom in a dense

The wash back at Blair Athol

The mash tun at Cardhu

The mash tun at Clynelish

bed. A full Lauter tun has arms that can move up and down while rotating, whilst the semi-Lauter arms rotate without vertical movement. The arms use a combination of rakes and blades to ensure maximum extraction of sugars. It also has continuous sparging, meaning to wash the extract from the mash. The sparging water is added continuously and not in batches as is traditionally done.

Two-and-a-half distillation

Stills at Clynelish

Usually, the wash and low wines are distilled consecutively in two stills (double distillation) or consecutively in three stills (triple distillation). In the two-and-a-half case, the low wines from the wash still are collected in the low wines receiver, at about 20% ABV, with the head or foreshots collected and kept separate. Then the low wines are fed from the low wines receiver and distilled once again in a spirit still, the larger of two spirit stills. Again, the heads or foreshots are collected and kept separate. The resulting spirit distillate is collected, at about 48% ABV, and diverted to a separate spirit still charger. Finally, the fluid that goes into the third still is mixed with the content of the separate spirit still charger and with the heads separated by the wash still distilling plus the heads separated by the first spirit still distilling. The proportion of the three mixed components and their different alcohol by volume (% ABV) is a function of the distillery's preference. The % ABV of the spirit resulting from this, the third, distillation is around 73 to 76% ABV, compared with traditional double distillation yielding 68 to 73% ABV. The head and tail from the last, the third, distillation is sent back to the spirit still charger holding the distillate from the second distillation. The philosophy is to have congeners returned that would have been stripped off in a traditional triple distillation process. This method is practised at Benrinnes, Mortlach and Springbank distilleries. It was also practised at now mothballed Rosebank distillery.

Shell and tube condensers and traditional worm condensers

The current and most common way to cool the vapours arising from the distillation process is by the use of the shell and tube heat exchanger/condenser. However, several distilleries have kept or reverted back to the classic worm tub method. This traditional method of cooling is by means of copper tube coils submerged in tubs, made of wood or sometimes cast iron or concrete, surrounded by flowing cooling water. The reason for retaining this method is its distinct contribution to a whisky's character. Technically, the surface area of copper in contact with the vapours in a worm tub is a fraction of that in a modern condenser. Hence, the whisky made in a distillery with worm tubs becomes much more meaty and sulphury in its character. The longer the alcohol vapours are in contact with copper, the lighter the whisky is likely to be. The worm tub method has only survived at a few distilleries: Balmenach, Benrinnes, Cragganmore, Dalwhinnie, Edradour, Glen Elgin, Glenkinchie, Mortlach, Oban, Pultney, Royal Lochnagar, Speyburn, and Talisker. Two distilleries use it partially: Springbank on their wash still only, and Linkwood on Linkwood A only. Cooling for Linkwood B is performed via conventional vertical copper tube condensers. It is interesting to learn that Dalwhinnie replaced their worms with modern condensers in the 1970s but reverted back to worms in 1996 as they noted that the style of the whisky had changed.

20

Copper and stills

Copper has an ability to influence flavour by acting as a catalyst, but also as a contributor; hence, the metal plays a significant role as an essential ingredient in the whisky formula. The patina, which forms on the copper's surface when exposed to spirit vapours, affects the formation of congeners, especially the esterification of organic acids by alcohols. It has also been demonstrated that the foul smelling, highly volatile sulphur compounds derived from the yeast are reduced and removed by the interaction with copper, especially in the wash still. Copper is therefore an essential element in producing clean spirit. Increased exposure to copper in the still and the condenser promotes a purer, lighter spirit. The exposure is achieved by various parameters such as the volume and shape of a still but also how full the still is charged – all factors forming an individual reflux pattern, contributing to a repeated contact with the copper. Others are the angle of the lyne arm or the lyne pipe and whether or not purifiers are fitted on the lyne pipe, or how slowly and how hot the stills are run.

Perhaps most important are the coolers or condensers. Traditional worm tub coolers give much less exposure to copper due to the rather short length of its coiled copper tube, whereas the modern shell and copper tube condensers, or heat exchangers, offer a substantially longer way for the vapours to travel. The lesser copper contact, offered by a worm tub cooler, contributes to a heavier and fuller spirit, and a longer contact contributes to a purer and lighter one.

Exposure to carbon dioxide, sulphur and direct heating wear away the copper. Areas subject to such attack need constant patching and eventually complete replacement. Directly heated stills (coal, coke, oil or gas) are built with thicker copper segments than indirect fired ones: 15mm versus 5mm. Life expectancy for indirectly fired stills are fifteen to twenty years for mash stills and ten to fifteen years for spirit stills; directly fired are worn out sooner. The predominant suppliers of distilling line equipment and maintenance are Abercrombie in Alloa and Forsyth in Rothes.

The shape of the still dictates its reflux, or re-distil, character. The shapes are categorised according to the shape of the neck and the lower pot or boiling vessel part: *normal shaped* – with a nearly circular shaped pot; *onion shaped* – with an onion-shaped pot;

Onion-shaped still at Caol Ila

lantern shaped – with a constricted neck which gives the still a lantern or lamp-like image; *pear shaped* – a short neck gives the still a pear shape. The various neck types add an extra dimension to the pot still's reflux profile. The necks are categorised as: *reflux balls neck* – its purpose is to separate heavier and lighter substances from the rising vapour by the means of adding cooling surface and increasing copper contact; *short neck* – contributes to thick, oily and pungent whiskies; *tall neck* – contributes to purer, lighter and relatively mild whiskies; *water jacket necks* – contributes to something in between of short and tall necks and is currently used at the Dalmore and Fettercairn distilleries only. An odd neck is installed at Allt á Bhainne; it is a straight, tall tube-shaped neck with parallel sides. It is the only one of its kind in the trade.

Heating of the stills was traditionally made by hand stoking a direct fire of anthracite, coal, peat or a mixture of the three. Later, the hand stoking became replaced by mechanical stoking equipment. After 1945 different indirect heating methods were introduced such as *steam pans* – pans placed in the bottom of the still, *steam coils* – tubes placed at the bottom of the still, *steam kettles* – hollow cylinders placed at the bottom of the still, *steam plate* – radiator-like units submerged in the pot still. External heat exchangers, pre-heating the wash, is another method combined with internal heating. Indirect heating eliminates the scorching, a frequent mishap during the old days.

Casks and the importance of oak

Cask management constitutes the single most important element of a whisky's creation. This includes factors such as time, type of casks, warehouse configuration and microclimate; however, the importance of the latter should not be stressed too much.

All Scotch whisky, whether malt or grain whisky, has to be matured in wooden casks for a minimum of three years. The size of such a cask may not exceed 700 litres. Since 1988, it has been prescribed by law that the wood used to build these casks must come from oak species. Further, the complete maturation cycle, regardless of its length, has to have occurred on Scottish soil. Prolonged cask maturation outside Scotland deprives the whisky its right to be identified as a *Scotch* whisky.

Scotch whisky, by tradition, never spends its full maturation cycle in fresh, new casks, though some minor experiments with finishing in such casks have been made. Finishing is the processes where a whisky is racked over to another cask to spend a fraction of its maturing cycle in a new environment.

Secondhand casks that had previously contained various types of sherry (amontillado, fino, oloroso, etc.) used to be the dominant type of vessel. However, the declining consumption of sherry after World War II made these casks a dwindling resource. A remedy came about when the coopers' union in the United States managed, in 1936, to get a ban on the re-use of 'barrels' that had once contained distilled alcohol. By that, they practically guaranteed themselves a never-ending job opportunity and the Scotch whisky makers a bottomless supply of casks. Not bound by US laws, the Scotsmen began in 1946 to import these secondhand casks, which previously had contained bourbon or rye whisky, *en masse*. An attractive factor is and was the price difference between sherry casks and US whisky barrels; a sherry cask

Casks at Mannochmore

• Nomenclature and Definitions •

How casks were once transported

Former content, like sherry, may also have an influence on the colour.

Not only will the oak and its character affect the flavours of the whisky, so will residuals from its previous usage. As the casks may be re-used for maturing whisky – the practical maximum is up to four times – this effect is gradually reduced by each reuse. A now-forbidden practice to overcome this was to rejuvenate the casks by pressure impregnating them with a syrupy concoction, consisting of grape juice and sherry leftovers, called Parajete.

Another vital factor that contributes to the metamorphosis of plain alcohol to whisky is the fire treatment that occurs during a cask's construction. When the staves are bent to form the cask they are heated. Heat alters the chemical structure of the inner surface of the casks. Without this treatment the alcohol will not

is approximately ten times more expensive than a whisky barrel from the United States. Today, 95% of all whisky produced in Scotland spends some time in whisky barrels from the United States. There is a difference in volume between the common casks used for maturation and American Standard Barrels (ASB). The ASB hold 181.7 litres and a common or hogshead cask about 250 litres. Hence, the ASBs are rebuilt in Scotland by expanding two casks with staves from a third. The enlarged casks are known as re-made or dump hogshead. Other sizes used are sherry butts, double the size of a hogshead, or about 500 litres, and puncheons that hold about 560 litres. In smaller casks, such as quarter casks (about 100 litres), the spirit-to-surface ratio is greater, which contributes to a faster maturation, but quality and character may be lost.

The oak wood used in Europe for most of the table and fortified wines are of the species *Quercus robur*, *Q. sessilis* and *Q. petrea*. American barrels are made of the local species, predominantly *Quercus alba*, or American White oak. The major difference is that *Q. robur* has higher tannin content, whereas the *Q. alba* develops vanillin-like flavour compounds by charring. *Q. alba* has a denser structure and, hence, becomes 'tighter' than a vessel made from the more porous *Q. robur* and its cousins, contributing to a different oxidation profile. As tannins add colour to the whisky, those matured in *Q. robur* are darker than those in *Q. alba*.

Casks being loaded at Port Ellen

change and become whisky as we know it. In Europe this fire treatment is gently applied stave by stave and is described as 'toasting'. The American cooper raises the cask and then heavily 'chars' its interior before bending the staves. The charring penetrates the surface one to two millimetres deep and not only caramelises the hemicelluloses but also converts the lignin to produce vanillin flavours.

Charles Doig and pagoda-roofed kilns

The well-known 19th-century distillery architect, Charles Doig of Elgin, is the 'father' of the pagoda-shaped kiln roofs, or the 'Doig Ventilator' as it is also called. They have become a signature for Scotch malt whisky distilleries. The aim of the construction was to provide the kiln with a stronger draught for the peat fire when drying the steeped barley for conversion to millable malt. Charles Doig installed his very first pagoda roof at Dailuaine distillery circa 1890.

Licence laws of 1644, 1784 and 1823

The first tax on spirits was imposed by the Scottish Parliament in 1644. This was intended to raise revenue for the Royalist army during the Civil War. In 1707, the Act of Union between England and Scotland led to the formation of the Board of Excise, which began to enforce the laws relating to excise duty quite rigorously.

Thus, the battle lines were drawn up, with the excise officers, or 'gaugers', versus the native whisky-makers, or 'smugglers'.

The growing numbers of backyard distilleries forced a reformation. The Wash Act of 1784 reduced the level of duty and simplified regulations and established a precise, geographical 'Highland Line' which separated the Lowlands from the High-lands for purposes of differential excise levels. The Act aimed to stimulate legal distilling in the Highlands and to reduce smuggling. Accordingly, lower rates of excise duty were applied to small-scale distilleries north of the line which used locally-produced barley. The Wash Act also led to a great expansion of legal Lowland distilling, as it encouraged distillers to produce more spirit from each batch of 'wash', with the licence fee being based on each distillery's capacity. Lowland whisky consequently gained a poor reputation as a result of being distilled very rapidly in extremely shallow stills.

This new tactic, however, did not serve its purpose, as the number of illicit stills constantly grew. No fewer than 14,000 were detected during the year of 1823 alone. The Duke of Gordon was a substantial landowner in north-east Scotland at the time. This was a corner of Scotland where the problem of illicit distillation was particularly serious. Gordon and some of his fellow landlords promised to help stamp out the illegal trade if the government provided an incentive for the smugglers to distil on the right side of the law. The proposed tool, the Excise Act of 1823, authorised production of malt whisky with the payment of a licence of £10,

A Wash Back declaration

and a tax by gallon of pure spirit. This Act was the end of moonshine distillation and provided excellent revenues for the government as well as for the distillers. The first new distillery to be licenced under the Act was built by George Smith of Glenlivet, one of the Duke of Gordon's tenants. As a consequence of the 1823 Act, the number of licenced distilleries in Scotland doubled in two years and the annual production of duty-paid whisky tripled. The 1823 Excise Act was the foundation of the Scotch whisky industry as we know it today.

Pattison crash of 1899

When the blended Scotch whisky concept took the world by storm the demand created a rush to increase production capacity. The blending of malt and grain whisky had been increasing significantly since Gladstone's Spirit Act of 1860 which permitted the blending of whisky to be kept under bond (deferred payment of spirit duty). Many new distilleries were built. In Speyside alone, twenty-one new distilleries were erected during the golden decade at the end of the century. The output of the Scottish distilleries virtually doubled in the years from 1889 to 1899. With this rapid growth, whisky came to be seen as a safe high-yield financial investment. The speedy build up led to an over-capacity and the bubble burst in 1899. This collapse had a cataclysmic impact amongst the Scottish distillers.

The Leith-based blending and whisky wholesale company Pattison's Ltd was one of the largest and certainly the most remarkable of the blending companies at the time. They were the leader of the game. 'Excess is everything' might well have been their motto, for excess typified virtually all they undertook. In 1898, for instance, they spent £60,000 (£3.5 million in today's purchase strength) on advertising not only in traditional media, but also via channels they invented. One innovation involved the purchase and training of 500 grey parrots, all of whom were taught to repeat the words 'Pattison's is best. Pattison's is best.' The parrots were set free in parks around Edinburgh at the end of a warm summer. They were all killed by the arrival of the first frost.

The Pattison brothers, Robert and Walter, had built their business on credit to finance a huge stock of malt whisky to be used in their blends. To finance their ongoing operation they used a minimum of the malt in their blends. The blends were simply based on cheap, immature grain whisky and a futile amount of malt whisky, adding little if any character to their blends. After a while, sale figures went into a downward spin. With a large amount of borrowed capital tied to the malt whisky stock Pattison's had no space to manoeuvre. However, several distillers were afraid they might lose out if they refused to deal with Pattison's and supplied them on a growing credit. In 1899, the bubble burst and Pattison's crashed owing £500,000, with assets of less than £250,000 (a £15 million loss in today's purchase strength). This was a grand bankruptcy and the collapse of the Pattison's empire sent shock-waves through the industry. A large number of individual investors were ruined and several distilleries were forced to close down as many companies were financially affected due to the complex network of credit arrangements within the industry. Pattison's had entered the marketing of blended whisky in an energetic and shrewd way, but behind the rapid rise to prominence was serious financial mismanagement and swindling on the part of the Pattison brothers, both of whom served prison sentences for fraud as a result of the firm's collapse.

The rise of Diageo

There are several tracks to follow that led to the formation of the Diageo Empire. The following explains a few.

When the output of whisky was greatly increased after the introduction in 1831 of the Coffey or Patent still, attempts were made to limit the near-flooding of the market. In October 1856, some Lowland grain distillers, all using the highly productive new still equipment, agreed to divide the trade in grain whisky among themselves, an agreement that lasted only a year. Another cartel attempt occurred in May 1865 with the formation of the organisation 'Scotch Distillers Association'. Membership was extended to a few Irish and English Patent still distillers, all with a substantial production. The Association lasted until 1876 and when it collapsed a group of the founding members decided to establish a commercial joint venture, a limited company. On 1 May 1877, the Distillers Company Ltd (DCL) was registered by the group. DCL started out as an amalgamation that involved six Lowland distilleries that all produced grain whisky by the use of the Coffey or Patent stills. The distilleries and their owners were *Robert Mowbray (Cambus), John Haig & Co. (Cameron Bridge), John Bald & Co. (Carsebridge), MacNab Bros. & Co. (Glenochil), Stewart & Co. (Kirkliston)* and *Macfarlane & Co. (Port Dundas)*. In 1885 the Caledonian distillery became a member. Not until 1886 were the DCL shares finally quoted on the London Stock Exchange. On DCL's initiative, to further protect their interests, a trade interest and lobby organisation, The United Kingdom Distillers Association (UKDA), nicknamed the 'Whisky Parliament' was established. This rather short-lived interest group, formed in 1878, did not survive the Great Depression (1878 to 1896) and ceased to exist in September 1888.

DCL went on with business as usual. Around 1925, DCL had taken over the three big blenders *James Buchanan*, *John Dewar* and *John Walker*. One branch of their business gained, in 1882, major control over the large yeast market for distillers and brewers. DCL standardised the popular 'Vienna' yeast strain to be sold as 'Pure DCL yeast' with central distribution on a daily basis. In the com-ing years, a diversification took place and DCL founded a division for the production of chemicals such as acetone and butanole. The importance of DCL shortly after the end of World War II was so great that it rose from rank thirty-nine to rank four of the fifty largest companies in Great Britain.

In July 1914, when A & J Dawson of the St. Magdalene Distillery ran into financial difficulties, DCL acquired control. Subsequently, DCL negotiated an amalgamation of five Lowland malt distilling firms forming a DCL-like structure. Besides *St. Magdalene* they were *Clydesdale, Glenkinchie, Grange* and *Rosebank*. The merger was highly successful; partly because they applied the same technique by using Coffey or Patent stills in their production of malt whisky, partly because they were old-fashioned and substantial economies were easy to achieve. The amalgamation was incorporated under the name 'Scottish Malt Distilleries Ltd' (SMD) with DCL as a substantial shareholder. During the years to come, SMD acquired several other malt distilleries merely to close them in order to limit production. In 1925, SMD's General Manager James Risk convinced the board of DCL to take full control over SMD, which they did. In October 1928, the DCL board discussed a transfer of all malt whisky production facilities they controlled into one single group to facilitate rationalisations. The embryo already existed; the SMD. For SMD, the re-organisation carried out from 1929 to 30, was a tidying-up operation in which it became the owner of forty-nine malt whisky distilleries. By 1935, fifty-one malt distilleries belonged to the SMD.

Guinness acquired the large blending firm Arthur Bell & Sons in 1985 and DCL the following year. By combining these two businesses, the United Distillers Ltd (UD) was formed in 1987, as a subsidiary to Guinness.

In 1962, W & A Gilbey, the famous gin maker, merged with United Wine Traders (Justerini and Brooks) to form International Distillers & Vintners (IDV). In 1972, Grand Metropolitan Hotels (Grand Met) acquired IDV.

An attempt to merge Guinness and Grand Met began in 1994. Before this merger could take place, Guinness and Grand Met had to fight against the resistance of the whole branch, especially the French luxury products company Louis Vuitton Moet Hennessy (LVMH) and its chairman Bernard Arnault. Arnault and Guinness had cross-shareholding of 34% in their respective companies (Guinness in LMVH's drink company Moet-Hennessy). The merger took place in 1997, and Diageo plc was the holding company created. Grand Met brought the International Distillers & Vintners Ltd (IDV) into the marriage, Guinness brought the United Distillers Ltd (UD), and from this point United Distillers and Vintners Ltd (UDV) emerged as a subsidiary company to Diageo plc.

The Distilleries

The RARE MALTS SELECTION

The Rare Malts originated from every part of Scotland, and as such they represented both her history and her geography. From Clynelish and Brora in the north to Bladnoch in the south, from Port Ellen in the west to Glenury Royal in the east, the Rare Malts embodied all that is rarest and best in malt-making tradition. The bottlings came from thirty-six distilleries, at least nine of which (underlined on the map) are now closed or 'silent'.

AUCHROISK

Pronounced '*othrusk*' meaning 'the ford of the red stream' in Gaelic, Auchroisk is located near Mulben, Banffshire. It is situated on a hilltop clearly visible from the village of Rothes. The name is borrowed from a neighbouring farm purchased by International Distillers and Vintners Ltd (IDV) in 1968. IDV was formed in 1962 by Justerini and Brooks together with W.A. Gilbey. This ultra modern, state-of-the-art distillery was designed in 1973 with great consideration and architectural skill to prevent the industrial complex and surrounding large warehouses, with their dark roofs and white-washed walls, from becoming an

Distillery details

REGION Highlands (Speyside)

OWNER Diageo

ADDRESS Mulben, Keith, Banffshire, AB55 6XS

ROADS B9103 on the Keith to Rothes Road

TEL 01542 885000

FAX 01542 885039

AUCHROISK

eyesore. Architectural and environmental awards received are testimony to the success of one of the last great distillery developments in Scotland. One was from the Angling Foundation for not interfering with the progress of local salmon as they swim upriver. The attractive distillery, built by George Wimpey and designed by Westminster Design Associates, has survived without any major renovations except for the introduction of energy-saving modifications.

When the decision was made to erect a new distillery, it was up and running within twenty-four months, with the first drops to flow on 4 January 1974. The objective of IDV was to guarantee a steady flow of whisky needed for its flagship J & B Rare, which was a major seller at the time. The distillery was taken over in 1975 by Watney Mann and by Grand Metropolitan Ltd later the same year. The merger in 1997 between Grand Metropolitan, owner of IDV and Guinness, owner to United Distillers and Vintners Ltd (UDV), made it part of the Diageo group.

Auchroisk draws its cooling water from the Mulben Burn and its process water from the generous Dorie's Well which has a flow rate of ten thousand litres an hour. The well is located halfway down a steep ravine. It is situated a few miles from the river Spey, on the Keith to

The entrance to Dorie's Well

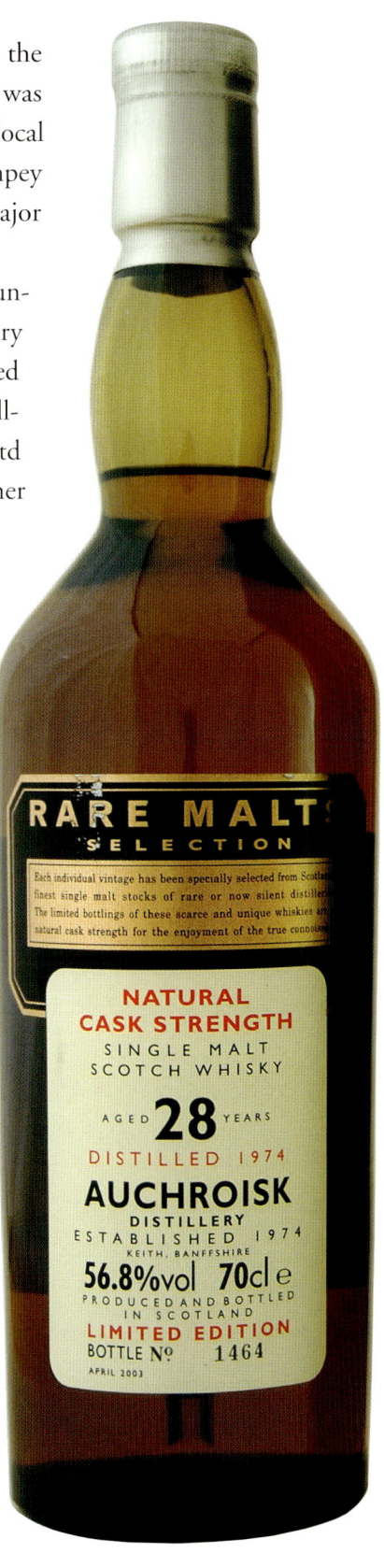

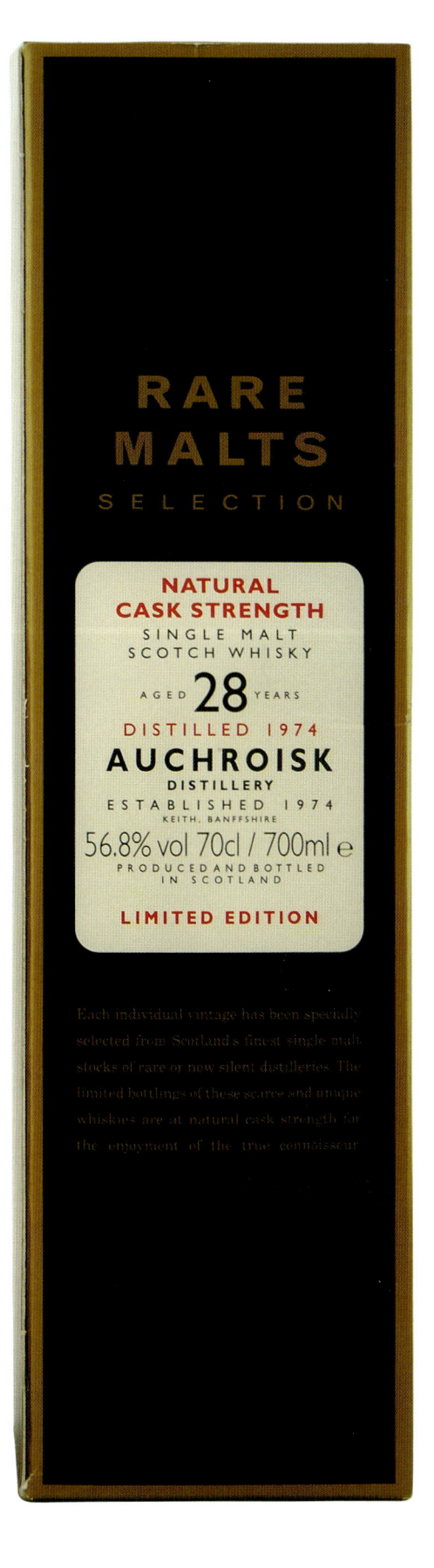

29

Rothes Road, and within the confines of the distillery. It was in fact the principal reason why IDV chose this site for a new distillery. Tests carried out in the 1970s by transporting water from the well to Glen Spey distillery for trial distillation made all concerned satisfied that the silky-smooth water which encountered granite as well as sandstone during its flow was suitable for the task. Hence, the water rights and additional land were purchased for a reputed £5 million. Today the well is secured inside a small stone building. If the 'key holder' is in a good mood he may open the door and let you water down your dram directly at the source. Own-floor maltings have never occurred; the malt is delivered on a daily basis from central maltsters, Burghead Maltings in Elgin. Malt used is non- to lightly peated and of Optic and Chalice varieties. Auchroisk's equipment is a reflection of modern technique: from the German-manufactured six-roller Buehler-Miag mill to the rather unorthodox stainless steel semi-Lauter mash tun and further to the eight 51,000-litre stainless steel wash backs. The large Lauter tun's capacity is 11.5 metric tonnes, from which twenty-one mashes are produced per week. Each mash produces almost foamless wort, hence, no switchers are needed. This is due to a local invention replacing the usual rotating motor and its propeller with four stainless steel bars above each wash back. As soon as foam reaches one of the bars, a mechanism triggers a release of a solution based on dietary fibres and the effect is immediate: the foam produced by the fermentation goes down. The yeast, a Distiller's yeast strain, is added to the wort line after the heat exchanger and before the wash back. One wash back serves all four wash stills. The vast, immaculate still house accommodates four paired, lantern-shaped stills. Each wash still has a capacity of 12,700 litres and the spirit stills 7,900 litres. All stills are indirectly heated by steam from oil-heated boilers and cooled by shell and tube condensers. The stills are larger-sized replicas of the ones found at the Glen Spey distillery and are manufactured by Archibald Macmillan of Prestonpans. They are fitted with nearly horizontal lyne arms, a prerequisite for the distillery's aim to produce a lighter, pale-coloured and gently peated sweet estery spirit. Capacity is 3,100,000 litres of alcohol per annum. Full throughput capacity is 300 tonnes of malted barley per week. The fermentation time is short, lasting about forty-four hours, and the distillation cycle lasts about seven hours per batch. New-make whisky is pumped over to casks for further maturation on site. Around 10% is reserved for bottling as single malt whisky.

Cask management is based on a ten-year maturation period, in ex-bourbon casks. A fraction of whisky is matured for twelve years in ex-oloroso casks. This portion is used as a 'spice' to create the special Auchroisk signature bottled as single malt under the label 'Singleton of Auchroisk'. The Singleton was introduced in 1986 after a concept formulated by the distillery's master blender at the time, Jim Milne. The maturing warehouses, with a combined capacity of near 300,000 casks are also used for whisky produced at other sites owned by the Diageo group. Auchroisk is also the 'assembly point' for Highland malt whiskies used in the J&B range. They are vatted together here, then sent to Glasgow for further blending with grain and non-Highland whiskies, and then returned to Auchroisk for a marrying period before bottling. Auchroisk is now managed by Justerini & Brooks (Scotland) Ltd and mainly produces blended whisky for the J&B brands such as J&B Rare, J&B Reserve and J&B Ultima. J&B Rare is today one of the largest brands of blended Scotch whisky. J&B is a subsidiary of the owner Diageo.

The distillery is open to visitors, by appointment. An old steam engine from the Strathmill distillery is on display in the visitors' hall. Worth a ride is the Keith and Dufftown Railway, an eleven-mile line linking the World's Malt Whisky Capital, Dufftown, to the market town of Keith. The line passes through some of Scotland's most picturesque scenery, with forest and farmland, lochs and glens, castles and distilleries.

AUCHROISK

Structural elements and their respective weights

Structure	Observations
Colour	7
Peaty/Phenolic	1
Sherried/Winey	
Fruity/Estery	2
Floral/Aldehydic	3
Cereal/Malty	2
Feinty	
Medicinal/Maritime	
Woody	2
Vanilla/Honey	2
Nutty/Creamy	1
Spicy	2
Sulphury	

Conclusive organoleptic sensations

	Observations
Colour	Baltic amber.
Nose	Gentle hint of peat, like a bonfire at a distance. Baked apples. Drying, newly cut grass. Malty, cereal and cooked mash. A whiff of beeswax and vanilla. Spicy, liquorice and crushed aniseed.
Palate	Light, clean and sweet. Creamy with traces of walnuts.
Finish	Woody edge, slowly erased by the vanilla and walnut notes.
Comment	A medium- to light-bodied, sweet and low-peat whisky with no pronounced sherry notes. Restrained, opens up with water. An after-dinner dram.

Issued versions

Distilled	Age	% abv	Size	Box	Version
1974	28	56.8	0.7		No versions

AULTMORE

Pronounced '*aultMORE*', from the Gaelic 'Allt Mohr' meaning 'the big brook'. 'Mohr' or 'Mór' is Gaelic for 'big' and 'Allt' is 'brook'. Aultmore is located in the hamlet of the same name situated 4km northwest of Keith, Banffshire. On display in the entrance hall is a 10 horsepower Abernethy steam engine. This was the power source for the distillery. The engine worked seven days a week, from the starting day in 1897 until 1969, without any interruptions other than maintenance, when a water wheel served as back-up power.

The sparsely populated tract around Aultmore, the many burns around and the peat from the Foggie Moss, perfect for illicit distilling, were incentive enough to erect a legal distillery here. Aultmore commenced production in 1897 and its product became an instant success. Therefore, in 1898, the distillery's capacity was doubled by improvements to equipment and extension of facilities. Reconstruction that occurred in the 1970s stripped most of the traces of its Victorian origin and charm. All warehouses were demolished in 1996 and the whisky produced in the hamlet of Aultmore is now matured elsewhere. Aultmore was closed from 1943 to 45 to comply with war restrictions. A pilot plant for experiments with recovering and converting solid remains from the malt whisky distilling process into high-protein feeding substance for livestock was set up here as early as 1952. This was not the first of such experiments. Alfred Barnard mentions a similar arrangement at the Loch Catrine distillery seventy years earlier. A full-size plant for dark grains was installed in 1972. Extensive modernisations were undertaken during 1971 and 1972. The number of stills was increased to four and they were all converted from direct coal-firing to indirect heating.

Distillery details

REGION Highlands (Speyside)

OWNER Bacardi

ADDRESS Keith, Banffshire, AB55 6QY

ROADS On A96 at turn-off to Buckie go B9016

TEL 01542 881800

FAX 01542 886467

EMAIL info@bacardi.com

AULTMORE

The distillery was built in 1895–96 by the great whisky entrepreneur, Alexander Edward, from Forres. Edward was at that time the owner of Benrinnes and had interests in the Craigellachie distillery. Edward later formed an industry group, the Oban and Aultmore-Glenlivet Distillers Company Ltd, which formally acquired Aultmore and Oban in early 1898. However, the group suffered like so many others at the time from the effect of the Pattison whisky bubble crash, a burst that occurred a year after their purchase. Bankrupted Pattisons of Leith had not only a stake in the group but had also contracted Aultmore as their main supplier of Speyside malt whisky. Furthermore, Pattison's agent, Mr Brickmann, was a board member of the Edwards group. No wonder that Aultmore's future was in doubt. The distillery managed to struggle on but experienced several setbacks during its first two decades of operating. Hardship combined with partial closures during World War I led to a forced sale in 1923. John Dewar & Sons Ltd acquired Aultmore for £20,000. John Dewar & Sons merged in 1925 with the now much-enlarged joint venture, the Distillers Company Ltd (DCL). DCL's subsidiary, Scottish Malt Distillers Ltd (SMD) took over the responsibilities for the distillery in 1930. In 1971 SMD licenced the operations of Aultmore to John & Robert Harvey Ltd. In 1992 the ownership was transferred to United Distillers Ltd (UD). Aultmore then became a part of the Diageo formation in 1997. A year later, Diageo sold the distillery, as part of a £1,150,000 billion deal, to the Bacardi-Martini group. At the same time the Bacardi group acquired the John Dewar Brands portfolio from Diageo, bringing the distillery back to its former owner John Dewar & Sons Ltd.

Aultmore draws its cooling and process water from the Burn of Auchinderran flowing from Foggie Moss to the River Isla. Water may also be taken from their own bores adjacent to the Moss. Aultmore abandoned floor malting in 1968. During the days of the operation of its own malting, peat from the Foggie Moss was used for the kilning process. Before the takeover by Bacardi the distillery was supplied by the UDV group's own malting resources. Now, Aultmore relies on Tweed Valley Maltings in Berwick-upon-Tweed who deliver an unpeated malt of the barley strain Optic. The mash bill previously included lightly peated Chariot and Prisma as well. Incoming malt is crushed by a traditional Porteus mill. A new stainless steel mash tun, a German Steinecker full Lauter mash tun, was installed in 2002. Its capacity is 10 metric tonnes. At full production fourteen mashes are produced per week, serving the six 46,500-litre wash backs made from

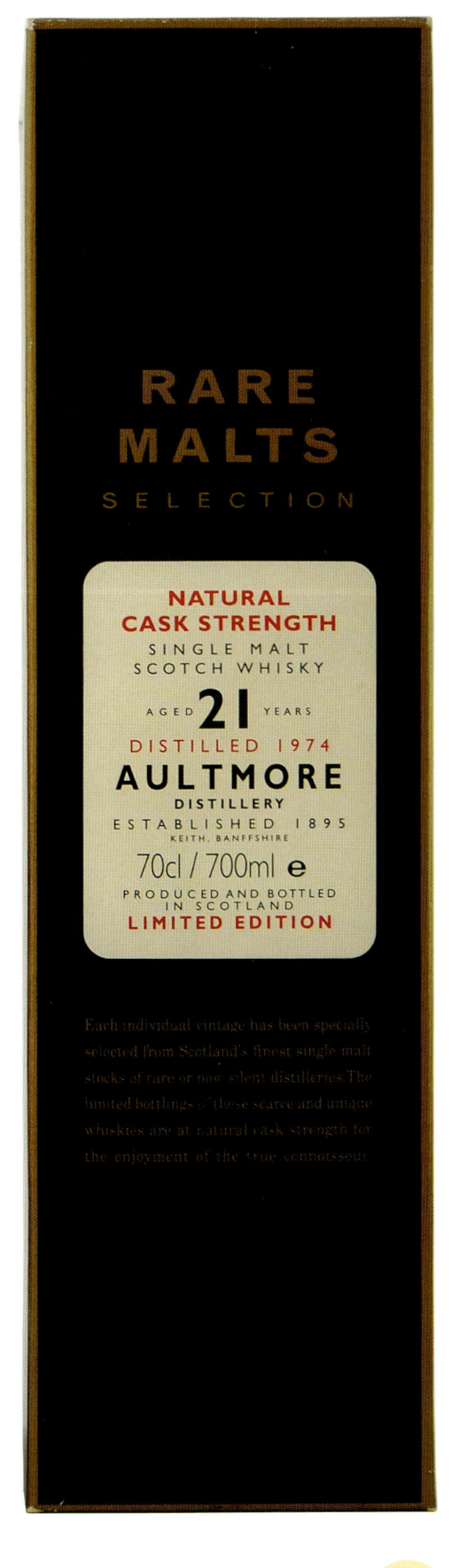

Scottish larch. Each wash back holds the volume for three wash stills. The yeast strain used is a special Distiller's yeast: Quest. The fermentation goes on for sixty hours, a bit longer than is required for 'short' fermentation, allowing some, but not full, malolactic conversion. The still house accommodates two onion-shaped wash stills and two lantern-shaped spirit stills with slight downward sloping lyne arms. All are indirectly heated by steam from oil-heated boilers and cooled by condensers. Capacity of the wash and spirit stills are the same: 15,500 litres. The stills were all manufactured by Archibald Macmillan of Prestonpans but are now maintained by Forsythes. The complete distillation cycle lasts about 12.5 hours per batch, and the full production capacity is 2.2 million litres of alcohol per year.

Cask management is based on a twelve-year maturation period, in ex-bourbon casks. A smaller volume matures in sherry butts. During the UDV era, since 1996, all newly filled casks were distributed mainly to UDV's central maturing warehouses located in Cambus, as well as to other neighbouring facilities – a practice inherited by the new owners. Aultmore, highly respected among blenders, is the backbone of John Dewar's White Label but is also included in VAT 69 and Johnnie Walker Black Label. A twelve-year-old official version of Aultmore was launched in 2004.

The distillery is open to visitors, by appointment. Nearby attractions are the well preserved Keith and Dufftown Heritage Railway and The Scottish Tartan Museum, both located in Keith.

AULTMORE

Structural elements and their respective weights

STRUCTURE	OBSERVATIONS
Colour	6
Peaty/Phenolic	2
Sherried/Winey	
Fruity/Estery	3
Floral/Aldehydic	3
Cereal/Malty	3
Feinty	
Medicinal/Maritime	
Woody	
Vanilla/Honey	1
Nutty/Creamy	
Spicy	
Sulphury	

Conclusive organoleptic sensations

	OBSERVATIONS
Colour	Rustic gold.
Nose	Aromatic, fragrant with gentle hints of bog gentians, peat and earthiness. Dried apple slices. Barley sugar. Roasted malt. Hay loft.
Palate	Dried fruit and floral notes. Gorse bushes and heather. Hint of honey.
Finish	Long, finishes slightly dry.
Comment	Medium to full bodied. Generous, delicate and attractive. Lacks a bit in complexity but not in class. A pre-dinner dram.

Issued versions

DISTILLED	AGE	% ABV	SIZE	BOX	VERSION
1974	21	60.9	0.7		No versions

BANFF

Pronounced '*bampf*' from the name of the neighbouring city in Banffshire. 'Banbh' is a poetic name for Ireland in Gaelic and is used as a place name around Scotland. This distillery is long since gone. Its last remaining buildings, a warehouse complex, were demolished after a fire broke out on 11 April 1991. The distillery has a history of being plagued by fires and explosions throughout time. Banff town was founded as a port community in the 1100s. Evidence shows that King Malcolm IV lived here around 1160. The town's harbour silted up and fell into disuse in the 1800s, leaving competing Macduff, on the east side of Banff Bay, to take up the role of principal commercial port along this stretch of coast.

DISTILLERY DETAILS

REGION Highlands (Speyside)

OWNER Last known Scottish Malt Distillers Ltd, a subsidiary to DCL, later UDV Diageo

ADDRESS Inverboyndie, Banff, Banffshire, AB45 2JJ

ROADS B9139, One mile west of Banff at the mouth of the Burn of Boyndie

TEL None

FAX None

The Banff distillery was built in 1863 in the village called Inverboyndie, located a mile west of Banff. It was called the Inverboyndie Distillery by the locals to differentiate it from the original Banff Distillery. The latter was located at the Mill of Banff near Colleonard and was founded in 1824 by James McKilligan & Co. It changed ownership in 1837 after the death of the company's founder Major James McKilligan. The new owner, Alex MacKay, operated the distillery until 1852. Mr James Simpson Sr (1796–1871) – married to Lilias MacKay, presumably a relative of Alex – and his son James formed a partnership and acquired the distillery in 1852. A decade later the partnership dissolved and the distillery closed. Simpson Jr had decided to pursue his career in the distillery trade, so he built himself a new one. He chose a site with a better water supply in proximity of the new railroad, the Great North of Scotland Railroad built in 1859. The Boyndie siding was added to facilitate transports to and from the distillery. Hence, Banff became the first rail-connected distillery. After the decease of Simpson's wife Janet Morrison at Colleonard in 1857, he married his second wife, Harriet Adam, in 1859. Harriet's father Thomas Adam (1806–1893) was a banker in Banff and Aberdeen and deputy chairman of the Great North of Scotland Railway Company. Perhaps this explains the investment in his son-in-law's distillery.

The distillery prospered until a devastating fire broke out on 9 May 1877. The main distillery building was gone but maltings and warehouses were left untouched. The distillery was rebuilt and back on track in October of the same year and its market position was rapidly reclaimed. As prevention an investment was made in a fire engine, which was kept permanently on the premises. The distillery prospered and expanded in the mid eighties. Banff went from one wash and two spirit stills to six stills, capable of delivering an annual output of 900,000 litres. The Simpson family formed a limited company with an estimated capital of £72,000 in November 1898. They kept full control over the company until 1921, when the family sold a large chunk of its equity to a London firm, the Mile End Distillery Company, a subsidiary of the brewers Taylor Walker & Co Ltd. A joint venture was formed and one of the warehouses was converted to a filling and bottling site. Financial problems, stemming from the depression, caused the London firm to let James Simpson & Co go into voluntary liquidation in 1932. SMD, Scottish Malt Distillers Ltd, a subsidiary of Distillers Company Ltd (DCL), bought Banff for £50,000 the same year and became the new and last owner of the distillery. SMD closed Banff immediately and kept the distillery closed until after the end of World War II but used the full capacity of all warehouses on the premises. The closure was in line with DCL's policy to control over-production of whisky by absorbing and closing.

Saturday, 16 August 1941 is a day that will never be forgotten at Banff. During late afternoon a solitary German Junkers Ju-88 blasted the building complex with machine gun fire, emptied its bomb cargo over the distillery and got a perfect hit at warehouse No. 12. The blazing fire that broke out was fed by the warehouses' highly flammable content of exploding whisky casks. Some casks, it was said, were propelled high up into the sky and crashed to the ground quite far from where they left. A river of burning whisky surrounded the place. Several hundred casks were lost that grim afternoon. Not all became victims of the flames. Thousands of litres found their way to farmlands and watercourses. Farmers claimed that the cows were not milkable days after due to unsteady feet, not the farmers but the cows. Waterfowls, wild and tame were found flapping drunkenly on the banks of the Boyndie Burn. A fireman passed his helmet, filled to the brim with rescued whisky, to colleagues and ended up in court accused of pilfering. Lord Haw-Haw (William Joyce) claimed in his daily propaganda bulletins, transmitted from Berlin, that a major ammunition depot, not a whisky depot, in northern Scotland had been destroyed by Luftwaffe. What was not disclosed to the public was that Banff was a training camp for future RAF pilots recruited from occupied countries like Norway and, hence, perhaps a strategic target for the Germans. The soldiers were billeted in the barley lofts and in Nissen huts on the site. Repair work occurred during the winter of 1941. In 1943 Banff formally became home to one of the RAF Strikewings.

The exterior was left almost untouched during Banff's lifespan but the interior underwent several updates over time. Banff was initially configured for triple distillation but was converted to the common and conventional double distilling practice some time after 1924, when the intermediate spirit still was removed. The last major renovation occurred just after the end of World War II, after which full production resumed. On 3 October 1959, a shattering explosion occurred when repair work on one of the spirit stills ignited contained fumes. The spirit still and a large part of the distillery were ruined by the explosion and it took a month to repair the damages. Luckily, no one was harmed, not even the coppersmith and his assistant. The two remaining stills were coal fired by hand until 1963, when mechanised stoking was installed.

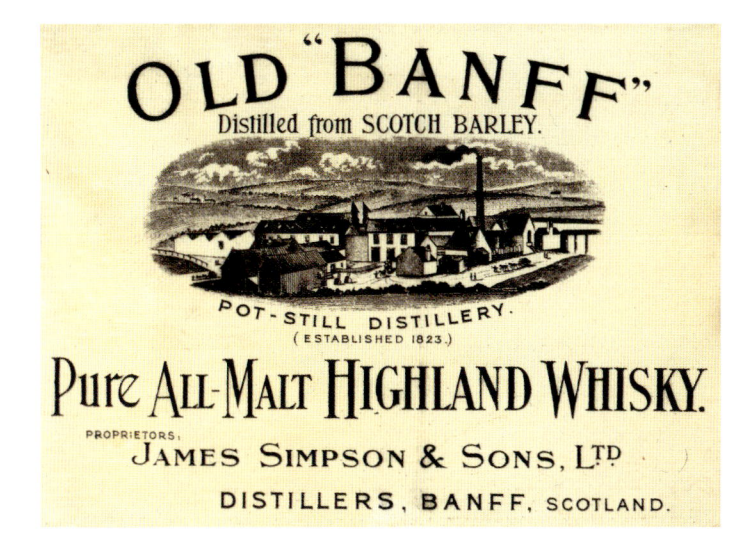

Banff cask store in the 1950s

A bottle label from Banff c.1915

The stills were converted to indirect heating by oil burners in 1970 and the number of warehouses was increased from eight to twelve. Banff finally closed 31 on May 1983 and was demolished section by section over the following years. The still house was knocked down in 1985 and the last remains were levelled in 1991 after a fire on 11 April. SMD had, in the mid sixties, applied for and obtained permission for a replacement distillery to be erected at the Inverboyndie industrial estate but never activated the plan. Hence, a group of investors some years later put forward a plan to revitalise the issue. Again permission was granted but again nothing materialised.

The process water was obtained from springs on Fiskaidly farm and the cooling water drawn from the Burn of Boydine. At the end of Banff's production barley was brought in from central maltsters, however a minor portion was malted on site. The strains of barley used toward the end are said to have been Golden Promise and Triumph. The yeast strain used was Brewer's. The mill is said to have been a 'King of Nailsworth'. In 1924 it was stated that it was the only of its kind in use at a whisky distillery. This was also the year when the production method was changed from triple to double distillation. Data concerning mash tun, wash backs and the size of the wash and spirit stills post-1924 is not known by the author. The stills were indirectly heated, fired by oil burners, and the cooling was by traditional submerged worms. The maximum annual production capacity was 900,000 litres of alcohol. For a period it was the 'house whisky' for the House of Commons. It also contributed to the blended whisky 'Slater Rodger'.

There are no remains of the distillery to visit. Other points of interest in the area are Duff House and its art gallery, situated in Banff. Duff House is one of Britain's finest Georgian houses.

BANFF

Structural elements and their respective weights

STRUCTURE	OBSERVATIONS
Colour	10
Peaty/Phenolic	2
Sherried/Winey	1
Fruity/Estery	4
Floral/Aldehydic	3
Cereal/Malty	2
Feinty	
Medicinal/Maritime	
Woody	
Vanilla/Honey	3
Nutty/Creamy	1
Spicy	
Sulphury	

Conclusive organoleptic sensations

	OBSERVATIONS
Colour	Copper with a slight reddish tinge.
Nose	Whiff of smoke like burnt damp hay. Astringent on the nose. Floral, like sun-dried grass and fruity with apple pie and orange peel in the background.
Palate	Butterscotch, slightly oily. Some nuttiness and distant sherry notes. Roasted chestnut and dry oloroso sherry.
Finish	Sweet, light smokiness and trace of vanilla.
Comment	Light bodied, gentle. Water adds an extra dimension. A pre-dinner dram.

Issued versions

DISTILLED	AGE	% ABV	SIZE	BOX	VERSION
1982	21	57.1	0.7		No versions

BENRINNES

PRONOUNCED '*ben RINnes*', this distillery gets its name from the mountain peak where it resides. 'Ben' is Gaelic for 'mountain' and the word 'rinn' means a sharp or promontory point. Ben Rinnes (840m) is the largest peak among the mountains overlooking Speyside and is used as a landmark by fishing boats in the Moray Firth. A dozen distilleries in its vicinity have drawn their water from the many springs here. The Benrinnes distillery is situated 213m above sea level on the northern shoulder of the summit.

The first Benrinnes distillery erected is said to have been founded in 1826 by Peter Mackenzie and originally called 'Lyne of Ruthrie Distillery'. It was a small combined farm and distillery situated on the premises of the Whitehouse farm (still in existence), a kilometre or so away from the present site. In 1829 the distillery was washed away in the great Speyside floods and had to be completely rebuilt. The distilling licence for the Lyne of Ruthrie Distillery was passed on to the landowner John Innes. He suffered economic hardship before a replacement distillery was established, so he sold the licence and surrounding farmlands to the firm William Smith & Co. Smith & Co. built the current distillery during the years 1834–35. The new distillery, designed to be larger and more efficient than its predecessor, had its name changed to Benrinnes and was located closer to the water sources. In 1864, the firm went bankrupt and Mr William Smith served time in Banff prison for his financial mismanagement. David Edwards and his son Alexander picked up where Smith left off in 1864. Alexander inherited not only the distillery but also the family estate near Forres when his father died in 1896. Alexander was also involved in founding the Dallas Dhu, Craigellachie and Aultmore distilleries and became a shareholder of Oban. The family went public in 1897 and sold the property, equipment and water rights for £78,930 to Benrinnes-Glenlivet Distillery Ltd. They kept a controlling interest until 1922, when the firm was absorbed by John Dewar & Sons Ltd. This was a forced sale due largely to losses accrued by the Pattison crash in 1899. John Dewar & Sons merged with Distillers Company Ltd (DCL) in 1925. DCL transferred operations to its subsidiary Scottish Malt Distillers Ltd (SMD) five years later. SMD further licenced the operation of Benrinnes to A & A Crawford Ltd of Leith, producer of

DISTILLERY DETAILS

REGION Highlands (Speyside)
OWNER Diageo
ADDRESS Aberlour, Banffshire, AB38 9NN
ROADS Between the A95 and the B9009
TEL 01340 872600
FAX 01340 872603

• RARE MALTS •

Crawford's blended whiskies range. Benrinnes became a part of Diageo with the Guinness/Grand Metropolitan merger.

After a ruinous fire in 1896 Benrinnes was largely rebuilt and three large stills and electric lighting were installed. In 1951 it ceased to produce its own electricity and it became linked to the national grid. A comprehensive renovation and modernisation work programme lasted from 1955–56, when the last traces of the old farm buildings were removed. Ten years later three additional stills were installed, increasing the number to six stills, occupying two separate still houses. Floor malting was abandoned in 1964 and became mechanized by the installation of a Saladin box. Since 1984, the Saladin box has been mothballed and malt is brought in from external sources. When the odd-looking kiln was used for onsite malting, the peat was brought in from the surrounding peat bogs. Direct coal firing was replaced with indirect heating in 1970. Benrinnes is one of the few remaining distilleries that still use traditional worms (spiralled tubes) submerged in a tub of flowing cold water to condense vapours of the distillate. Benrinnes was closed between 1932 and 1933 and from 1943 to 1945.

Cooling and processing water is drawn from the Scurran and Rowantree burns. The burns are fed by melted snow (or 'snow bree' as the locals say) passing over granite and filtered through mossy banks and gravel before reaching the distillery. Water used for cutting down the distillate to maturing strength is tapped from a domestic supply. The malt is brought in from Burghead and Roseisle Maltings in Elgin. The barley strain Decanter is favoured. It is dried to the specification 'non- to lightly peated'. For the milling a traditional Porteus mill is used.

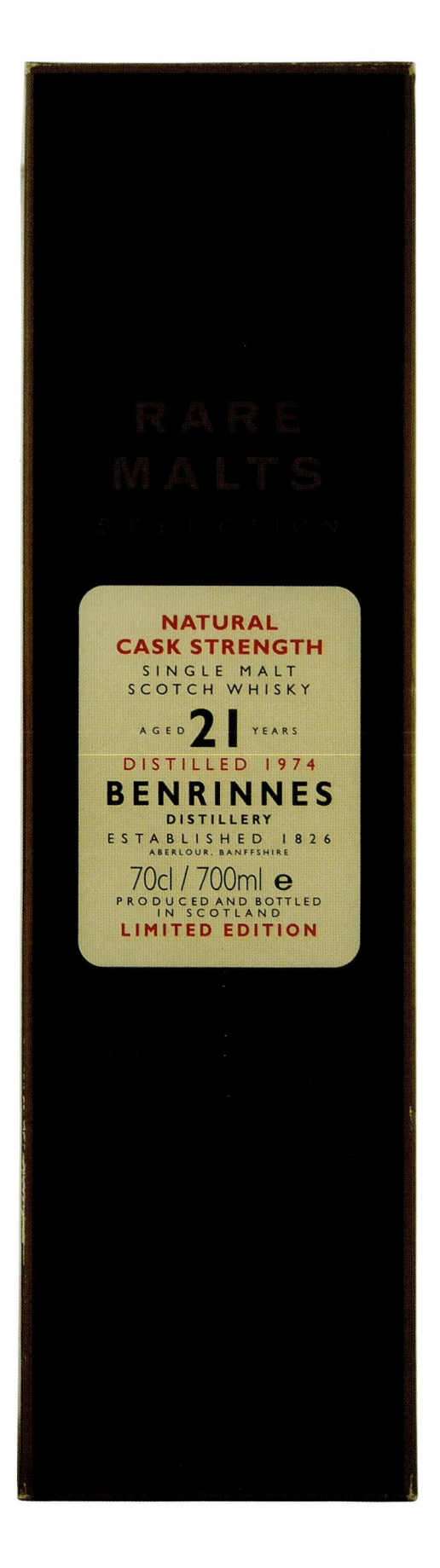

• BENRINNES •

Mashing is performed in a stainless steel full Lauter mash tun. Its capacity is nine metric tonnes and the mashing cycle lasts for six hours. The fermentation occurs in eight wooden wash backs made from Scottish larch, each with a capacity of 50,000 litres.

Distiller's Mauri yeast is used and short fermentation (weekdays) lasts for sixty hours and long fermentation (weekends) for 110 hours. The stills are grouped in trios, not paired. Capacity of the two wash stills is 22,935 litres each (charge is 20,000 litres). Two of the spirit stills have a capacity of 9,292 litres (charge is 7,099 litres) and the other two (intermediate) spirit stills hold 6,364 litres (charge is 5,243 litres). Each trio is housed in its own still house. The shape of the stills is the traditional onion shape. However, the angle of the lyne arms varies from the spirit stills' straight angle to descending degrees. Cooling is by traditional worm tubs. Distillation is rather unconventional, popularly defined as a two-and-a-half distillation, and the new-make spirit has 76% ABV. For explanation of two-and-a-half distillation see the 'Nomenclature and Definitions' chapter. The capacity is sixteen mashes per week and 2,600,000 litres of alcohol per year. Pot ale and draff are sent to the dark grains plant at Dailuaine distillery to be converted to animal food. The lion's share of the production is earmarked for the blending trade and goes into Johnnie Walker Red and Black labels, J&B and the Dewar's range.

Cask management is based on a varied maturation period, in ex-bourbon casks. A smaller volume matures in sherry butts.

The distillery is not open to the public. When in the heartland of malt whisky production, take time to follow the whisky trail and stop for a rest at the Craigellachie Hotel and its bar with 550+ single malt whiskies to sample, including several of the versions covered in this book.

BENRINNES

Structural elements and their respective weights

STRUCTURE	OBSERVATIONS
Colour	8
Peaty/Phenolic	2
Sherried/Winey	1
Fruity/Estery	3
Floral/Aldehydic	3
Cereal/Malty	
Feinty	
Medicinal/Maritime	
Woody	
Vanilla/Honey	
Nutty/Creamy	3
Spicy	1
Sulphury	

Conclusive organoleptic sensations

	OBSERVATIONS
Colour	Polished old gold.
Nose	Faint smoke. Grassy and flowery. Fresh lemon and lime aromas.
Palate	Striking a hazelnutty and barley sugar sweet note. Creamy. Slight oily texture.
Finish	Rich, long lasting. Light peppery finish.
Comment	Robust, medium bodied, sweet to some extent. Behind fragrant citrus notes a hint of tallow which contributes to a 'meaty' edge. A pre-dinner dram.

Issued versions

DISTILLED	AGE	% ABV	SIZE	BOX	VERSION
1974	21	60.4	0.7		No versions

BENROMACH

Pronounced 'ben ROmach', the distillery gets its name from Romach, the lesser mountain range, or rather hills, where it resides. 'Ben' is Gaelic for 'mountain' and the word 'romach' means 'hairy', 'towsy' or 'speckled'. It may stand for a hill covered in trees or bushes or simply 'shaggy mountain'. The distillery is located on the outskirts of the Royal Burgh and ancient market town of Forres in Morayshire and is the smallest working distillery in the Speyside area. It was also the first distillery to install direct oil firing of pot stills. Benromach was mothballed for years and stripped of vital parts, with only the spirit safe left, when the remains were purchased by the famous independent bottler Gordon and McPhail (G&M). After a complete refurbishing of the distillery it was officially inaugurated by HRH Prince Charles on 15 October 1998.

DISTILLERY DETAILS

REGION Highlands (Speyside)

OWNER Gordon & McPhail

ADDRESS Inverness Road, Forres, Morayshire, IV36 3EB

ROADS On the Aberdeen-Inverness A96 road. Turn off at the signpost for Waterford

TEL 01309 671733, visitor centre 01309 675968

FAX 01343 540155

EMAIL info@gordonandmacphail.com

WEB www.benromach.com

• BENROMACH •

The story begins when a promoter of whisky ventures, Alexander Edward, set aside land for a new distillery. A partnership was formed involving Duncan MacCallum, owner of Glen Nevis Distillery in Campbeltown, and F.W. Brickmann, a whisky broker from Leith. Their firm, the Benromach Distillery Co., commissioned Charles Doig for the design of the new and, for its time, ultra-modern distillery. Charles Doig was designer of the pagoda-shaped kiln rooftops which were in fashion among malt whisky distilleries at the end of the nineteenth century. Benromach was built from 1898 to 1900. The first drops should have been processed in spring 1899 but test runs were postponed until May 1900. Sadly, the distillery had to close almost at once as one of its directors, F.W. Brickmann, was directly involved in the Pattison crash. Brickmann's firm was suspended in October 1899 with liabilities exceeding £70,000. Benromach instantly became a victim of this debacle and over the years suffered badly from the aftermath. Hence, distillation proper did not start until around 1907. Duncan MacCallum, who was left to carry on alone, operated the distillery under the name of Forres for a period. By 1909 the ownership had been transferred to the London firm J.E. Jameson Ltd and in 1911 further transferred to Harvey, McNair & Co. The latter ran full production until the general closing of distilleries due to the outbreak of World War I.

Immediately after the end of the war, R.J. Calder acquired the distillery. In November 1919, Calder sold his interests to a newly formed venture, the Benromach Distillery Ltd (not Co. this time). Investors were regional brewers in England and the firm of MacDonald, Greenlees & Williams in Leith. This group abandoned the name Forres and reinstated Benromach as the name for the distillery. During the years from 1931 to 1937, as a result of the depression, Benromach was silent. Revived in July 1938 by Joseph Hobbs and his venture, the Associated Scottish Distillers Ltd (ASD), Benromach went into production again. Hobbs shortly thereafter sold off his stake in the firm for a nice profit. A US-based corporation, the National Distillers of America (NDA), became the new owner. In its portfolio it carried famous Kentucky names such as Old Grand Dad, Old Crow and Old Taylor. The new ownership awakened hopes and expectations for stability and orderly progress for this bruised distillery. However, they failed to materialise. It seemed like a bad spell had been put on this establishment. The distillery was shut down again shortly after the takeover until 1953, when Distillers Company Ltd (DCL) added Benromach to its vast portfolio of malt whisky distilleries. DCL appointed its subsidiary Scottish Malt Distillers Ltd (SMD) as custodian for Benromach. SMD licenced the daily production to J.&W. Hardie Ltd (owner of the brand Antiquary). Over time the production remained constant except for 1966 and 1974. During these years Benromach underwent much-needed modernisation and refurbish- ment. However, the annual throughput of the distillery remained low (maximum 900,000 litres) due to its configuration – just two pot stills. Hence UD decided in 1983 to again make the distillery dormant. The hibernation period that began on 24 March 1983 lasted until 1993, when the Elgin-based merchant firm and independent bottler Gordon & McPhail (G&M) bought the nearly empty distillery. For instance, the 14,000-litre wash still and the 12,000-litre spirit still were gone, and the six wash backs, each with a capacity of 28,000 litres, were badly damaged. After comprehensive restoration work the distillery was up and flying again, and distilling officially commenced on 15 October 1998. A few test runs had already occurred from 1997 to October 1998. G&M's move probably saved Benromach from demolition.

G&M invested in an insulated stainless steel mash tun with a copper top. It is of semi-Lauter type and holds 1.5 metric tonnes of grist, producing 7,500 litres of wort. The tun was pre-owned by a British brewery. Four new wash backs, each with a capacity of 11,000 litres and made from Scottish larch taken from the six old wash backs, a malt hopper and filling vats were installed at the same time. An item that survived from the previous owner is an elegant spirit safe manufactured by Abercrombie of Alloa in 1980. The costliest part of the new equipment is the brand new, indirectly heated, straight-necked and onion-shaped pot stills. They were made by Forsyths in 1997. Heating is by steam plate and cooling by condensers. The spirit still has a boiling ball added to its neck. The wash still has a capacity of 7,500 litres and the spirit still 5,000 litres. The distillery is now set up to handle an annual production of up to 250,000 litres of alcohol.

The process water is obtained from the Chapelton Springs, situated 3,200m away in the Romach Hills, and the cooling water used to come from the Burn of Mosset, also in the Romach Hills. Water may also be drawn from the Forres town supply, the Romach Loch. The days when malting was performed on site are long gone, having ceased during the DCL era when malt was brought in from DCL's central malting in Burghead situated a few kilometres from Forres. Today malt is brought in from various sources, including Moray Firth Maltings, and the most common barley strain used is Chariot; Optic and Golden Promise are also used. According to G&M's specifications the major part of the malt bulk is lightly peated (8ppm) but, unusual for a Speyside, some is heavily peated (30ppm) to be used for special releases. The malt is milled by a four-roller Boby Mill. The yeast strains used are a mix of Brewer's and Distiller's. Benromach operates with long fermentation periods of three to five days. The distillation period lasts for about six hours, resulting in a new make at 70% ABV.

Cask management is based on maturation in ex-bourbon casks from Jack Daniels. A smaller volume matures in sherry (oloroso) butts and some finishing occurs in casks that previously contained other spirits, fortified wines and table wines. All newly filled casks are matured in traditional dunnage-styled warehouses on site. Filling occurs at G&M's bottling plant in Elgin. The whisky is an important part of the blends Avonside, Glen Calder and Spey Cast. It ought to be noted that there is a distinct difference in the house styles found in whiskies made before 1983, the closing year compared to whiskies made in the new production line that came on stream in 1998.

The distillery is open to visitors and since 1999 has had a visitor centre and shop. For up-to-date information regarding admission fees and time of operation, consult the Benromach web site. Worth visits are Brodie Castle and the Pictish Rodney's Stone on the castle's premises.

BENROMACH

Structural elements and their respective weights

Structure	Observations
Colour	12
Peaty/Phenolic	1
Sherried/Winey	1
Fruity/Estery	3
Floral/Aldehydic	1
Cereal/Malty	2
Feinty	
Medicinal/Maritime	
Woody	2
Vanilla/Honey	
Nutty/Creamy	1
Spicy	
Sulphury	

Conclusive organoleptic sensations

	Observations
Colour	Golden brown, chestnut.
Nose	Malt and mealy cereal notes. Fruity/estery aroma. Pear drops. A floral, perfume note with a shade of geranium and apricot. A hint of drying herbs and heather. The spirit has a tendency to show some aggressiveness.
Palate	Oak wood notes and mellowing tannins. Trace of peat in sync with layer of apricot, cinnamon and sweet sherry. Recognisable tannins.
Finish	The finish is very long and scented. Slightly fruity. A lingering trace of burnt peat becomes a pleasant finale.
Comment	Medium bodied. A splash of water dampens the slightly aggressive alcohol. The herbal-floral notes contribute to a fresh, crisp palate. Pleasing pre-dinner dram.

Issued versions

Distilled	Age	% abv	Size	Box	Version
1978	19	63.8	0.7		No versions

BLADNOCH

Pronounced '*bladNOCH*', this distillery gets its name from the river and village of the same name. Bladnoch is the most southerly operating distillery in Scotland and one of the last surviving Lowland distilleries. The original grey-stone and slated-roof buildings and the malting kiln with authentic pagoda roof are still standing. The distillery is located about 100km south of Glasgow on the Machars peninsula, in the heart of Galloway. Or, to be precise, 2km south of the Burgh of Wigtown, at the north end of a bridge crossing the Bladnoch River. Wigtown is known as Scotland's National Book Town and is home to several antiquarian bookshops. After closing in 1993, Bladnoch distillery was reopened in December 2000, however on a very modest scale as production is limited to 100,000 litres of

DISTILLERY DETAILS

REGION Lowlands

OWNER Co-ordinated Development Services Ltd

ADDRESS Bladnoch, Wigtown, Wigtownshire, DG8 9AB

ROADS From Newton Stewart take the A714 to Wigtown Before entering the town go right on the A746

TEL 01988 402235, visitor centre 01988 402605

FAX 01988 402605

EMAIL enquiries@bladnoch.co.uk

WEB www.bladnoch.co.uk/index.htm

alcohol per year. The credit for this revival goes to the energetic Irishman Raymond Armstrong, whose enthusiasm and hard work overcame all obstacles to make Bladnoch operational again.

Bladnoch was founded in 1817 by the industrious brothers John and Thomas McClelland. It would remain in the hands of the family until 1912. In 1872 Charles McClelland, son of John, became the proprietor. Under his supervision the distillery was substantially enlarged from 1877 to 1878 to contain two kilns, six wash backs (two 27,000 litres and four 16,000 litres), three pot stills of older models, one 59,000-litre wash still and two 18,000-litre spirit stills. In 1905 the distillery became dormant and remained so until 10 October 1911, when William Dunville & Co. Ltd of Royal Irish Distilleries in Belfast purchased Bladnoch for £10,775. The new owners traded as T & A McClelland Ltd from 1911 until 1937. Bladnoch is a Lowland distillery but refrained from the 1920s practise of the traditional triple distillation method which is standard for the area. On 31 March 1937, due to hard times, the distillery closed until 1956. During this period the non-producing distillery shifted hands a couple of times. Shortly after World War II it was purchased by the whisky broker Ross & Coulter of Glasgow who in 1956 sold it to A.B. Grant, another Glasgow based firm. Ross & Coultner dismantled the distilling equipment and sold the three stills to the producing arm of the Swedish Alcohol Monopoly. These stills were put into work in the city of Sodertalje from 1955 until March 1966. They were instrumental in the production of a malt whisky aimed for the domestic blend 'Skeppet'. Its barley came from the province Scania (home of the vodka Absolut), peat from the province Smaaland and water from Sodertalje mains. The malting occurred in a copy of a Charles Doig kiln erected on the premises. Bladnoch was revived in 1956 by A.B. Grant and the newly established Bladnoch Distillery Ltd.

A total modernisation of the facilities during 1957 included four new long-necked single onion-shaped pot stills, manufactured at Blair of Glasgow. In 1964 the company was acquired by Ian Fisher, chairman of the Glasgow blender McGown & Cameron Ltd. In 1973 the distillery was sold to Inver House, a subsidiary of the US firm Publicker Industries Ltd of Philadelphia. During this time a decision was taken to cut the production by half by mothballing two of the stills. When Arthur Bell & Sons plc acquired Bladnoch in 1983 it had been closed for a year. Full production commenced in 1984. Bell became absorbed by Guinness in 1985 and transferred to their subsidiary United Distillers Ltd (UD) in 1989, which later became a part of Diageo's subsidiary United Distillers and Vintners Ltd (UDV). UD mothballed the distillery in June 1993, for probable demolition in the near future. In November 1994 Bladnoch estate was sold to the Irish entrepreneur Raymond Armstrong. He had plans to convert the estate to a recreation centre and holiday accommodation. A condition for the transaction was that it would never again be used as a distillery. However, Armstrong realised Bladnoch's potential as a working distillery and therefore as a part of his recreational village. After lobbying from the local community and Armstrong, Diageo gave permission for a limited revival of the distillery. The agreement, reached in 2000, permitted Bladnoch to produce a maximum of 100,000 litres of alcohol per year. As UD had left only stills and wash backs, Armstrong had to re-equip the distillery. He spent about £250,000 installing new and second-hand equipment and had Bladnoch up and running again on 18 December 2000.

Bladnoch's process and cooling water is obtained from a dam upstream of the Bladnoch River, situated 2500m away. The dam was not only built to overcome the tidal effect on the river but also, via a mill lade, to carry water to a Pelton wheel which delivered power to the distillery. Floor malting and kilning onsite were abandoned years ago. Malting of the barley is performed by Simpsons of Berwick and is lightly peated to Bladnoch's preference. The barley strains used vary but are generally Optic and Chariot. The malt is milled with a Boby mill. Mashing occurs in an old stainless steel, 8-tonne semi-Lauter mash tun equipped with new paddles. Its previous owner was the Moffat Centre at Inver House Distillery. Fermentation, which lasts for about forty-eight hours, is performed in six wooden wash backs made from Oregon pine with a capacity of 40,000 litres each. The yeast strain used is cultivated by Quest and is of their 'M' variety. Only one pair of the Blair of Glasgow stills is left and in use. They are indirectly heated and cooled by condensers. The large 13,500-litre wash still almost joins the roof and its lyne arm had to be curved in order to fit. The 10,000-litre spirit still was initially designed as a wash still, which is evident by the typical inspection portholes. The lower part of the neck is widened to boiling balls. The boil balls help to partially cool the vapours so that the heavier volatiles fall back (reflux) and a lighter spirit results. The spirit safe is, oddly, made of stainless steel like a few other components. The (revived) triple-distilled new make runs off the still at around 63% ABV. When, occasionally, a 2.5 distillation is practiced the run of the still is a bit higher, around 71% ABV. For an explanation of two-and-a-half distillation see 'Nomenclature'. The annual production is theoretically 1,300,000 litres but is limited to 100,000 litres and a maximum operation of thirty weeks per year.

Cask management is based on ten years' maturation in new and re-used ex-bourbon casks. A smaller volume matures in sherry butts. Maturation occurs in eleven warehouses of dunnage type, on-site. Some filling from older Bladnoch stock is administered by Signatory in Edinburgh. Previously, Bladnoch contributed to the blend brands The Real Mackenzie, Bell's and Inver House.

The distillery is open to visitors and has a visitor centre, shop and inn. For up-to-date information regarding admission fees and time of operation, consult the Bladnoch web site. Bladnoch is also home of the 'Whisky School', where several three-day courses are run during the year. Information may be obtained from the school's website www.whiskyschool.co.uk. Close to the distillery is Baldoon Farm, where stands the ruined castle to which Janet Dalrymple, the 'Bride of Lammermoor', came to die after her marriage to David Dunbar of Baldoon.

BLADNOCH

Structural elements and their respective weights

Structure	Observations
Colour	2
Peaty/Phenolic	
Sherried/Winey	
Fruity/Estery	3
Floral/Aldehydic	3
Cereal/Malty	2
Feinty	
Medicinal/Maritime	
Woody	
Vanilla/Honey	2
Nutty/Creamy	
Spicy	2
Sulphury	

Conclusive organoleptic sensations

	Observations
Colour	Pale straw.
Nose	Reveals a fragrant-floral and a fruity aromatic character that progressively leads to lemon peel and lemon grass. Moist hay. Barley grist.
Palate	Delicate. Lemon sherbet. A shadow of fino sherry.
Finish	Sharp, not peppery but chilli hot and concentrated. Grappa-grapey.
Comment	Light bodied and with finesse. Not so demanding and dominating. A perfect pre-dinner dram.

Issued versions

Distilled	Age	% abv	Size	Box	Version
1977	23	53.6	0.7		No versions

BLAIR ATHOL

PRONOUNCED '*blair ATHol*' from the Gaelic 'blair' meaning 'a plain', and the name of a vale, 'athole', which may have been derived from the Gaelic 'ath Fodhla', 'new Ireland'. So it may be translated as 'Plain of the new Ireland'. The distinguished-looking Blair Athol distillery is located on the southern edge of the picturesque, Victorian town of Pitlochry and is one of the oldest working distilleries in Scotland. The land occupied by the distillery was owned by the Dukes of Atholl. Nearby Blair Castle, the seat of the Dukes, is the meeting place for the illustrious and exclusive whisky society 'Keepers of the Quaich'. Membership is available for those who have made a significant contribution to the Scotch whisky industry. The castle is also

DISTILLERY DETAILS

REGION Highlands (Southern)

OWNER Diageo

ADDRESS Perth Road, Pitlochry, Perthshire, PH16 5LY

ROAD Pitlochry is situated next to the A9, about 40km north of Perth. Blair Athol is located on the southern edge of Pitlochry, 800m from the town centre

TEL 01796 482000, visitor centre 01796 482003

FAX 01796 482036

BLAIR ATHOL

home to the Duke's 'Atholl Highlanders', the sole remaining private army in the UK. Note, the distillery spells its name with a single 'l' whereas the village, Blair Atholl, in which the distillery is not located, uses two 'l's.

The first trace of a distillery on the premises of Blair Athol, as we know it, goes back to 1798. That year John Stewart and Robert Robertson founded a distillery by the name of 'Aldour', after the burn from where the distillery obtained its water. Its source is found on the nearby Ben Vrackie. The Gaelic spelling of the burns name is 'Alt na dour' translated as 'burn of the otter'. The distillery may initially have been an illicit operation during its rather short-lived existence as no formal registration documents have been found. Another explanation may be that it did not manage to survive the heavy burden of the day's taxes. However, taxes were reduced by the 1823 Excise Act and the distillery was revived again, in 1825, by John Robertson, who also decided to change its name from Aldour to Blair Athol. Robertson leased the land from the Duke of Atholl. Later, in 1826, the land lease and the distillery were acquired by the Connachar family, via their Alexander Connachar & Co. firm. It stayed within the family for more than fifty years, although it was dormant for many years around 1830. From 1860 the control of the distillery was in the hands of the heir, Elizabeth Connachar, until it was sold off in 1882. The new owners, P. Mackenzie & Co., enlarged the distillery significantly. A new malting floor and malt bins were added, which altogether with other improvements contributed to an increased annual output of nearly 450,000 litres. P. Mackenzie & Co. reconstituted itself in 1897 as P. Mackenzie & Co. Distillers Ltd, and shortly thereafter acquired the Dufftown-Glenlivet Distillery. P. Mackenzie & Co. closed Blair Athol in 1932 and in 1933 was taken over by J. Arthur Bell & Sons. Arthur Bell & Sons continued to keep Blair Athol mothballed until 1949. An ongoing, comprehensive modernisation and improvement programme was launched that year: two new stills were installed in 1973, a dark grain plant in 1975, four stainless steel wash backs in 1982, and a visitor centre in 1987. The distillery has been up and running without interruption other than for preventive maintenance since 1949. Arthur Bell & Sons became a part of Guinness in 1985 and was transferred to their subsidiary United Distillers Ltd (UD). UD merged with Grand Metropolitan in 1997 to form Diageo. Blair Athol proudly proclaims to be the 'Home of Bell's Whisky' and Bell's line of blended whiskies, to which 96% of its production goes.

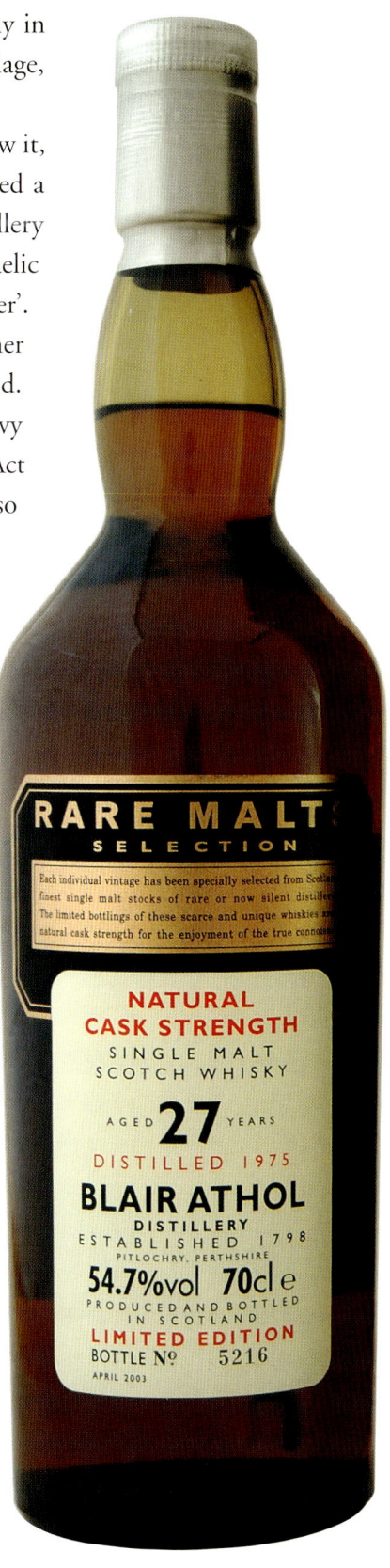

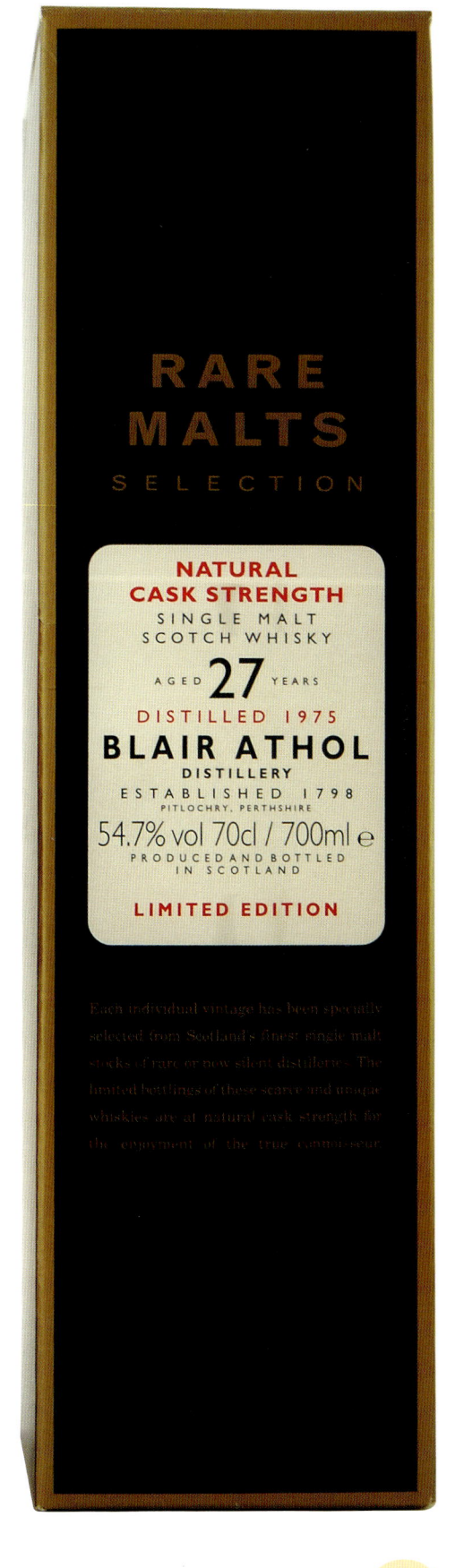

Wash backs at Blair Athol

Distilling water is obtained from Blair Athol's own burn, the Allt na dour, which runs through the distillery on its way to the River Tummel. Process water flows from Loch a Choire, situated five kilometres high up on the heathery southern slopes of Ben Vrackie. Floor malting used to be performed on site until 1960 and the malt was dried with peat from the Orkneys. The malted barley is now lightly peat-smoked to Blair Athol's specification by Glen Ord's central malting operations. Prisma and Optic are the barley strains of preference. As storage space is limited at the distillery, the malt is usually delivered twice daily. The malt is milled by a traditional Porteus mill. Batches of eight metric tonnes at a time are mashed in the large stainless steel semi-Lauter tun. The wort is distributed to the four 18,000-litre larch wood wash backs and the four stainless steel wash backs, two holding 25,000 litres and two 30,000 litres. Yeast for the fermentation is a Distiller's yeast produced by Kerry. The fermentation is long, lasting for two to three days, however short fermentation is also applied. The pot stills, including the two added in 1973, are all of traditional onion shape with straight necks and lacking boiling balls. Heating is indirect via steam pans and cooling is by condensers. The wash stills' volumes are 33,000 litres each, and the spirit stills are 11,500 litres. The distillation cycle lasts for about four hours per batch. The configuration of the stills' integrated heating and cooling system makes the distillery the most energy efficient in the trade. Capacity is 2,000,000 litres of alcohol per annum, but it is not operated at full capacity.

Cask management is based on an eight-year maturation period, in ex-bourbon casks. A smaller volume matures in sherry butts. All whisky intended for sale as single malt is matured in the five bonded warehouses on the premises, whereas whisky intended for Bell's and other blends are matured on other, not so romantic, sites. Bottling occurs in plants in Leven and Glasgow.

The distillery is open for visitors and has a visitor centre with audiovisual exhibitions and a shop. Worth visiting are Kinnaird Cottage and Birnam Wood, the latter with King Duncan's castle and other Macbeth associations. During a stay at Kinnaird Cottage, near Moulin, Robert Louis Stevenson wrote some of his short stories, including *The Merry Men* and *Thrawn Janet*. The Fish Ladder, an artificial waterfall with glass-fronted viewing chambers, gives visitors underwater views of salmon and other fish making their way up and down the river that runs through the town.

The Blair Athol visitor centre

BLAIR ATHOL

Structural elements and their respective weights

Structure	Observations
Colour	9
Peaty/Phenolic	1
Sherried/Winey	1
Fruity/Estery	3
Floral/Aldehydic	
Cereal/Malty	2
Feinty	
Medicinal/Maritime	
Woody	2
Vanilla/Honey	2
Nutty/Creamy	3
Spicy	1
Sulphury	

Conclusive organoleptic sensations

	Observations
Colour	Amontillado sherry.
Nose	Sawdust from oak, chestnut purée, butter, chocolate chip cookie and honeyed biscuits. Fading fragrant smokiness.
Palate	Hazelnut spread. Chocolate. Lemon peel. Restrained sherry. Creamy and malty.
Finish	Complex. Long, lively gingery, spicy and sweet. Ripe banana intertwined with spicy gingery confectionary.
Comment	Medium body. All the sumptuous fruit makes it a perfect after-diner dram.

Issued versions

Distilled	Age	% abv	Size	Box	Version
1975	27	54.7	0.7		No versions

BRORA

Pronounced '*BROra*', and formerly called Clynelish Distillery (see the chapter regarding the new Clynelish), it is located 3km inland, north of the town Brora at the mouth of Strait of Brora. It is believed that brora or 'bru'r aa' is Norse for 'the bridge across the river'. Some historic sources claim that the township of Brora was hastily founded when the Duke of Sutherland evicted almost overnight 15,000 crofters and burned 500-plus crofts. The reason, it is said, was simply that the Duke wanted free and open space for his herd of cheviot sheep. The ones who refused to leave were brutally forced away, either to the shantytown of Brora or elsewhere. Others emigrated to America and Australia. This period in Scottish history is known as the 'Highland Clearances'.

DISTILLERY DETAILS

REGION Highlands (Northern)

OWNER Diageo (Historic Scotland)

ADDRESS Brora, Sutherlandshire, KW9 6LR

ROADS A9, 3km north of the village Brora, follow Balnacoil Road

TEL 01408 623000 (new Clynelish)

FAX 01408 623004 (new Clynelish)

Other sources argue that the Duke was working in the interest of the locals who lived in extreme poverty and erected improved living conditions for the suffering ones.

A few years after the Clearance, in 1819, the Duke decided to give some support to the starving population in Brora. He simply, for £750, erected a distillery on one of his farms. At the distillery the poor could convert their meagre harvest of barley into a fluid which could be traded for a higher profit. It was also a move to provide competition against the illegal distilleries creating social unrest in the area. The ready availability of cheap, local workers forced to dig coal from the nearby Brora coalfields (opened 1529) was another factor. The coal turned out to be of rather poor quality and not fit to fire the pot stills and had to be mixed with peat from nearby bogs. The first licenced manager for the distillery, by now named Clynelish Distillery, was a Midlothian man, James Harper. He suffered hardship and went broke in 1827. Harper left John Matheson in charge until he had recovered financially and resumed control of the distillery from 1828 to 1834. The lease and licence was thereafter transferred to Andrew Ross, who continued operations without any major improvements or noticeable success. In 1846 he sold his licence to industrious George Lawson, who initiated an expansion and improvement programme, including replacement of the stills. Later, in 1878, Lawson launched George Lawson & Sons Co., which operated the distillery until 1896. That year George Lawson & Sons sold the distillery to Glasgow-based Ainslie & Co., which continued to carry out a revamping and extensive modernisation of Clynelish, including new warehouses. As another victim of the Pattison adventure, Ainslie & Co. had to declare bankruptcy in 1912, whereafter the distillery became the joint property of James Risk, former owner of Bankier Distillery, and influential in The Distillers Co. Ltd (DCL). A holding company, the Clynelish Distillery Co. Ltd, with a capital of £20,000, was set up by the joint owners the same year.

Ainslie & Co. was later reconstructed and transformed from the distiller's trade to the blender's, merged with DCL and, hence, became a part of Diageo's United Distillers and Vintners Ltd (UDV). In 1916 John Walker & Sons Ltd acquired a minority stake in the holding company. The same year operations were expanded as the Coleburn Distillery was acquired. During 1925

DCL became the sole owner by acquiring all stocks. In 1930 DCL transferred Brora to its subsidiary Scottish Malt Distillers Ltd (SMD). Clynelish was silent from March 1931 to September 1938. Wartime restrictions forced another closure, this time lasting from May 1941 until November 1945. Unproven rumours claim that a low volume production did occur during the war years. Nearly two decades later, in the early 1960s, some minor improvements and refurbishment occurred. Power generated by the Pelton water wheel and the Shanks of Arbroath steam engine were replaced with electricity. Oil-fired burners replaced the hand-stoked coal furnaces, which had been supplied with coal from the nearby Ross Pit, and the stills became indirectly heated. As these modernisations were not enough to increase production, a decision was taken to add a second distillery on the premises. The new and super-modern distillery, begun in 1966, was ready in August 1967. It was erected on a hilltop a few hundred metres away from the old one. Both distilleries produced in parallel from August 1967 until August 1968 when the old Clynelish was closed. During this short overlapping period casks with whiskies from either distillery were wrongfully stencilled as 'Clynelish'. However, internally they were recognised as Clynelish A (the new) and Clynelish B (the old). In 1969 the old Clynelish was reopened with the intention to produce a heavy, peated Islay-like whisky. Caol Ila was, incidentally, closed for refurbishing at this time. Production of this highly peated whisky earmarked solely for the blending industry occurred until 17 March 1983, when the distillery formally closed – hopefully not forever. It is believed that distilling for maintenance purposes may have occurred beyond the formal closing date. As only a few easy-to-replace elements, like the spirit safe and receiver, are missing a resurrection of the distillery may be possible. In the 1990s this Victorian distillery was declared, and hence saved, as a national treasure. It is now placed in the custody of Historic Scotland.

When the old Clynelish re-opened in 1969, a problem arose with the two distilleries carrying the same name. The proprietor was forced by the Scotch Whisky Association (SWA) to change the name of one of the two Clynelish distilleries, so the old one reverted back to a name it was said to have carried on and off for short periods during its early history: Brora. A similar incident had occurred at the end of nineteenth century when Glen Grant operated two different distilleries under the same name (the other one was renamed Caperdonich). Authorities at that time formulated a rule, still in effect, making it illegal to apply the same name to two or more distilleries.

A previous water source, according to A. Barnard, was a small stream that originated in a loch some miles away amongst the hills and collected in a stone cistern on the premises. Water was later taken from the same source used for the new distillery: the Clynemilton Burn. It is situated on the shoulder of Col Bhein and flows over bare red sandstone to a dam. Floor malting occurred on site until 1967. Golden Promise and Triumph seem to have been the barley strains of preference during this period. The kiln, with its classic pagoda roof, is still standing. The ppm level (phenolic level) oscillated from time to time and went from 7ppm to as high as 45ppm, peaking in 1970–77. During this period Brora received its malt from the same maltster used by Caol Ila and Talisker. Caol Ila was closed from 1972–74 and Brora served as a backup for this and others of the distillery group's Islay distilleries. The malt was milled with a traditional mill. The mash tun had a capacity of 31,500 litres feeding six wooden wash backs, each with a capacity of 29,500 litres. The yeast strain used was Distiller's yeast. The wash still accommodated 22,500 litres and the spirit still 17,700 litres. Both were onion shaped, equipped with boiling balls, indirectly heated with oil burners, and cooled with traditional submerged worms. Annual maximal output was 1,000,000 litres of alcohol. Spent grain went to a local piggery. The whisky was a component of Johnnie Walker Red Label.

The distillery and its old stills can be viewed when visiting Clynelish. However, almost all the plant and equipment has been removed. Only the oil-fired stills, receiver and the two worm tubs remain in place. See the chapter regarding Clynelish for further information.

• BRORA •

BRORA

Structural elements and their respective weights

STRUCTURE	OBSERVATIONS
Colour	3
Peaty/Phenolic	3
Sherried/Winey	
Fruity/Estery	3
Floral/Aldehydic	2
Cereal/Malty	1
Feinty	2
Medicinal/Maritime	4
Woody	2
Vanilla/Honey	
Nutty/Creamy	1
Spicy	2
Sulphury	

Issued versions

DISTILLED	AGE	% ABV	SIZE	BOX	VERSION
1972	22	58.7	0.7	None	
1972	22	60.02	0.7		
1972	22	61.1	0.7		
1972	22	54.9	0.7		
1972	22	59.1	0.7		
1974	20	57.5	0.7		
1975	20	60.75	0.2	Box 2	
1975	20	54.9	0.7		
1975	20	59.1	0.75		
1975	20	59.1	0.75	None	USA
1977	21	56.9	0.7		
1977	24	56.1	0.7		
1982	20	58.1	0.7		

Conclusive organoleptic sensations

	OBSERVATIONS
Colour	Pale gold.
Nose	Seaweed and iodine. Clean and unspoiled peat smoke. Citrus notes on the top layer. A hint of leather, like car seats and saddles. Some veils of barley and peaches and tropical aromas like coconut.
Palate	The peat sensation on the palate is more intense than on the nose. The impression of salt (however non-existent) is immense and stylishly balanced. Spicy, with prickling peppery feeling, combined with refreshing lemon notes. Slight oily with some waxiness. Gentle, near silky oaky tannins.
Finish	The peat returns for an impressive finale and the oakiness is present as a perfect counterpoint. The permanence of its attributes fades out in a very slow and pleasing pace.
Comment	Full bodied, big, robust and richly flavoured malt with unadulterated maritime character. A perfect after-dinner dram, or for solitary contemplation.

CAOL ILA

Pronounced '*kaal eeela*', it is Gaelic for 'the sound of Islay', the sound that separates Islay from the island Jura. Caol Ila is situated on the brink of a sheltered bay on the northern side of Islay and is not only the largest distillery on the island but also one of the largest in Diageo's portfolio. On the other side of the narrow sound the Isle of Jura's famous, towering Paps of Jura are clearly visible. The distillery's production building is a rather unattractive contrast to the beauty of the surrounding area. However, this is much compensated for by the views from the panoramic window-framed still hall. The breathtaking view is undoubtedly one of the best of any Scottish distillery, with the exception perhaps of Scapa. There is a nearby (500m) ferry port in Port Askaig, serving Islay and Jura. When the distillery was built, the houses erected on the hillside overlooking the distillery were set aside for its workers. This small community had its own shop and Mission Hall. Several of the houses still stand and are used by today's distillery personnel, some of whom are the third generation to work at Caol Ila. As most of the production goes to the blending trade, Caol Ila has not been in the spotlight as much as its Islay relatives.

DISTILLERY DETAILS

REGION Islay

OWNER Diageo

ADDRESS Port Askaig, Isle of Islay, Argyllshire, PA46 7RL

ROADS Main A846 from Bowmore turn off just before Port Askaig

TEL 01496 302760

FAX 01496 302763

CAOL ILA

The site where Caol Ila was built was previously used as a lead ore washing work because of the large supply of water running off the nearby Loich nan Ban. When Hector Henderson started looking for a site for his new distillery in early 1840, it was the plentiful supply of water that led his tracks to this sheltered bay. Henderson, a former partner to the Littlemill Distillery Co. in Dunbartonshire and in business with some Campbeltown distilleries, had sold out and moved to Islay. Industrious but restless, he decided to return to the trade by building himself a new distillery on the island. His plans materialised when he created Henderson, Lamont & Co. in 1846 and inaugurated its jewel, the Caol Ila distillery. By parallel investments, not only in the Islay distillery Lochindaal but also in the Camlachie in Glasgow, Henderson overspent his financial resources and had to sell out. In 1852 the distillery was sold to Norman Buchanan, owner of the Isle of Jura distillery. The distillery is situated a few kilometres away from Caol Ila on the other side of the strait. A decade later, in 1863, Buchanan encountered financial troubles and had to sell. The new owner was Bulloch, Lade & Co., a blending firm based in Glasgow and owner of the Catrine Distillery in Glasgow. Bulloch, et al. carried out an extensive modernisation of the distillery in 1879. The upgrade extended Caol Ila's output to 650,000 litres. When the new buildings were erected in 1879 a new substance was used: concrete. These were the first buildings on the island to use concrete and were a novelty for its time. The partnership was converted to a limited company in 1896. During the Bulloch era, a small pier was built in front of the distillery to cope with the rise and fall of the tide. Hence, cargo ships could bring in supplies of coal and barley directly to the distillery and return with matured whisky to the mainland, unhindered by the shift of tides. A later owner had its own little transporter, a so-called 'puffer' named *Pibroch*. *Pibroch* was in regular use until she was retired in 1972. Today, malt is transported by lorry from Port Ellen Maltings and road tankers are sent via the regular passenger ferry to the mainland for cask filling and maturation off Islay.

Again the aftermath of the Pattison era and wartime hardships had a distillery on its knees. Hence, in 1920, Bulloch, Lade & Co., decided to go into voluntary liquidation. J. B. O'Brien acquired the limited company in 1920 and in 1921 sold it to the newly formed Caol Ila Distillery Co. Ltd, which acted as a subsidiary to Robertson & Baxter Ltd, with Dewar's Ltd and Distillers Company Ltd (DCL) as joint investors. DCL took complete control as the sole owner in 1927.

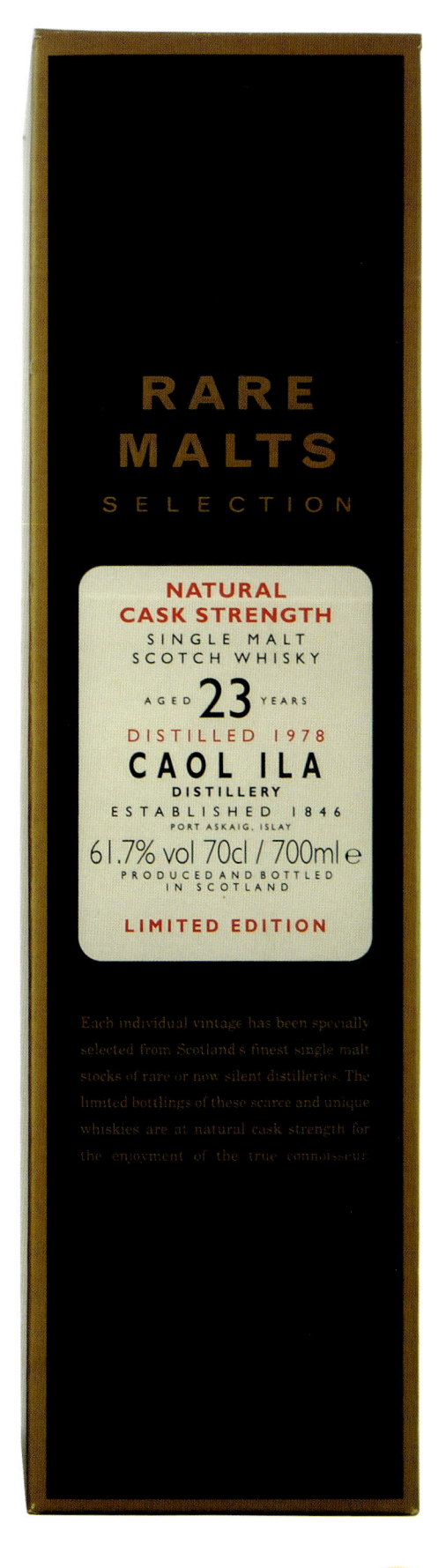

In 1930 the responsibilities for daily operations were transferred to DCL's subsidiary Scottish Malt Distilleries Ltd (SMD). Via mergers and acquisitions, through Guinness and the United Distillers Ltd (UD), Caol Ila finally ended up in the Diageo group in 1997. For two periods Caol Ila was dormant, first from 1930 to 1937 and then from 1941 to 1945. After the war, when the restrictions were lifted, Caol Ila was producing at full steam again. During the first dormant period the Island Creamery used a few of the buildings and some of the equipment was removed. Since neither preventive maintenance nor ongoing modernisation had occurred since the early 1920s, it was decided in the early 1970s to completely replace everything old and worn out at Caol Ila, except the warehouses. A vast sum for its time, £1,000,000 was allocated for the task. The result was a modern, effective production site where the architecture is sadly discordant with the surrounding landscape. The rebuilding, which occurred from April 1972 to January 1974, led to a supply problem for the blending industry. The rich flow of malt whisky with an Islay twist became simply a trickle. Hence, the Highland distillery Clynelish (see the chapter for Brora) was quickly converted to mimic Islay characterised malt whisky and serve as a backup site for Caol Ila. When Caol Ila reopened in 1974 its paired old stills had been replaced with six new replicas of the two old ones. Push-button control panels had been installed and all equipment was of the optimum size to allow for maximum efficiency. Floor maltings were abandoned in 1970 and malt has been brought in from Port Ellen since 1974. Minor updates have occurred since 1974. The mash tun, for instance, was lately converted to a semi-Lauter. An interesting historical aspect is that Caol Ila has always had indirectly heated spirit stills but direct coal-fired wash stills. The wash stills were updated with automatic stoking in the 1960s and later converted.

Process water comes from the Loch Torrabolls or Loch nam Man (meaning 'the Lady's loch' in Gaelic) situated in the hills above the sound, 1.5km away from the distillery. The water arrives via a small waterfall, which in older days drove a waterwheel delivering power to the distillery. Cooling water is drawn directly from the sea. Malt, peated to various specifications as high as 35ppm, is delivered by nearby Port Ellen central maltings. Caol Ila does not operate with a fixed ppm attached to its mash bill. Even unpeated barley has been processed here since 1999. The barley variety used for the weekly sixteen mashes is basically Chariot, but others may be used as well. Each batch uses eleven metric tonnes of malt, which is milled by a traditional Porteus mill, made in the 1950s. The grist goes to a cast-iron semi-Lauter mash tun, painted cream with a copper canopy. With a diameter of nearly seven metres and capable of swallowing 11.5 metric tonnes of grist, or 55,000 litres, it is the largest mash tun in the trade. The tun, the pot stills and the spirit safes were built by Abercrombie of Alloa in 1974. It is said that the eight 60,000 litres and 5m high wash backs, built by a work crew on site and made from Oregon pine, have never leaked a drop. Yeast for the fermentation is Distiller's yeast from Mauri's. Caol Ila practice short (80 hours) and long (120 hours) fermentation cycles. The magnificent still house contains a parade of six large, shining and broad-necked onion-shaped stills. Their gently sloping lyne arms, with different angles for the wash and spirit stills, all have a condenser attached. The pots are all now indirectly heated by steam – steam pans for the wash stills and steam coils for the spirit stills. The hatches trim on the three 35,345-litre wash stills are painted red, and on the three 29,549-litre spirit painted blue. The charge is 18,000 litres for the wash stills and 12,000 litres for the spirit stills. The average time for distillation is seven to eight hours. With a maximum annual production of 3,500,000 litres of alcohol, Caol Ila is one of Diageo's top producers. Most of the spirit produced goes to the blend industry – mainly Johnnie Walker and Bell's, but also to the 'own label' brands trade, such as Tesco, Sainsbury, etc. Caol Ila was not available as a distillery-bottled single malt whisky until 1988.

Cask management is based on a maturation period of ten years. Primarily all maturation occurs in ex-bourbon casks of second and third refills. A smaller volume is, for experimental reasons, matured in sherry casks. There are warehouses on the premises, limited to 6,000 casks. Nearby are a few other dunnage-type warehouses left over from the defunct Lochindaal distillery, which closed in 1929. They are used for storing and maturing Caol Ila whisky earmarked for bottling as single malts, but also by others such as Port Ellen. The lion's share of the production is, however, transported by road tanker to Diageo's mainland warehouses in

Blackgrange at Cambus and Carsebridge at Menstrie where casks are filled and matured. Bottling is performed at Leven in Fife. Caol Ila adds it marks to blends such as Bell's, Johnnie Walker's different labels, White Horse, Black Bottle and Swing.

The distillery is open to visitors, by appointment. There is a visitor centre and shop on the premises. Worth visits are all the Islay distilleries, and when on a whisky pilgrimage to the island include the nearby Isle of Jura (ferry from Islay via Port Askaig). Another highlight is the ruined Dunyvaig Castle, a fortress of the MacDonalds, the 'Lords of the Isles' before James IV asserted his authority in 1493. The Big Strand is a superb seven mile stretch of beach along the west-facing Laggan Bay.

CAOL ILA

Structural elements and their respective weights

Structure	Observations
Colour	4
Peaty/Phenolic	4
Sherried/Winey	
Fruity/Estery	2
Floral/Aldehydic	1
Cereal/Malty	1
Feinty	2
Medicinal/Maritime	4
Woody	
Vanilla/Honey	
Nutty/Creamy	2
Spicy	2
Sulphury	

Conclusive organoleptic sensations

	Observations
Colour	Golden with greenish tinge.
Nose	Fragrant peaty smoke. Medicinal, iodine and sea spray. Hint of citrus, a lemony whiff. Crushed barley.
Palate	A flow of peaty, smoky notes that escalate. Nuts, citrus fruit and dark chocolate. Olive oily. Gently interspersed with prickling pepper and salty-feeling markers.
Finish	The peaty, smoky note pitches towards the finale. Oaky, tannic dry. Long, complex, and in perfect balance.
Comment	Full bodied. Dry, pungent. Distinct maritime character. A classy replacement for, or a complement to, the after-dinner tobacco.

Issued versions

Distilled	Age	% abv	Size	Box	Version
1975	20	61.12	0.75		
1975	20	61.12	0.75	None	USA
1975	20	61.12	0.2	Box 2	
1975	20	61.18	0.75		
1975	21	61.3	0.7		
1977	20	61.3	0.75		
1977	21	61.3	0.7		
1977	21	63.1	0.7		

CARDOW (formerly CARDHU)

Pronounced '*kar doo*', the Gaelic spelling is Creag dubh, corrupted as Cardow, meaning 'the black rock'. This may refer to the nearby Mannoch Hills, which look rather black from a distance. The distillery has oscillated between the names Cardhu and Cardow over time, which has confused consumers believing it to be two different whiskies. Recently, in 2004, it was decided that the name should revert back to that of the farm on which the distillery is built: Cardow. The Cardow distillery, situated on a hill, offers a stunning view of Speyside. The old kiln, no longer in use, was recently equipped with an ornamental pagoda roof.

DISTILLERY DETAILS

REGION Highlands (Speyside)
OWNER Diageo.
ADDRESS Knockando, Aberlour, Morayshire, AB38 7RY
ROADS B9102, off the A941 Elgin to Grantown road
TEL 01340 872550, visitor centre 01340 872555
FAX 01340 872556

• CARDOW •

The first distillery linked to the Cardow farm, which is situated on the north bank of the river Spey, was an illegal operation. With easy access to peat and water, remotely located from the nearest village and hidden among the Mannoch Hills, it was perfectly situated. From here, small casks were transported nightly by pony to the black markets in Elgin and Forres. John Cumming, the shrewd and infamous whisky smuggler, founded the still in 1811. He simply decided to control the production link in the chain from barley ear to brim-filled clay crocks. Over time he encountered several clashes with the 'gaugers' (Excise officers) on their never-ending chase for production sites not paying taxes. After having been convicted three times for illegal distilling, Cumming decided to get legal. He applied for and received a distilling licence in 1824. The court judgements are framed and hung proudly on the wall of the distillery manager's office today. The illegal days, now over, were lined with amusing stories of how Cumming and his wife Helen tried to fool the authorities. Fumes from the nearby distillery were masked by Helen's intensive cooking and baking. Randomly visiting Excise officers were routinely invited to lodging and sumptuous dinners, giving Cumming time to hide traces of his activities. Moreover, a red flag was hoisted on the barn as a pre-arranged signal to alarm and warn neighbours and fellow moon-shiners to hide their equipment and casks. 'Over-the-counter', or rather 'through-the-window', sale was another source of income. It is said that bottles, or crocks, were passed trough the farm's kitchen window for a shilling apiece.

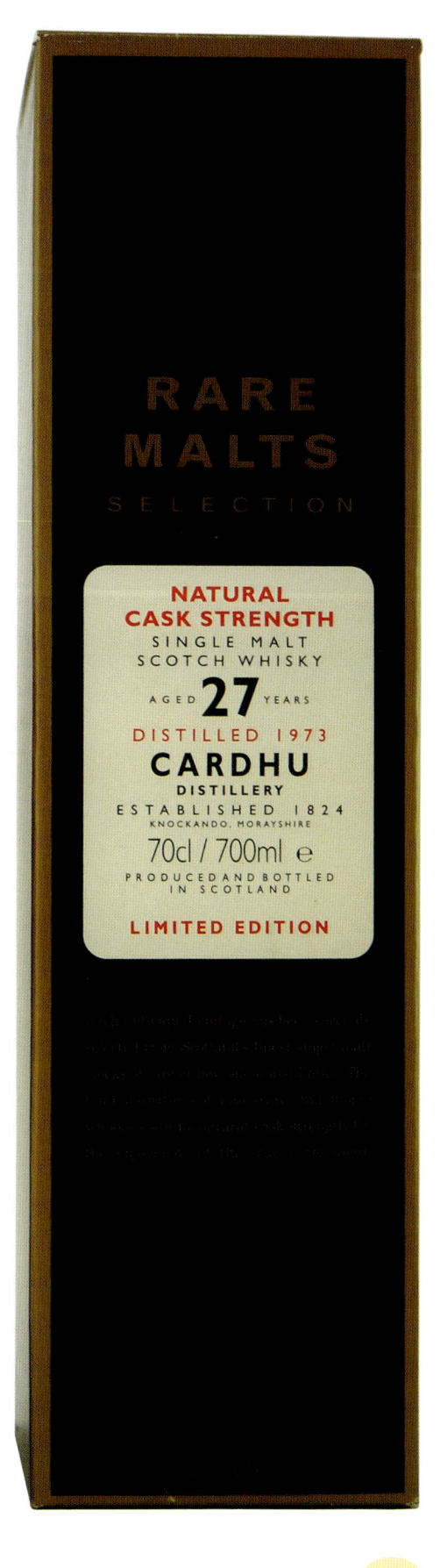

Cumming met his maker in 1846 and the oldest son, Lewis, who inherited the lease jointly with his brother Hugh, took over the responsibilities for managing the distillery. Helen, who lived to be ninety-five years old, outlived her son. Sadly, Lewis passed away in 1872, leaving the daily operations to his wife Elisabeth (née Robertson). She, probably the first woman distiller in Scotland, managed to keep production up until 1884, with the help of three hired hands. The farm lease, with the still attached, had to be renewed every nineteenth year. The Cummings, uncertain of lease renewal, neither invested in the distillery nor performed preventive maintenance. Managing a nearly worn-out production facility, the dynamic and talented Elisabeth had to make a decision: either step out of the trade or invest. She opted for the latter, bought land from an adjacent farm, and invested in a state-of-the-art distillery, which she had up and running with annual capacity of 270,000 litres in 1884. She sold her old patched and thin-skinned pot stills to William Grant, then managing director at Mortlach Distillery, for the enormous sum of £102.97. With Elisabeth's pot stills as foundation, William Grant established the legendary Speyside distillery Glenfiddich in Dufftown. Elisabeth adopted Cardow as the trademark for her new distillery and claimed to be the only Speyside distillery to not profit by adding 'Glenlivet' to its name. Cardow proudly stood on its own and demonstrated its consistent quality, a quality that was recognised and sought after among whisky blenders of the time. Cardow sold the lion's share of its whisky to the blender John Walker of Kilmarnock; the whisky became the major malt whisky blended into the Walker's global success 'Johnnie Walker' and is still going strong as the core of the blend. Elisabeth became recognised as 'The Queen of the Whisky Trade' and managed the distillery first by herself and later with the assistance of her son John until he took full responsibility. In 1893 Cardow's largest customer, Johnnie Walker, presented an offer that could hardly be refused: the distillery shifted hands for £20,500. The deal also included that the Cumming family was granted the responsibility for the daily operations of the distillery. John became a director of Johnnie Walker and managed the distillery for several years. He retired in 1924 and his son Ronald continued as Johnnie Walker's export manager; he became chairman of Johnnie Walker and ended up as chairman of the Distillers Company Ltd (DCL). A name change was decided and the whisky became 'Old vatted Cardhu'. This change lasted until 1908 when the name reverted back to Cardow. In 1981 the name changed back to Cardhu, and in 2004 it reverted to the initial Cardow – probably the last name change within the foreseeable future. The new owners expanded the distillery in 1897 by upgrading from two to four stills. Johnnie Walker went public in 1923 and was absorbed by the Distillers Company Ltd (DCL) in 1925. In 1930 their subsidiary Scottish Malt Distillers Ltd (SMD) took over the licence.

The distillery went through a rebuilding and modernisation phase in 1960–61, when the rows of pot stills were again expanded, from four to six. At the same time power sources like the old water wheel and the 32 hp. steam engine were removed and replaced with electric power from the grid. The coal-fired pot stills' direct heating system was replaced with indirect heating in 1971. From 1922 to 1924, enterprising experiments with indirect heating were

Spirit safe at Cardow

carried out but were found to be too expensive. These were probably the first stills equipped with what is the standard of today. A new, gleaming (polished daily) copper spirit safe was installed in 1999.

Water for cooling comes from the Lyne Burn and the process water is brought in from the nearby Mannoch Hill spring. The malt comes from a central maltster, Burghead Maltings in Elgin. In the old days when floor malting occurred on site, the peat for the kiln was harvested in the Mannoch Hills and, therefore Cardow's whisky was different compared to today's. Malt strains used are Chariot and Optic and are generally brought in unpeated. The malt is milled by a traditional Porteus mill. Mashing occurs in a mash tun made of stainless steel with a polished copper canopy and a capacity of 56,000 litres or seven metric tonnes. The wort is diverted to eight wooden wash backs, each made from Scottish larch. Their capacity is 50,000 litres each. For the sake of visitors, one has a window and a wiper, which make it possible to study the process without inhaling the strong fumes generated by the fermentation. The yeast strain used is a mix of Distiller's and Brewer's. A short fermentation period, lasting sixty hours, is maintained. The still hall is occupied by three larger wash stills and three smaller spirit stills. They are all onion shaped with tall necks and sloping shoulders and indirectly heated via steam coils. The capacity for the wash stills is 9,200 litres and the spirit stills 7,200 litres. Their long, sleek, swan necks, ending in copper condensers, contribute to a reflux that gives a special character to Cardow. Capacity is 1,900,000 litres of alcohol per annum.

Cask management is based on a maturation period of twelve years. Only ex-bourbon casks are used for the whisky earmarked for the blending trade. These casks may be re-used up to five times. A smaller volume is matured in sherry casks. Maturation occurs in bonded warehouses located on site. Bottling is performed in Kilmarnock, where about 70% goes to the blending trade, especially to Johnnie Walker's range of brands and the Swing.

The distillery is open for visitors and has a visitor centre and shop. Worth a visit is Balvenie Castle and Mortlach Parish Church, one of the oldest churches in Scotland. It claims to have been in regular use since about AD566.

CARDOW (formerly CARDHU)

Structural elements and their respective weights

STRUCTURE	OBSERVATIONS
Colour	3
Peaty/Phenolic	1
Sherried/Winey	
Fruity/Estery	3
Floral/Aldehydic	3
Cereal/Malty	3
Feinty	
Medicinal/Maritime	
Woody	
Vanilla/Honey	2
Nutty/Creamy	2
Spicy	1
Sulphury	

Conclusive organoleptic sensations

	OBSERVATIONS
Colour	Pale gold.
Nose	Trace of peat smoke. Fragrant and flowery, violets stick out from the bouquets. Fruity, peaches and sweet tangerines. Honey sweetness and cinnamon. Distinct malty notes.
Palate	Fresh, clean sweetness. Hints of smoke and spice. Cinnamon again. Nuttiness, slightly bitter, as from combined almond and peach stone flavours.
Finish	Distant veils of peat smoke that drift away. Rather sweet with tangerine notes kept through the finale.
Comment	Light bodied, and refreshing. A super dram at a garden party. If gender may be used as a descriptor then this is certainly feminine.

Issued versions

DISTILLED	AGE	% ABV	SIZE	BOX	VERSION
1973	25	60.5	0.75		
1973	27	60.02	0.7		

CLYNELISH

Pronounced *'klyn leesh'*, it is Gaelic for 'fertile plain'. Clynelish is a rather new distillery, located 3km inland. It is situated north of the town of Brora and close to the old Clynelish distillery, which was renamed 'Brora' in 1969 (see the chapter regarding Brora). Clynelish, which was erected in 1966–67 in response to the 1960s whisky boom, was in full production in August 1967. It is a large and very modern glass, steel and concrete structure that contrasts sharply to the older, rather smaller traditional distillery. When the licensee Scottish Malt Distillers Ltd (SMD) needed increased production capacity, a decision was taken to construct a brand new, ultramodern distillery rather than expand the old one. Extra land from the Clynelish farm was acquired and a new water source had to be located. The water is now taken from the Clynemilton Burn, once the water supply for the town of Brora. The new distillery was erected a few hundred metres from the old one, which closed a year later, in August 1968.

Distillery details

REGION Highlands (Northern)

OWNER Diageo

ADDRESS Brora, Sutherlandshire, KW9 6LR

ROADS A9, 3km north of the village Brora, follow Balnacoil Road

TEL 01408 623000

FAX 01408 623004

• CLYNELISH •

When the old Clynelish reopened in 1969 a problem arose by having two distilleries carrying the same name, and the proprietor was instructed by the 'Scotch Whisky Association' to change the name of one of the two Clynelish distilleries. The candidate became the old one which reverted back to a name it was said to have carried on and off for shorter periods during its history – Brora. A similar incident had occurred at the end of nineteenth century when Glen Grant operated two different distilleries under the same name.

The cooling as well as the process water is obtained from the same old reliable burn that has been in constant use by the town of Brora since 1819. It is the Clynemilton Burn, which flows over red sandstone slopes to a collecting dam and is fed to the distillery by gravity. The malt is provided by Glen Ord in Muir of Ord. The preferred peat level specified by Clynelish is about 5 ppm and the barley varieties used are Chalice and Optic, cultivated in Scotland. The malt is brought in by lorries almost daily and milled by a traditional Porteus mill. The capacity of the stainless steel full Lauter mash tun is 12.5 metric tonnes. It has a typical copper canopy as a lid. The wort is passed from the mash tun to a cluster of eight wash backs, each made of Oregon pine, with a capacity of 58,600 litres each. All wash backs have switchers. On its way the wort passes a large open stainless steel underback and an Alfa-Laval heat exchanger. The configuration is set up to sustain sixteen mashes per week. The yeast strain used is

Spirit safe at Clynelish

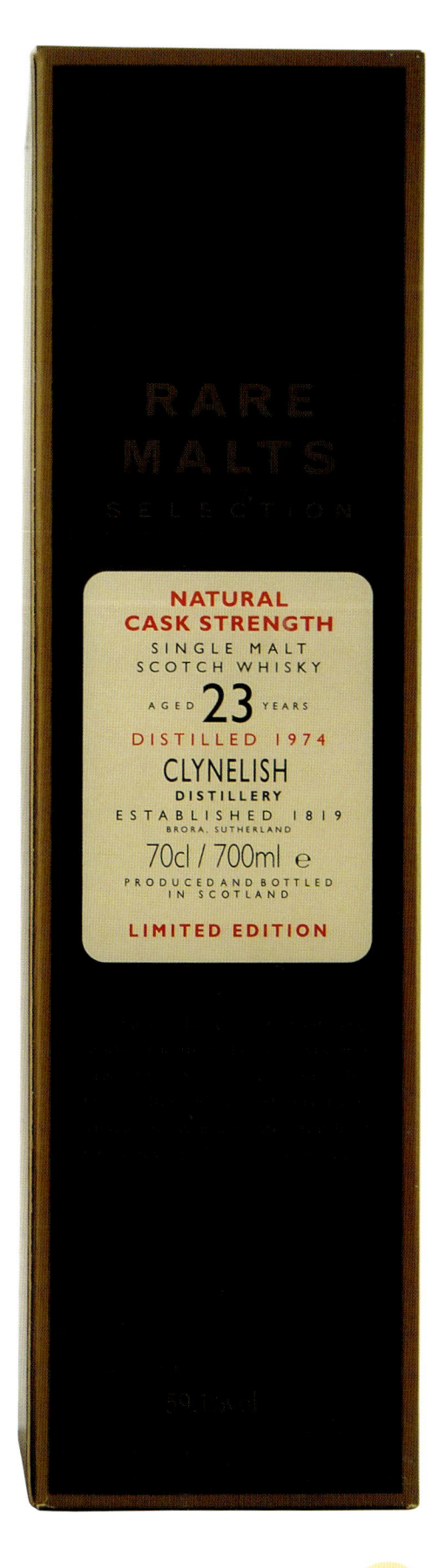

Distiller's yeast, from Kerry. The still hall is magnificent with its large polished copper pot stills, parading in a line. There are three wash stills, with a volume of 25,050 litres each, and three spirit stills, with a volume of 26,241 litres each. All six are paired and their necks taper to straight lyne arms that end at copper condensers. Their necks are rather short and thick. All are onion shaped, equipped with boiling balls and heated indirectly by steam pans. The stills and the two spirit safes are the work of Abercrombie of Alloa's coppersmiths. Annual maximum output is 3,400,000 litres of alcohol.

Cask management is based on a fourteen-year maturation period, in ex-bourbon casks. A smaller volume matures in small and large sherry casks. Maturation occurs principally in the two traditional dunnage warehouses located on site, the oldest from 1896. They have a combined capacity of 7,000 casks. Overflows are transported to the Diageo group's central warehouses in Cambus. Bottling is performed in Leven in Fife. The licensee is Anslie & Heilbron (Distillers) Ltd, a subsidiary of Diageo. Most of the whisky goes to the blending trade, especially to Johnnie Walker's range of brands.

The distillery is open to visitors and has a visitor centre and shop. The old Clynelish distillery (renamed Brora) can be viewed when visiting Clynelish. Worth a visit is nearby Dunrobin Castle, seat of the Dukes and Earls of Sutherland.

Filling casks at Clynelish

CLYNELISH

Structural elements and their respective weights

STRUCTURE	OBSERVATIONS
Colour	4
Peaty/Phenolic	3
Sherried/Winey	
Fruity/Estery	2
Floral/Aldehydic	3
Cereal/Malty	1
Feinty	1
Medicinal/Maritime	3
Woody	
Vanilla/Honey	
Nutty/Creamy	1
Spicy	2
Sulphury	

Issued versions

DISTILLED	AGE	% ABV	SIZE	BOX	VERSION
1972	22	58.95	0.2	Box 1	
1972	22	58.95	0.75		
1972	22	58.64	0.75	None	USA
1972	23	57	0.75	None	B297
1972	23	57.1	0.75		
1972	24	61.3	0.7		
1974	23	59.1	0.7		

Conclusive organoleptic sensations

OBSERVATIONS	
Colour	Ripe corn.
Nose	Fresh, leafy, grassy. Toasted digestive biscuits. Smoky and sweet, like molasses. Spicy. Brackish.
Palate	Bitter lemon fruitiness, spiced with tamarind. Malty. Leaves a slight oily coating on the palate.
Finish	Slightly smoky, dry finish. Peppery and brackish saltiness present through the last round.
Comment	Full bodied, firm. An uncomplicated pre-dinner dram.

COLEBURN

PRONOUNCED '*kolburn*', this is probably a non-Gaelic site name. Its meaning is lost but believed to be 'a burn where charcoal was made nearby'. The distillery, which closed in 1985, is located in the village of Longmorn, near Elgin. It was built in a valley between a railway line (closed 1966) and the road from Elgin to Rothes. The buildings, almost unchanged since their erection, are still in good condition, but whisky will probably not be produced here again. Some of the long-lived equipment still remains on the site. It is known that during the heyday of the whisky trade Coleburn served as laboratory for the testing of different whisky production methods. When Coleburn became

DISTILLERY DETAILS

REGION Highlands (Speyside)

OWNER Dale and Mark Winchester

ADDRESS Longmorn, Elgin, Morayshire, IV38 8GN

ROADS A941 on the Rothes to Elgin road, 2km from Glen Elgin.

TEL None

FAX None

COLEBURN

dormant United Distillers Ltd (UD) had plans to convert the complex to apartments and got local approval but decided not to carry on with the project. Instead it was later sold to other developers by Diageo. Brothers Dale and Mark Winchester, involved since childhood with Scottish folk music and who starred in the film *Local Hero*, became the new proprietors in 2004. Their multi-million-pound project, with plans for a conversion including a concert hall, hotel, restaurant and shops, was approved by Moray Council in October 2004.

Coleburn, founded in 1897, during the Pattison hype, was designed by the architect then in fashion, Charles Doig. Doig is remembered for his pagoda-shaped kiln rooftops, which have become a signature for Scotch malt whisky distilleries. Doig supervised the construction for the work, which was commissioned by the investor John Robertson & Son Ltd, a Dundee whisky blender. Its first manager, John Grant, supervised the distillery for thirty years. Coleburn was in production until 24 May 1913 and left dormant until 1916, when it was sold to the Clynelish Distillery Co., a partnership consisting of John Walker & Sons, John Risk and Distillers Company Ltd (DCL). Clynelish Distillery Co. revived the distillery and operated Coleburn from 1917 until 1930. In 1930 it was decided that Coleburn should be transferred into the custody of DCL's subsidiary Scottish Malt Distillers Ltd (SMD). That same year, SMD licenced the distillery to Mitchell Brothers Ltd and later to J & G Stewart Ltd (Usher's Green Stripe). The licence was traded for 8,000 casks of immature whisky, the largest transaction performed in the trade at the time. Stewart held two Royal Warrants as supplier of whisky to Her Majesty the Queen and to the late King Gustav Adolph VI of Sweden. Several upgrades were implemented during the years of operation; in 1962 the direct coal firing was replaced with indirect heating and the old worm tubs were replaced with condensers. Floor malting was abandoned in 1968, the mash tun replaced in 1959 and again in 1976. The spirit still was replaced in 1950, followed by wash still replacements in 1955, and again in 1971. The distillery finally closed in 1985 and the last spirits run occurred on 28 March 1985. The licence to distil was cancelled in 1992.

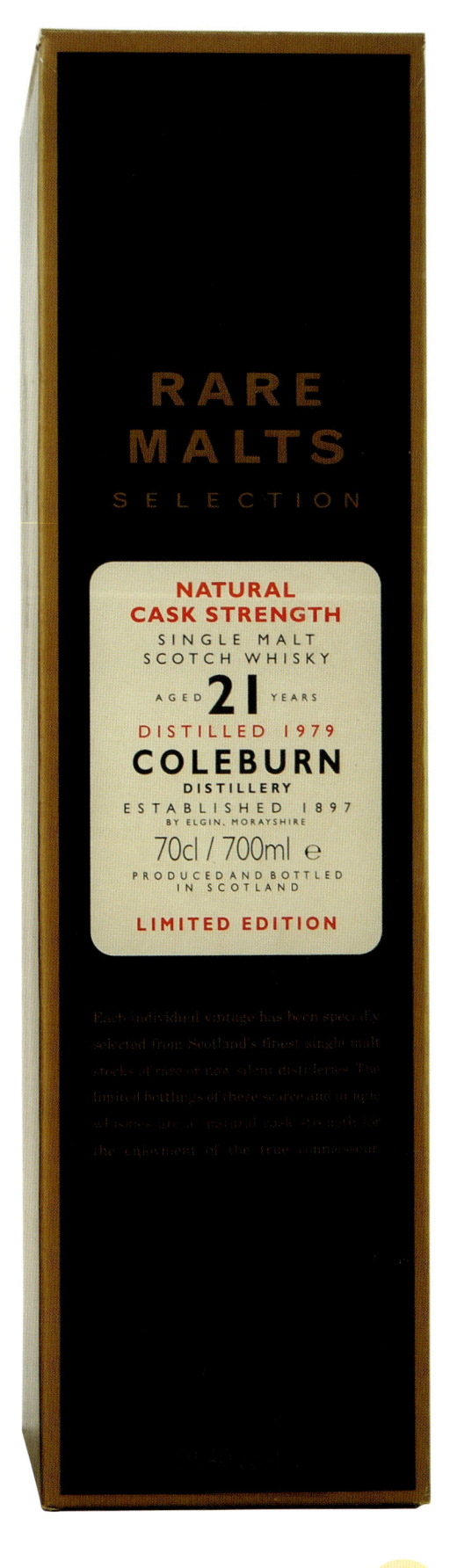

Cooling water was obtained from the Glen Burn near Glen of Rothes and situated on the slopes of Brown Muir. Process water was drawn from a calcium-rich spring nearby. At the end of Coleburn's life cycle barley was brought in from central maltsters. The strains of barley used are said to have been Golden Promise and Triumph. The yeast strain was Brewer's. The type of mill and the capacity of the mash tun and the four wooden wash backs are not known by the author. The wash still had a capacity of 18,185 litres and the spirit still 14,548 litres, both cooled by shell and tube condensers. Annual maximum production was estimated at 1,000,000 litres of alcohol, based on nine mashes per week.

Cask management was based on a varying maturation period. All of the production went to the blend industry; however, a few casks have found their way to the independent bottling trade. Maturation occurred primarily in ex-bourbon casks. All maturation occurred on site. The one and only warehouse on the site accommodated 4,500 casks.

The distillery is closed but can be viewed, at least from the outside. Worth a visit is the Elgin Cathedral ruin.

COLEBURN

Structural elements and their respective weights

Structure	Observations
Colour	5
Peaty/Phenolic	2
Sherried/Winey	
Fruity/Estery	3
Floral/Aldehydic	
Cereal/Malty	
Feinty	3
Medicinal/Maritime	1
Woody	1
Vanilla/Honey	1
Nutty/Creamy	
Spicy	
Sulphury	1

Conclusive organoleptic sensations

	Observations
Colour	Gold, ripe lemon.
Nose	Smoky with a faint whiff of burnt rubber. Restrained fragrance, like wild flowers on a meadow. Drying lemongrass.
Palate	Smoke and salt from a hint of Japanese, roasted seaweed. A meandering tone of ginger and tangerine zest. Trace of butterscotch. Slightly oily and a bit tannic/woody.
Finish	Departing rather quickly. Short and dryish. No trace of the initial sulphury-rubbery whiff.
Comment	Light bodied. With some water it becomes a fitting libation to match sushi.

Issued versions

Distilled	Age	% ABV	Size	Box	Version
1979	21	59.4	0.7		No versions

Convalmore

Pronounced '*konvall more*', it is named after the nearby Conval Hills, which probably got their name from St Conval, patron saint of Cumnock. 'More' is from the Scottish Gaelic 'mór' meaning 'big'. The pretty, grey-stone distillery with its classic pagoda roof has been dormant since 1985. The distillery is nearly intact but it is said that Convalmore will not be put into production again. The distillery is situated in the heart of Speyside, just north of the small town of Dufftown and between the William. Grant & Sons-owned Glenfiddich, Balvenie and Kininvie distilleries. Convalmore was the fourth distillery to be built in the area. The saying 'Rome was built on seven hills; Dufftown was built on seven stills' describes the rather high concentration of distilleries in the area. William. Grant & Sons saved Convalmore from being demolished or converted, a fate other distilleries suffered during the big shake up in the 1980s. They found the complex useful for their operations and utilised it as a maturation and storage warehouse.

The distillery was a project that started on 23 June 1893 with the formation of the Convalmore-Glenlivet Distillery Co. The initial 1,200 shares offered were all purchased by Glasgow brokers and merchants. The buildings, designed by the architect Donald Mackay, were speedily erected and Convalmore reached full production in February 1894. The first managing director appointed was Peter Dawson, a whisky merchant from Dufftown. As financial problems arose, fresh capital was necessary so reconstruction after a capital increase occurred in 1896. Eight years later, in 1904, the company went into voluntary liquidation as yet another distillery suffering from the wake of the Pattison crash. In March 1905 the Glasgow blender W.P. Lowrie & Co. purchased all the stocks for £6,000 and became the new owners. Mr Lowrie, a former manager from Port Ellen Distillery on Islay, had started his own business as a whisky broker in 1869. It is argued whether he or Andrew Usher was the first one to practise and commercialise the blending

Distillery details

REGION Highlands (Speyside)

OWNER William Grant & Sons Ltd

ADDRESS Dufftown, Keith, Banffshire, AB55 4DH

ROADS A941, 1km north of Dufftown

TEL 01340 820000, visitor 01340 820373 (Glenfiddich)

FAX 01340 820805

EMAIL pr@wgrant.com

WEB www.williamgrant.com

· RARE MALTS ·

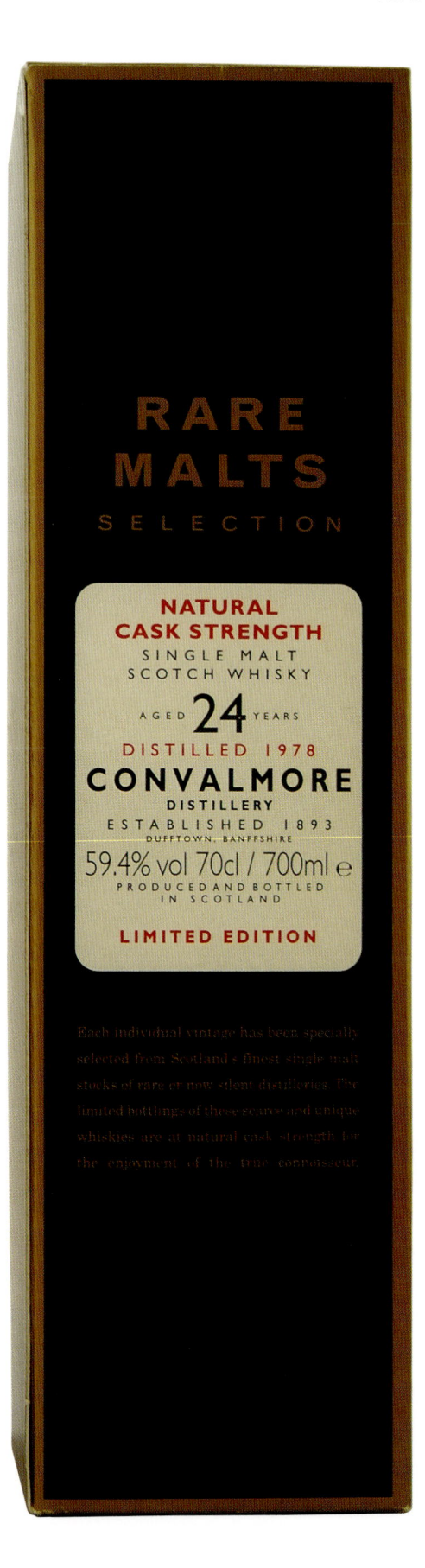

of grain and malt whiskies. Beyond a doubt, it was Usher who made the concept of blended whisky a commercial success. Lowrie's business idea was to operate as a producer, bottler and blender for merchants lacking such facilities. In 1906, Lowrie ran into financial troubles. Lowrie's largest customer, James Buchanan & Co. Ltd, was on the verge of losing its best supplier, so it stepped in and bought the company. Lowrie retired and James Buchanan & Co. continued the expansion to meet the demand for its blend, the Black & White brand.

Convalmore was almost destroyed by a devastating fire that broke out in the middle of a raging snowstorm at midnight on 29 October 1909. It is said that the fire blocked access to the connection point for the hoses and had to be fought by a line of locals passing buckets of water. The still house was saved but everything else lost. Damages were estimated at £8,000. Rebuilding started immediately and Convalmore was in full production the following year. At that time it was also decided to experiment with modern distilling equipment and investment was made to expand the production line from two stills to include a large column (Coffey) still. Its continuous capacity was 2,300 litres of wash per hour, but the malt whisky produced was of unstable quality, poorer than grain whisky produced by this type of still and the project was cancelled five years later. The column still, or continuous still, was removed in 1915. It is still legal to produce Scotch malt whisky by the use of patent stills instead of traditional pot stills. The last use of such equipment for malt whisky occurred during the 1960s by Strathmore Distillery. Others who have carried out similar experiments were Lochruan Distillery, a Campbeltown Distillery closed in 1925, and Glentauchers. Buchanans were absorbed by the Distillers Company Ltd in 1925 and transferred to its subsidiary Scottish Malt Distillers Ltd in 1930. During World War II Convalmore was dormant. The capacity was doubled by the installation of two new pot stills in 1964–65. All four were at the time converted to indirect heating. Two new wash backs plus a new boiler were also added. A dark grain plant serving neighbouring distilleries was built in 1972 (closed 1983). The bonded warehouses were expanded the same year. The last improvement occurred in 1975 when a new mash house was built and a stainless steel wash tun installed, replacing the old cast iron one. Later, via merger and acquisition DCL joined the United Distillers Ltd and in 1985 UD mothballed the distillery. In 1992 the silent distillery was sold to Wm. Grant & Sons never to be reopened, which probably may have been a part of the deal. Wm. Grant & Sons now use Convalmore's production complex and warehouses for storage and maturing their own Glenfiddich, Balvenie and Kininvie malt whiskies.

Process water came from an area called Burnside located in the Conval Hills; its water was collected in a dam 1km away from the distillery. Cooling water was drawn directly from the river Fiddich. Barley was floor malted and lightly peated on site. Toward the end of production, the barley strain for the six weekly mashes of 6.5 metric tonnes each were the ones popular for the time: probably Golden Promise and Triumph, but others may have been used as well. Close to its finale the distillery operated well below its capacity. The grist went to the new stainless steel mash tun which replaced the old cast iron one in 1975. The wort was fermented in the six wooden wash backs under the influence of Distiller's yeast. Distillation occurred in the two onion-shaped wash stills and two onion-shaped spirit stills, all four of almost identical volume and indirectly heated by steam coils. Cooling was provided via the old-fashioned method of a worm, or coiled pipe, submerged in an outer tank. The annual production was less than 1,000,000 litres of alcohol per annum.

Cask management was based on a varying maturation period. All of the production went to the blend industry; however a few casks have found their way to the independent bottler trade. Convalmore used to be included in Black & White and Lowrie's blends. Maturation occurred primarily in ex-bourbon casks, on site. The warehouse capacity was, and still, is 17,000 casks and is now used by William Grant & Sons for their various distilleries.

The distillery is closed but can be viewed, at least from the outside, when visiting the Glenfiddich and Balvenie distilleries. Contact Glenfiddich visitor centre for further information.

CONVALMORE

Structural elements and their respective weights

Structure	Observations
Colour	8
Peaty/Phenolic	1
Sherried/Winey	3
Fruity/Estery	2
Floral/Aldehydic	1
Cereal/Malty	2
Feinty	
Medicinal/Maritime	
Woody	2
Vanilla/Honey	
Nutty/Creamy	2
Spicy	
Sulphury	

Conclusive organoleptic sensations

	Observations
Colour	Deep gold.
Nose	Malty, fruity aroma. Cream sherry, vanilla and chocolate. Fading peat smoke. Hint of sun-warmed saw dust.
Palate	Fruity. Hints of sherry and peat smoke. Some traces of dark chocolate and cocoa butter. A slight lemony sting.
Finish	Nutty. Sherryish. Oak notes.
Comment	Medium bodied. An after-dinner dram.

Issued versions

Distilled	Age	% ABV	Size	Box	Version
1978	24	59.4	0.7		No versions

CRAIGELLACHIE

Pronounced '*kray KHEL lachi*', it is Gaelic for 'rocky hill' and was first applied to the majestic Craigellachie cliff on which much of the village is sited, overlooking the convergence of the River Spey and River Fiddich. The distillery is built on and around the north-facing bluff defined by the two river valleys and has a spectacular view of the gracefully flowing rivers. The small village of Craigellachie and the nearby famous hotel of the same name with its famous Quaich Bar can also be viewed from this vantage point.

Due to the proximity of the new railway junction and the quality of the plentiful local water, the village of Craigellachie was

DISTILLERY DETAILS

REGION Highlands (Speyside)

OWNER Bacardi

ADDRESS Craigellachie, Aberlour, Banffshire, AB38 9ST

ROADS A95, between Rothes and Aberlour

TEL 01340 872971

FAX 01340 872970

EMAIL info@bacardi.com

chosen as the site for this distillery. Craigellachie's original buildings and layout were designed by the well-known nineteenth century distillery architect, Charles Doig of Elgin. Craigellachie stood in place and ready for full production in the summer of 1891. Sadly, nothing of the original 1891 buildings is left except the kiln, with its pagoda roof, and a few warehouses. Some of the old dwellings, called the 'mud houses', which were in existence long before the distillery was erected, were incorporated into the site. For a time they were in use as storage rooms. The distillery was financed by the Craigellachie Distillery Co. Ltd, a partnership established in 1888 and restructured in 1896 as the Craigellachie-Glenlivet Distillery Ltd. One of its founders was the industry legend and owner of the Benrinnes distillery, Alexander Edward. Another of the founders was the energetic and dynamic Peter Mackie, nicknamed 'Restless Peter' by his contemporary. Mackie was the creator of the famous White Horse blend and he inherited the Lagavulin Distillery on Islay from his uncle J.L Mackie. Restless Peter was involved in numerous other adventures such as a tweed factory, a factory manufacturing concrete slabs, and a mill specialising in fortified flour. Edward, who had also been involved in the operation of the Aultmore, the Dallas Dhu and a few other distilleries, retired in 1900, leaving Mackie as the major owner of the company. Mackie had formed a holding company, Mackie & Co. (Distillers) Co., to administer his successful brand, White Horse, named after the White Horse Inn at Canongate in Edinburgh.

In 1916, when Mackie had gained full control of the shares, he formally transferred his stake in Craigellachie to his holding company. In 1923 he organised transport by train and boat around Scotland to the newly acquired warehouses in Campbeltown. When Mackie died in 1924 the holding company changed its name to White Horse Distillers Ltd. In 1927 the company merged with the Distillers Company Ltd (DCL) and was in 1930 transferred to DCL's subsidiary Scottish Malt Distillers Ltd (SMD). In 1997, when Diageo was formed to create one of the world's largest drinks companies, it was decided that the distillery did not fit into Diageo's portfolio and was sold to its present owner, the Bacardi-group. Craigellachie was known for years as 'The Home of White Horse Whisky', which was in bold letters on the wall of the still house.

Craigellachie has undergone several updates and modernisations since it sprung into full production in 1891. Electricity was installed in 1948. Comprehensive rebuilding was carried out from 1964–65 when the still house, mash house and tun room were all replaced. The new wash backs were all built in 1965. The massive iron hoops and the staves made from Oregon pine (not larch as some sources claim) arrived in a ready-to-assemble shape. The assembly was a painstaking and arduous task carried out by a locally scrambled workforce under the supervision of a master cooper from Glasgow. At the same time the water wheel delivering power to the rummager for the wash still was dismantled, and the line of pot stills was expanded from two to four with indirect heating installed on all four. The new still house was the first to be built from a striking design that exposes the pots stills through huge windows. At night the stills are lit by spotlights, providing a spectacular view to passersby. During the period from 1966 to 1973 the same concept was introduced at Clynelish, Glen Ord, Teaninich and others. When UD abandoned floor malting on site, as many others did at the time, a new, highly efficient mash tun replaced the old cast-iron vessel. The new stainless steel and full Lauter tun is extremely efficient in sugar extracting and is able to discharge its content of 9.5 metric tonnes of draff in seven minutes. The latest change occurred in 1995 when nearly all on-site cask fillings were abandoned. The distillate is simply sent by road tankers to UD's central filling stations. That same year several of the warehouses were demolished.

Water for the process comes from a spring on Little Conval situated on the granite Conval Hills. The water is collected in the large, deep Blue Hill dam and from there drawn to the distillery. Cooling water is obtained directly from the River Fiddich. Malt, rather distinctly peated to be used by a Speyside distiller, is brought in from the central maltster, Glen Esk Central Malting, in Montrose. The barley strain used is predominantly Decanter. The malted barley is crushed to grist by a traditional Porteus mill. Each week 9.5 metric tonnes of grist goes into thirteen mashes. It is mashed in a modern full Lauter stainless steel mash tun, a German Steinecker. Fermentation, under the influence of the Distiller's yeast strain Mauri Quest MX Blend, occurs in eight wooden wash backs, made of Oregon pine with a capacity of 60,000 litres each. The wash is diverted from the wash backs into four, indirectly heated pot stills for a common two-step distillation. These are basically onion shaped but the shoulders incline considerably, deviating from the traditional geometry. Each of the two wash stills and the two spirit stills has an equal volume of 22,730 litres. The wash stills are heated by steam kettles and the spirit stills by steam coils. The stills are equipped with straight, long necks and lightly slanted lyne arms. It is claimed Craigellachie's character is mainly achieved by retaining the traditional cooling worms, or copper coils, submerged in tubs with flowing cooling water. Capacity is 2,800,000 litres of alcohol per annum.

During the earlier UD era cask management was based on a maturation period of fourteen years, a bit longer than usual for Speyside whiskies. All maturation occurred on site. Primarily ex-bourbon casks were used, however a smaller volume was matured in sherry casks of different sizes. The warehouses on the premises were limited to 7,000 casks. The lion's share of the production was earmarked for the White Horse and Dewar's blends. The spirit was, at the end of the UD era, sent by road tankers to UD's central maturation and filling site in Cambus. Today it is mainly Dewar's White Label, a brand which is owned by Bacardi, who is the recipient of the whisky produced.

The distillery is not open to visitors. It may, however, be possible to arrange visits. Contact the distillery for further information regarding times and conditions.

The village of Craigellachie is at the heart of Speyside. The whisky pilgrim wishing to see the most distilleries by the least amount of travelling should choose this as the base for excursions. The road out of the village leads to the famous whisky towns Aberlour, Dufftown, Elgin, Keith and Rothes. A large number of distilleries are within a 25km radius. One of the most famous landmarks in Speyside is Thomas Telford's cast iron bridge over the River Spey at Craigellachie, built in 1814. Telford is recognised as one of Britain's finest civil engineers.

CRAIGELLACHIE

Structural elements and their respective weights

Structure	Observations
Colour	8
Peaty/Phenolic	3
Sherried/Winey	
Fruity/Estery	3
Floral/Aldehydic	3
Cereal/Malty	3
Feinty	
Medicinal/Maritime	
Woody	1
Vanilla/Honey	
Nutty/Creamy	1
Spicy	
Sulphury	

Conclusive organoleptic sensations

	Observations
Colour	Old gold.
Nose	Cereal sweetness as from fresh malt grist. Fruity, flowery and fragrant with an orangey and citric hint. More fruity than flowery with distinct fresh Golden Delicious apple notes. Meandering peat smoke, more blurry than in focus.
Palate	Apples and sweet citrus, tangerine and mandarins. Cereal notes reminiscent of shortbread. Oily mouthfeel.
Finish	Long, aromatic and harmonious finish, slight woody. The peat smoke returns, now in good order. Slight tannic dryness.
Comment	Medium bodied. After-dinner dram.

Issued versions

Distilled	Age	% abv	Size	Box	Version
1973	22	60.2	0.7		No versions

DAILUAINE

Pronounced *'dall-yewan'*, this stands for 'the green valley' and is a combination of the Norse 'dal' meaning 'valley' and Gaelic, spelled as 'An Dail Uaine'. Dailuaine is situated near the town of Aberlour, between the slopes of the mountain Ben Rinnes and the valley of the River Spey. Inspired by the beautiful surroundings, Alfred Barnard, the late nineteenth century author who documented the malt whisky distillers, wrote: 'Here the whole glory of the scenery below suddenly burst upon us, and new points of beauty presented themselves, never was there such a soft, bright landscape of luxuriant green, of clustering foliage, and verdant banks of wild flowers, ferns and grasses'. Barnard was so impressed that he dedicated seven pages and two sketches to this distillery. However, it was the incoming railway and the abundance of superior water that were the primary reasons to select this site for a distillery, not its beauty. Charles Doig, the 'father' of the pagoda-roofed kilns, or 'Doig Ventilator', had his very first pagoda roof installed at Dailuaine in 1889. The aim of its construction was to provide a stronger draught for the peat fire. The walls of the building, still standing, are composed of granite skilfully carved from a local quarry.

In 1851 William Mackenzie, a local farmer from Carron, built the distillery at Drum Wood, a hollow by the Carron Burn, naming it Dail-Uaine. When the expected 'whisky railway' of the Highlands arrived in 1863 to Carron, only 5km away, Dailuaine

DISTILLERY DETAILS

REGION Highlands (Speyside)

OWNER Diageo

ADDRESS Carron, Aberlour, Banffshire, AB38 7RE

ROADS Off A95 Aberlour to Granton road, 2km south of Aberlour

TEL 01340 872500

FAX None

• DAILUAINE •

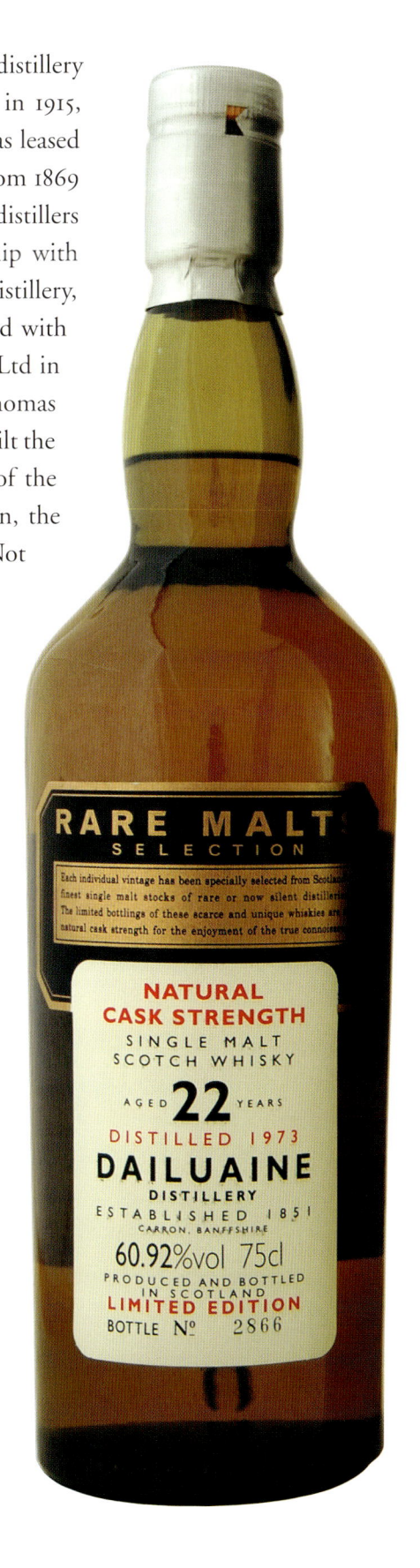

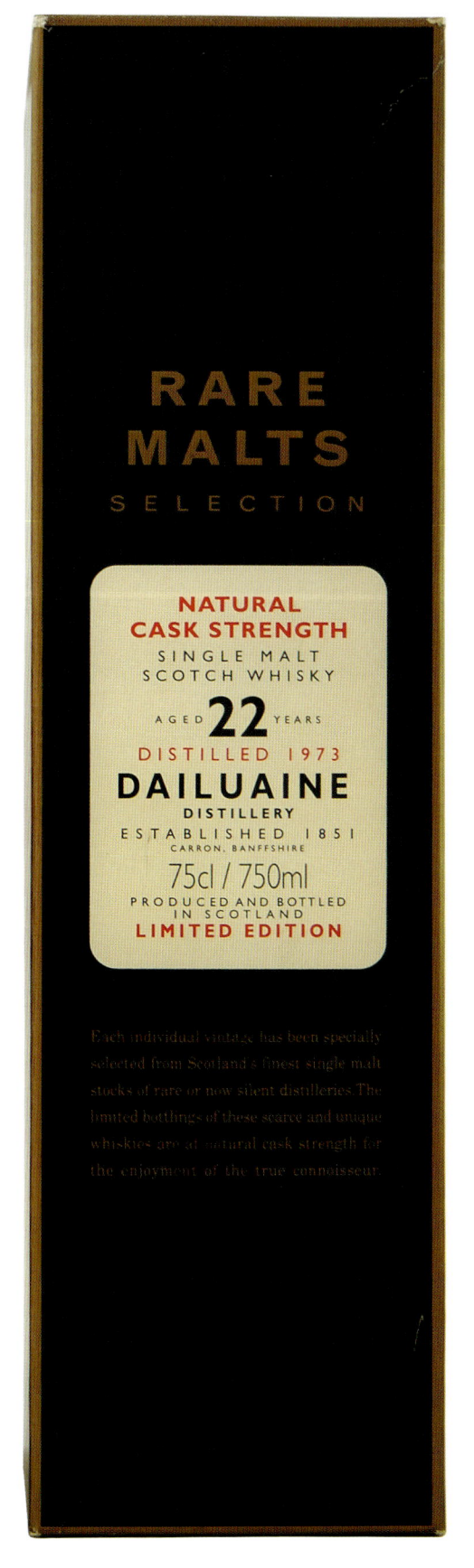

Distillery was eventually linked to the network by its own siding. The distillery remained in the family's possession until William's son Thomas died in 1915, leaving no heirs. When Mackenzie passed away in 1865 the distillery was leased by his widow Jane to the banker James Flemming, a lease that lasted from 1869 until 1879. For a while, Janet joined the ranks of early Scottish women distillers like Elizabeth Lewis at Cardow. In 1879 Thomas formed a partnership with James Flemming to set up Mackenzie Co. to control the Dailuaine Distillery, which became the Dailuaine-Glenlivet Distillery Ltd in 1891. It merged with the Talisker Distillery Ltd on Skye in 1896 and the Imperial Distillery Ltd in Caron in 1898 to form the Dailuaine-Talisker Distilleries Co. Ltd. Thomas Mackenzie had a substantial interest in the Talisker Distillery and had built the Imperial Distillery. He became the chairman and managing director of the new company, which also owned a grain whisky distillery in Aberdeen, the Bon Accord Distillery. Bon Accord was renamed 'North of Scotland'. Not long afterward the whisky industry was affected by the Pattison adventure and a following recession. Hence, the company traded at a loss and went on to suffer a series of misfortunes due to heavily reduced demand, lawsuits and the destruction of their Aberdeen distillery by a fire. In 1916, the year after Mackenzie died, a group of customers tried to steer the company out of difficulties by forming a consortium. The group, lead by John Dewar & Sons Ltd and John Walker & Sons Ltd took over control and responsibility for the company. In 1925, it joined James Buchanan & Co. and Distillers Company Ltd (DCL) to form a larger DCL, which became the whisky giant of its time. In 1930, Dailuaine was transferred to DCL's subsidiary, Scottish Malt Distillers Ltd (SMD). From 1884 to 1887, a major renovation modernised and expanded Dailuaine to one of the largest Highland distilleries, with an increased annual output of 730,000 litres of alcohol. In 1907, a railway siding was built linking Dailuaine with Imperial and Carron warehouses. A devastating fire in 1917 caused extensive damage by engulfing nearly all of the distillery's buildings and equipment, including the unique pagoda roof, the first of its kind. Substantial rebuilding lasted until 1920, when the distillery resumed full production. At that time electric light was installed with power generated by steam engines. The production lasted uninterrupted until 1959, when another fire broke out. This fire triggered a long-needed refurbishing of the distillery. The modernisation, which was completed in 1960, included the expansion of the pot still line from four to six. The on-site floor malting was discontinued, and replaced by a Saladin box – mechanised malting equipment rarely installed at a distillery, but generally at central maltings. A dark grains plant, common for several distilleries in the neighbourhood, was also constructed. It is the fumes from this plant that meet the visitor to the area. All six pot stills were converted to indirect heating in 1965 and malting on site by the Saladin box was abandoned in 1983. Conversion from coal to oil firing of the boilers occurred in 1970. A new mash tun was installed in 1993. Dailuaine was connected to the national electric grid in 1950, but kept its four steam engines and two water wheels, working in tandem, as backup and as a complementary power source until 1961.

Water for the process comes from the Bailliemullich Burn, situated on the lower slopes of granite Ben Rinnes. The cooling water is obtained from the Green Burn. When floor malting was performed on site the steeping water was drawn from the Burn of Derrybeg. All three burns are situated on the Ben Rinnes. Today, the lightly peated malt is brought in from the central maltsters Burghead Maltings in Burghead and Roseisle Maltings in Roseisle. The barley strains of preference are Chariot and Optic. The malted barley is crushed to grist by a four-roller Porteus mill. Each week 8.25 metric tonnes of grist goes into eight mashes to be mashed in a full Lauter stainless steel mash tun with a peaked canopy. The tun has a capacity of 9.5 metric tonnes. Fermentation, under the influence of Distiller's yeast occurs in eight wooden wash backs, with a capacity of 55,000 litres each and made from Scottish larch. The fermentation cycle is sixty hours on weekdays and is extended to a long cycle on weekends. The wash is diverted from the wash backs to the pot stills for a common two-step distillation. The distillation occurs in three lantern-shaped wash stills, with a capacity of 19,000 litres each, and three onion-shaped spirit stills, with an equal volume of 21,000 litres. All six are indirectly heated. The wash stills are heated by steam pans and the spirit stills by steam coils. Both the wash and spirit stills have features which would cause additional reflux – the tucked neck on the lantern-shaped wash stills and the inclined lyne arm on the onion-shaped spirit stills. There are separate receivers for the low wines and the feints and foreshots. Set quantities are mixed in the charger prior to pumping the 'low wines' to the spirit still. Condensers are used for cooling the spirit vapours. The original configuration was a three-still system consisting of one wash still in tandem with two spirit stills. This was changed in the early 1950s to a two-pair set up and later (1959–60), the line of four pot stills was expanded to six. Capacity is 2,500,000 litres of alcohol per annum.

The cask management is based on a maturation period of sixteen years, longer than usual for Speyside whiskies. All maturation used to be on site. Sadly, all the classic granite and double-storey dunnage warehouses now lie empty as all Dailuaine whisky is sent away by road tankers to be filled into casks at the central warehousing complex in Cambus. Primarily ex-bourbon casks are used; however a smaller volume is matured in sherry casks of different sizes. The lion's share of the production is earmarked for different blends of the Johnnie Walker brand.

The distillery is not open to the public.

Dailuaine's second steam locomotive, christened *Dailuaine no. 1* was bought from Barclay of Kilmarnock in 1939. The first one was bought in 1897 from the same source and was later used for hauling goods back and forth from the Carron railway station via Dailuaine's own siding. Locomotive no. 1 was donated to the Strathspey Railway Museum in Aviemore when British Railways axed the Strathspey Railway Line in 1967; it was returned to United Distillers and is being restored for display at Aberfeldy Distillery. Its last official run was in 1970.

DAILUAINE

Structural elements and their respective weights

Structure	Observations
Colour	8
Peaty/Phenolic	2
Sherried/Winey	3
Fruity/Estery	3
Floral/Aldehydic	1
Cereal/Malty	1
Feinty	
Medicinal/Maritime	
Woody	
Vanilla/Honey	1
Nutty/Creamy	1
Spicy	2
Sulphury	

Conclusive organoleptic sensations

	Observations
Colour	Deep gold, orange.
Nose	Light, elegant peat and peat reek. Spicy, peppery. Pronounced malty. Marked trace of sweet, succulent sherry influence. Vanilla.
Palate	Orange fruity and a floral hint of violets. Malty sweetness. Oak woody background harmonic balanced by the sherry.
Finish	Slight tannic dry and astringent with a nutty twist.
Comment	Medium bodied, sherried and fruity. A dram to finish a dinner with. On its own or with the puddings.

Issued versions

Distilled	Age	% abv	Size	Box	Version
1973	22	60.92	0.75		
1973	22	60.92	0.75	None	USA
1973	22	61.8	0.2	Box 2	

Dallas Dhu

Pronounced '*dallas doo*', it stands for 'valley of the black water', which in Gaelic is spelled as 'Dall eas Dubh'. Dallas Dhu, initially named 'Dallasmore Distillery', is situated near the ancient town of Forres, which is believed to be the village called 'Varris' by the invading Romans. The distillery was designed by Charles Doig and therefore got the typical pagoda roof in fashion at the time. Dallas Dhu ceased to produce whisky in March 1983 and was later converted to a museum. It is so well preserved and unique that it was proclaimed a protected Ancient Monument and was placed by its owner at the time, United Distillers Ltd (UD), in the custody of Scottish Historic Buildings and Monuments in 1988. William de Ripley bought the estate and the

Distillery details	
REGION	Highlands (Speyside)
OWNER	Diageo. Caretaker is Historic Scotland
ADDRESS	Mannachie Road, Forres, Morayshire, IV36 2RR
ROADS	Off A940, 2km south of Forres in direction of Rafford
TEL	01309 676548 (museum visitor centre)
FAX	None
EMAIL	hs.website@scotland.gsi.gov.uk
WEB	www.historic-scotland.gov.uk

hamlet from the Crown in 1279. Another version is that the land was given to him by King William the Lion. Ripley's descendants added 'of Dallas' to the family name, spelling Dallas differently over the years. A story told is that Dallas, Texas, is indirectly named after this hamlet. Legend says that a desendant of William de Ripley, George Miffin Dallas (1792–1864), who was US vice-president in 1845, named the Texas metropolis.

As a response to the exploding demand for Scotch Highland whisky, Dallas Dhu was erected in 1898–99. Completed and in production in April 1899, its name was changed from Dallasmore to Dallas Dhu in December of that year. Dallas Dhu was one of several distilleries located on land owned by the local laird and Victorian entrepreneur Alexander Edward and is situated in a delightful, tiny hamlet on Sanquhar Estate. Its own siding connected the distillery with the Highland Railway. Edward supervised the construction. The time for the inauguration of Dallas Dhu was poorly chosen because of a recession that emerged from the Pattison crash the same year and severely wounded the whisky industry. Edward managed to transfer the formal ownership of the distillery to the Glasgow blender Wright & Grey Co. the following year. The fact that Edward was a member of the board may have helped to carry out the transaction. Wright & Grey, owner of the popular blend of its day, the Roderick Dhu, sold Dallas Dhu in 1919 to a Glasgow-based blender colleague, J.P. O'Brien & Co., who also controlled the Caol Ila Distillery for a short period. J.P. O'Brien sold Dallas Dhu in 1921 to the English limited partnership Benmore Distillers Ltd, which already owned the distilleries Benmore, Lochhead and Lochindaal. Benmore Distillers was absorbed by the Distillers Company Ltd (DCL) in 1929 and, in 1930, transferred to its subsidiary Scottish Malt Distillers Ltd (SMD). Dallas Dhu was finally closed in March 1983 but kept intact.

SMD kept Dallas Dhu closed from 1930 until 1936. A few years later there was another silent period. It started on 9 April 1939 when a fire engulfed the still house and its contents. Forres fire brigade spent five hours trying to control the blaze. They successfully managed to enclose the fire and block it from spreading to the other buildings limiting damages to £7,000. A few months later war broke out and Dallas Dhu remained closed during the period due to the restrictions in force. The distillery was restored but did not go into full production again until 1947. It is said that some minor production runs were performed from 1945 to 1947. Dallas Dhu's compact size and limited water supply kept the distillery disqualified as a primary candidate for

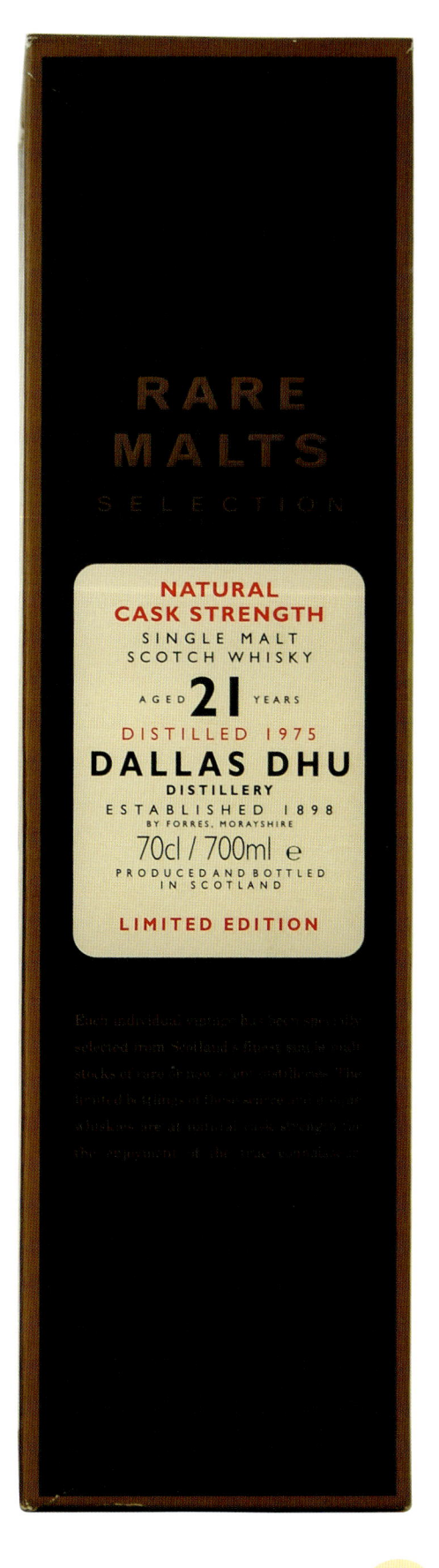

DCL's ongoing major renovation and modernisation programme, a post-war programme applied to its extensive string of distilleries. Minor updates occurred, however. In 1950, Dallas Dhu was connected to the national electric grid and the distillery's main power source, a steam engine, was replaced with electric motors. However, the water wheel, driven by the overflow of water for cooling worm-tubs, was not taken out of service until 1971. Its task was to generate power for driving the rummager in the wash still. The hand-firing of the stills was mechanised by an automatic coal stoker in 1963 and replaced with oil-fired indirect heating in 1971. Floor malting was abandoned in 1968. The last cask was filled on 16 March 1983. The distilling licence was cancelled in 1992.

The cooling water was obtained from the Blair's Burn. Water for the process came from the Altyre Burn, locally called the Scourie Burn. The Altyre Burn's soft foundation contributed to cave-ins so had to be dug out and stabilised. During the era when floor malting was practised on site all the barley brought in was locally cultivated. This district is considered to be the core of the top-producing Scottish barley farms. After floor malting was abandoned, lightly peated, malted barley was brought in from DCL's central maltsters, consisting of barley strains that varied over time. At the end of the era Golden Promise and Triumph came into use. The barley was crushed to grist by a Vickers mill, a converted Boby mill. Each week, during full production, 3.3 metric tonnes of grist went into twelve weekly mashes. The large stainless steel mash tun, with its copper lid, had a capacity of 9.5 metric tonnes or 13,000 litres. The wort went from the tun into the six wooden wash backs for fermentation. They were made from Oregon pine, each with a capacity of 17,000 litres. The yeast strain used was Distiller's yeast. The distillation occurred in two traditional, onion-shaped stills: the wash still had a capacity of 18,000 litres, and the spirit still had a near equal volume. Both were indirectly heated by steam coils. The wash and spirit stills had features which contributed to a unique reflux profile – steep slanting shoulders and narrow, nearly horizontal lyne arms. Cooling was traditional, by submerged worms. Capacity was 750,000 litres of alcohol per annum.

The cask management was based on maturation periods of ten and twelve years, normal for Speyside whiskies. A mix of ex-bourbon and sherry casks, of different sizes, was used. During the heyday the warehouses accommodated around 8,000 ex-bourbon casks. The whisky contributed to the Roderick Dhu and Benmore blends.

The distillery, fully operational, is now a museum and is open for visitors. Contact the museum for details and schedule. A famous landmark nearby is the Sueno's Stone – a tall, upright stone carved with Pictish symbols dating from the ninth century and believed to have been erected by Kenneth MacAlpin, the first king of the Scots after he defeated the kings of seven northern Pictish kingdoms. Another stone to visit may be the Witches Stone, thought to date from Pictish times and to have been used as an altar to the Sun God. It marks the landing place of three whisky casks in which three witches were rolled down Cluny Hill and put to rest.

DALLAS DHU

Structural elements and their respective weights

Structure	Observations
Colour	8
Peaty/Phenolic	1
Sherried/Winey	
Fruity/Estery	3
Floral/Aldehydic	3
Cereal/Malty	3
Feinty	
Medicinal/Maritime	
Woody	1
Vanilla/Honey	2
Nutty/Creamy	
Spicy	1
Sulphury	

Conclusive organoleptic sensations

	Observations
Colour	Deep old gold.
Nose	A floral aromatic scent, orange flowers, dominated by malted barley and burning heather.
Palate	Seville oranges, candied fruits, heather honey. Traces of peat and barely grist. Sugary summer apples on a bonfire. Silky tannins.
Finish	Sliding from a slight spicy peppery note to toffee and sweet sugary vanilla, toasted, as on a crème brûlée.
Comment	Light bodied. A refreshing pre-dinner dram for an open-air midsummer buffet.

Issued versions

Distilled	Age	% abv	Size	Box	Version
1970	24	60.54	0.7		
1970	24	60.6	0.7	None	
1970	24	59.91	0.7	None	
1970	24	58	0.7		
1975	21	61.9	0.7		

Dufftown-Glenlivet

Pronounced '*daffin*', initially the town was named Balvenie and built to give employment after the Napoleonic Wars. Eventually, the name of the town was changed to the name of its founder, James Duff, 4th Earl of Fife, who founded the town in 1817. Duff stands for 'black', which in Gaelic is spelled 'Dubh'. Several distilleries in the area added the geographic descriptor Glenlivet to their names, probably to jump on the fame of the original and legendary distillery, The Glenlivet. Glenlivet stands for 'the valley of the River Livet'; 'glen' is 'valley' in Gaelic. The town is the home of seven distilleries and is indeed the centre of Scotch malt whisky distilling. The Dufftown distillery is located in the beautiful Dullan Glen. It is a short distance from the Mortlach and Pittyvaich distilleries and the sixth to be erected here. It is the largest malt whisky distillery within the Diageo empire.

Dufftown-Glenlivet is housed in a stone building that was converted from the Pityvaich saw and flour mill in 1895. The old mill was acquired by a group of investors who had formed a partnership, the Dufftown-Glenlivet Distillery Co., the same year. The main investors were the two wine merchants Peter Mackenzie and Richard Stackpole, both from Liverpool. Others were John Symon (original owner of the mill) and Charles MacPherson, a local solicitor. The first whisky flowed from the stills in November 1896, after the first mash on 10 November. The local cultivated barley was malted in the new, pagoda-roofed kiln. Charles Doig seems to have been involved in its design. Later, disputes regarding the rights to the water supply arose. The landowner, George Cowie, also owner of nearby Mortlach Distillery, used the same well as the Dufftown distillery. Cowie not

Distillery details

REGION Highlands (Speyside)

OWNER Diageo

ADDRESS Dufftown, Keith, Banffshire, AB55 4BR

ROADS A941 towards Dufftown, Dullan Glen just outside Dufftown

TEL 01340 822100

FAX None

Dufftown-Glenlivet

only claimed sovereignty over the well but also had its flow diverted. A fight broke out that went on for some years. The flow of the well was diverted and re-diverted via nightly expeditions, from both sides. Eventually an agreement was reached and settled in court. Delivery of barley for the own-floor malting was for a long time secured via John Symon and his farm in Pityvaich. Peter Mackenzie had years before formed another limited partnership, the P. Mackenzie & Co. (Distillers) Ltd. He now used this company to acquire all the shares of the Dufftown-Glenlivet Distillery Co. a year after its start-up. In addition, his holdings in the Blair Athol Distillery in Pitlochry were transferred to this company at the same time (1897). The distilleries produced first-rate malt whiskies which all went into the Mackenzie brand blends. These were highly popular in the US, which became the major market for the company. During the US prohibition era the profitability of the company suffered severely. Hence, in 1933, Mackenzie & Co. Ltd was forced to sell to avoid bankruptcy. The company and its two distilleries were acquired by J. Arthur Bell & Sons Ltd in the same year for £56,000. Blair Athol was immediately mothballed and stayed so until 1949. The Dufftown-Glenlivet distillery became the backbone of the successful Bell blends, and still is. J. Arthur Bell & Sons Ltd later merged with the Distillers Company Ltd (DCL). Bell and DCL joined Guinness the United Distillers Ltd (UD) in 1985.

Wartime restrictions led to a silent period that lasted from 1941 until 1946. Several modernisation and upgrading works were performed during the sixties and the seventies, a period when the Bell blends experienced an explosive growth. To meet the demand a sister distillery, Pittyvaich, was built nearby in 1974. It had its pot stills and production flow identically duplicated to simulate the whisky flowing from Dufftown-Glenlivet. Hence, Dufftown/Pittyvaich could be classified as a tandem distillery such as Brora/Clynelish and Mannochmore/Glenlossie. Dufftown-Glenlivet's on-site floor maltings were abandoned in 1968 and at the same time the old worm tubs were replaced by condensers. Oil-fired boilers for indirect heating were installed, too. The line of pot stills was expanded from two to four in 1974. In 1979 the line was again expanded, from four to six pot stills. A modern full Lauter mash tun was installed, and three older wooden wash backs were replaced with five stainless steel wash backs to make a total of twelve. In spite of all the modernisation, the distillery's old power source, a water wheel, was left intact and still remains.

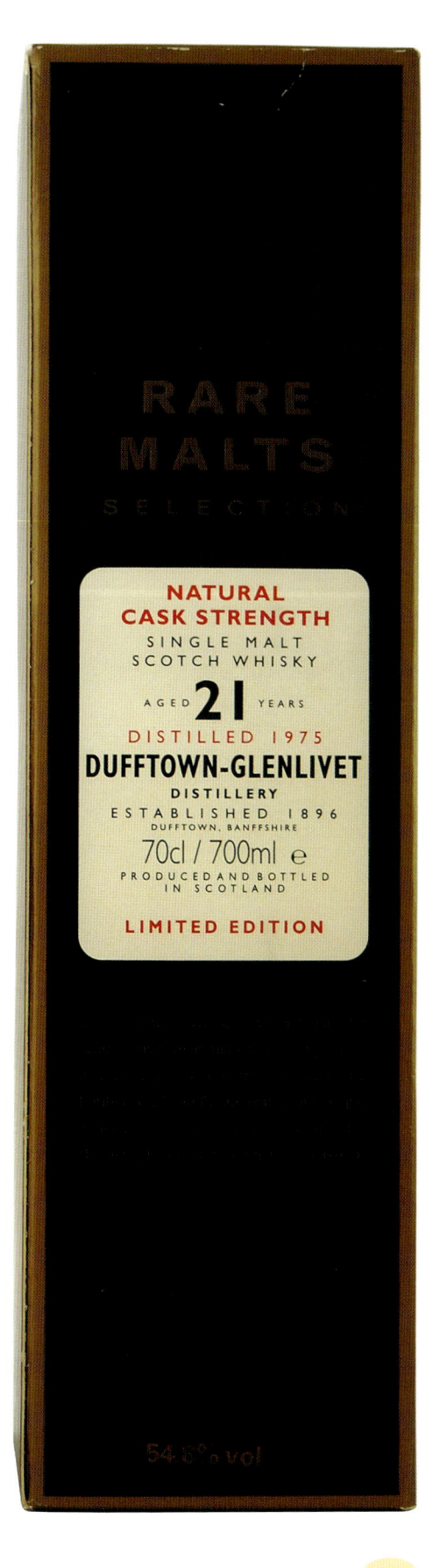

Water for the process is piped from the generously flowing springs of Jock's Well in the Conval Hills. The cooling water is obtained from the River Dullan. Supplemental process water is also obtained from nearby Balliemore and Convalley Springs. When on-site malting was abandoned in 1968 unpeated malted barley was brought in daily from local sources. Now, Diageo's central maltings, Burghead in Elgin, provides unpeated malt. The barley strains are Chariot and Decanter varieties. The malt is crushed to grist by a Vickers mill, a rebuilt Boby mill. At full production, twenty-two mashes are processed per week. Each mash consists of 11 metric tonnes of grist. The mash tun is a full Lauter tun and made of stainless steel. The capacity of the stainless steel wash backs is 51,000 litres each. Yeast used for the fermentation is a mix of Brewer's and Distiller's. The fermentation period is of the short type only, lasting sixty-five hours. The distillation occurs in six hours, by steam coils indirectly heating pear-shaped stills. They are all equipped with broad, straight necks and descending lyne arms. Two of the wash stills each hold an equal volume of 19,775 litres, and the third slightly more. The three spirit stills hold a volume of 24,000 litres each. All stills are cooled by shell and tube condensers with sub-coolers added. Capacity is 4,000,000 litres of alcohol per annum and makes Dufftown the largest malt whisky distillery in Diageo's portfolio.

Cask management is based on a ten-year maturation period, in ex-bourbon casks. A smaller volume matures in sherry butts. The warehouses, on site, are shared with neighbouring but now mothballed Pittyvaich Distillery. The warehouses are non-dunnage and rather modern shelf type. The bottling is centralised and occurs at plants in Leven and Glasgow. Dufftown-Glenlivet contributes to the Bell's blends and The Real Mackensie.

The distillery is open to visitors, by appointment. Worth a visit is the nearby Balvenie Castle, founded during the thirteenth century. The Dufftown Highland Games, held during the summer months, is a highly popular activity to watch and participate in.

DUFFTOWN-GLENLIVET

Structural elements and their respective weights

STRUCTURE	OBSERVATIONS
Colour	1
Peaty/Phenolic	1
Sherried/Winey	
Fruity/Estery	3
Floral/Aldehydic	3
Cereal/Malty	1
Feinty	1
Medicinal/Maritime	
Woody	
Vanilla/Honey	
Nutty/Creamy	
Spicy	2
Sulphury	

Conclusive organoleptic sensations

	OBSERVATIONS
Colour	Young Chardonnay with greenish tinge.
Nose	Heather honey. Fruity, sweet melony. Mineral oil. Malty.
Palate	Fudge, toffee and shortbread. Cane sugar, sweetish.
Finish	Ginger, peppery, and a hint of smokiness. Dryish.
Comment	Medium bodied. A pre-dinner dram.

Issued versions

DISTILLED	AGE	% ABV	SIZE	BOX	VERSION
1975	21	54.8	0.7		No versions

GLEN ALBYN

PRONOUNCED '*glenn ALbin*', 'glen' is the anglicised version of the Gaelic word 'gleann' meaning 'valley'. 'Albyn', 'Alba', or 'Albion' is an old name for Scotland. The Great Glen of Albin, also known as Glen Mhor (see the distillery with the same name), or simply the Great Glen, cuts across Scotland from the northeast to the southwest. Glen Albyn was situated beside the Caledonian Canal, at the Muirtown basin opposite the Glen Mhor distillery. A shopping centre with two supermarkets now occupies Glen Albyn's and adjacent Glen Mhor's sites. A pub in the city centre pays homage to the old distillery, having adopted its name.

DISTILLERY DETAILS

REGION Highlands (Northern)

OWNER Last owner was DCL before it became part of the UD-Guinness group

ADDRESS Telford Street, Inverness, Inverness-shire, IV3 5LD

ROADS A9, north-west side of Inverness near the Caledonian Canal

TEL None

FAX None

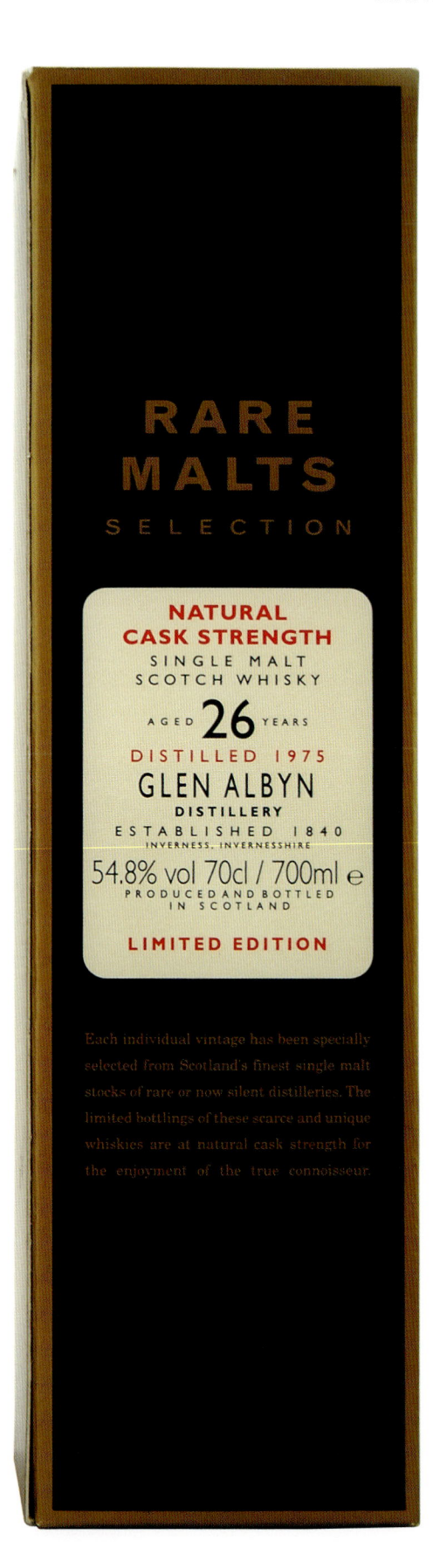

James Sutherland, the Provost of Inverness, founded Glen Albyn. The demand for whisky in the 1840s exceeded supply and capital, generated from the profitable barley and malt trade, was readily available. Inverness was the main shipping port for barley and malt to the brewing industry. The location chosen for Glen Albyn, the site of the ruined Muirtown Brewery, situated near the Caledonian Canal and the Great North Road, were perfect from a logistical point of view. Easy access to water from Loch Ness was another factor. The official inauguration date was 10 October 1844; however, full production was not recorded until 1846. The distillery was severely damaged by a fire that blazed through the complex in November 1849. The reconstruction was a swift operation as the distillery was up and running again by February 1850 and reached full production in 1852. Three years later James Sutherland was bankrupt and the distillery was closed and put up for sale. No investors were interested and the idle distillery remained unsold for several years.

Glen Albyn was converted to a flour mill from 1866 to 1884, when a new owner emerged. Gregory & Co., owned by the local grain merchant A.M. Gregory, purchased the site and buildings with the aim of restoring it as a working distillery. The site was expanded and a new distillery building was erected closer to the Caledonian Canal. The annual output was increased to 340,000 litres. A few years later the distillery was transferred to the newly formed Glen Albyn Distillery Co. Glen Albyn was reconstructed as a limited partnership in 1885, now as Glen Albyn Distillery Co. Ltd. When its appointed manager John Birnie was refused share capital in the company by the owners, he left and founded, in 1892, the Glen Mhor distillery across the street. Production continued except during part of World War I and a few post-war years until 1920. Between 1917 and 1919, the distillery was used as a US Naval base and also as a mine factory. The owners were not interested in resuming distillery production after the years of alternative usage so they put it up for sale.

In 1920 Glen Albyn was purchased by the owners of Glen Mhor, Mackinlay and Birnie Ltd. For decades the two distilleries were run in parallel. In 1954 Glen Mhor pioneered mechanised maltings as opposed to traditional floor maltings. Some sources claim the installation of the Saladin box to be as late as 1961, which may have been a replacement of an older box version in operation from 1954. The modern Saladin box is a screw version, whereas the older one was a stir version. There are also notes that both original stills were replaced with indirectly heated oil-burner fired stills with a larger capacity. The replacement may have occurred when the Saladin box was installed or replaced in 1961. In 1972 DCL, who via its subsidiary John Walker & Sons Ltd controlled 43.5% of Mackinlay and Birnie Ltd, decided to take full control. That year DCL bought all the stocks of the company and transferred it to its subsidiary Scottish Malt Distillers Ltd (SMD). SMD kept production ongoing for some years and then mothballed Glen Albyn and Glen Mhor in the early 1980s. Both distilleries were closed in 1983 and were demolished in 1986.

Water for the process and cooling was obtained from Loch Ness. Glen Albyn abandoned floor malting on site in 1954 by installing a mechanical germination device, a Saladin box or similar piece of equipment. Glen Albyn used its Saladin box until 1980 when it was replaced by malt brought in by lorry from the group's central maltsters. This went on for the remaining three years of the distillery's life span. It is believed that the barley strains brought in from the central maltsters in Ord were Golden Promise and Triumph, peated to the preferred level. The barley used during the floor as well as during the Saladin box malting era was cultivated locally and the versions varied through the years. When the kiln drying was performed on site the heat and smoke were generated by a mix of peat and coal and also coke. Mixing coal, coke and peat was not an uncommon habit among maltsters in those days. The peat was cut on the Dava Moor but was later replaced with peat from the Pitsligo in Aberdeenshire. The coal in the stoke mix added an oily/peaty character to the whisky. The malt was crushed to grist by a Porteus mill. Around 10 metric tonnes of mash went into the mash tun, but the number of mashes per week varied over time. The mash tun was made of Scottish larch and not equipped with any stirring gears, except wooden oars. The wort was moved to three wooden wash backs, also made from larch. Each had a capacity of 21,000 litres. It is believed that the yeast strain used for the fermentation was Distiller's yeast, at least during the SMD days. The distillation occurred in two traditional onion-shaped stills. The original pot stills were built by a lesser-known Glasgow producer of stills: Fleming, Bennet & McLaren. Volumes of the old stills were wash 8,128 and spirit 6,819 litres. The new wash still held a volume of 13,600 litres, and the new spirit still a volume of 11,360 litres. The original stills were all equipped with odd lyne arms which were said to cool the fluid more quickly and improve its flavours. The lyne arms did have a circular cross section but were flattened, giving a capital D-shaped cross section, with the flat side lying down. Each still had a 100m-long coil or submerged worm to cool the vapours and was indirectly heated by steam coils. The maximum annual output was 1,125,000 litres of alcohol; however during the later years of production volume was limited to 330,000 litres of alcohol per annum.

Cask management was in ex-bourbon casks only and is believed to have been based on a ten-year maturation period. The warehouses, on site and shared with Glen Mhor, had a capacity of 60,000 casks. In 1986, the warehouses held a mix of Glen Albyn, Glen Mhor and other distilleries, amounting to about 40,000 casks. These casks were distributed to other warehouses within the United Distillers Ltd (UD) group at the time of demolition. Several of the few remaining Glen Albyn casks are now in the possession of independent bottlers. Most of the whisky was used by various blenders. However the only official bottlings, besides the RMS bottlings, are from one cask which found its way to the Italian market during the 1970s

All the distillery buildings have been demolished. The site is now the home of two supermarkets. Worth a visit near Inverness is Urquhart Castle standing on a promontory overlooking Loch Ness – the long, thin, dark and deep loch that's said to be the home of Nessie, the monster. East of Inverness is Culloden Moor where the rebellion lead by Charles, the pretender to the crown, was brought to a bloody halt in 1745.

GLEN ALBYN

Structural elements and their respective weights

Structure	Observations
Colour	3
Peaty/Phenolic	1
Sherried/Winey	
Fruity/Estery	1
Floral/Aldehydic	1
Cereal/Malty	1
Feinty	2
Medicinal/Maritime	
Woody	
Vanilla/Honey	
Nutty/Creamy	
Spicy	1
Sulphury	

Conclusive organoleptic sensations

	Observations
Colour	Pale gold/lemon.
Nose	Very light and restrained. Flowery, pear fruit. Hints of malt and peat. Discretely spicy. Acidic.
Palate	Sweet, slight oily. Touching on pears and acidic summer apples. Gentle malt notes.
Finish	Short to medium in length. Herbal and fruity. Lightly peaty. Delivering a dry woody finale.
Comment	Light bodied and uncomplicated. A garden party dram.

Issued versions

Distilled	Age	% ABV	Size	Box	Version
1975	26	54.8	0.7		No versions

GLEN ESK (formerly HILLSIDE)

Pronounced '*glen ESK*', this stands for 'valley of the water' in Gaelic. 'Glen' is the anglicised version of the Gaelic word 'Gleann' meaning valley. 'Esk' is the anglicised form of the Gaelic word for water, 'uisge'. Esk is also the name given to the divided river that flows through the valley. Glen Esk distillery, now dormant, is situated in the hamlet of Hillside, which stands on a sloping ground just 3km north of the seaport and Royal burgh of Montrose. Danish Vikings violently and repeatedly attacked Montrose around the end of the first millennium. The distillery has changed names several times: from Highland Esk to North Esk, to Montrose, to Hillside, to Glenesk and finally to Glen Esk. It has had the most names of any distillery in the history of Scotch malt whisky. Glen Esk's two kilns topped with classic Charles Doig pagodas are still standing, but all the

Distillery details

REGION Highlands (Eastern)

OWNER Greencore Group/Pauls Malt Ltd

ADDRESS Pauls Malt Ltd., Kinnaber Road, Hillside, Montrose, Angus, DD10 9EP

ROADS A90 or A92, Hillside is north of Montrose, (A937, intersect Kinnaber Road)

TEL 01284 772060

FAX 01284 753349

EMAIL george.irving@paulsmalt.co.uk

WEB www.paulsmalt.co.uk

• RARE MALTS •

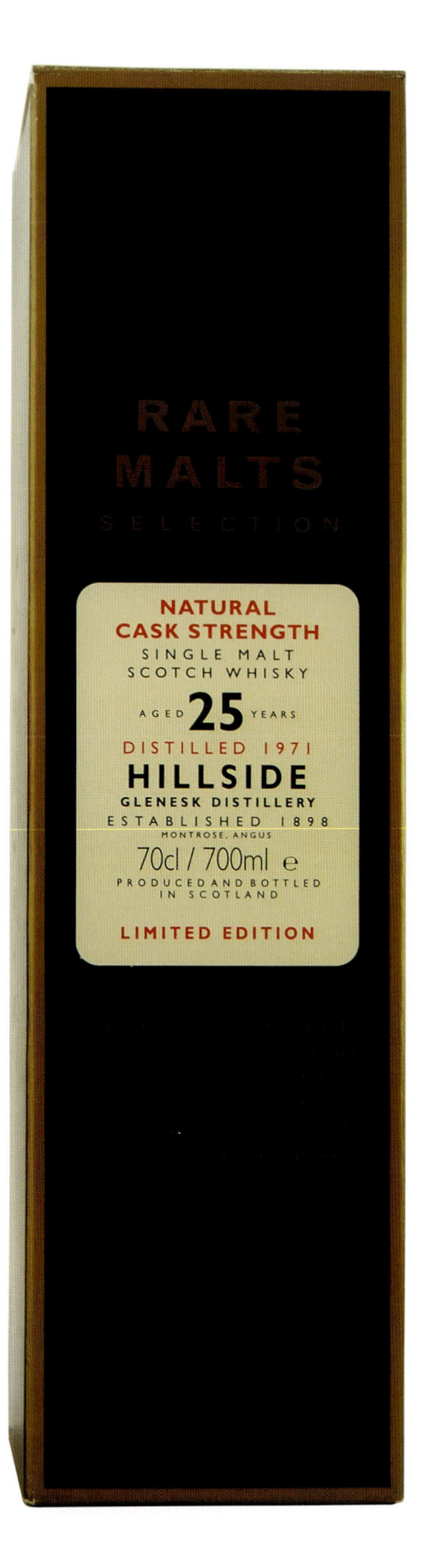

distillery equipment is removed. Today the premises are used for a large-scale malting operation, the sixth largest of its kind in the world.

Highland Esk Distillery was founded in 1897 by Septimus Parsonage and James Isles, a wine merchant from Dundee. They had formed a limited partnership, the Septimus Parsonage & Co. Ltd, which bought the premises of an old flax spinning mill and converted it to a distillery. The founders did not survive the Pattison crash, which occurred shortly after the inauguration of the distillery, and they were forced to sell in 1899. They sold their partnership to John F. Caille Heddle, who renamed the distillery 'North Esk Distillery' and kept it running until the outbreak of World War I. In 1910 several of the distillery buildings were destroyed by fire but the distillery was quickly rebuilt. When war broke out in 1914 North Esk Distillery was closed and its premises converted to billet troops. The distillery did not resume operation until 1938. In 1919 Thomas Bernard & Co. purchased the facility, changed the name to North Esk Maltings and used it for malting operation only. In 1938 Thomas Bernard & Co. sold the entire property to Associated Scottish Distillers Ltd (ASD), a subsidiary of Train & McIntyre Ltd, itself a subsidiary of National Distillers of Americas Inc. (NDA). A major shareholder in ASD was Joseph H. Hobbs, owner of Ben Nevis, Benromach, Bruichladdich, Glenkinchie, Glenury and Lochside distilleries. ASD completely changed the scope of the distillery by converting it (by installing a continuous still) from a malt whisky to a grain whisky distillery. ASD also changed the name to Montrose Distillery. From then until the mid-sixties the distillery was a grain whisky distillery.

Again the distillery was called into service to billet troops, providing accommodation for soldiers from 1941 to 1945. Post-war plans to expand the distillery fell through due to economic hardship and ASD, with Montrose included, was sold to Distillers Company Ltd (DCL) in 1954. DCL downgraded operations at Montrose shortly after the takeover and used the warehouses and the malting facilities only. In 1959 it was decided that the grain whisky distillation should be temporarily resumed due to a shortfall in DCL's production of grain whisky; although Montrose's capacity and operations were considered to be un-economic for long-term production, it lasted until 1964. In 1965 Montrose was

Glen Esk

transferred into the custody of DCL's subsidiary, Scottish Malt Distillers Ltd (SMD). SMD reverted the operation back to malt whisky production the same year and changed the name to Hillside Distillery. It produced malt whisky from its four new pot stills, starting in November 1965 and continuing until it closed in 1985. During the SMD era large drum malting machinery was installed, capable of providing this distillery, as well as others, with malted barley. The new drum maltings, initially installed in 1968 on an adjacent site, was enlarged in 1973. The upgrade included an increase to twenty-four germination drums, each with a capacity of thirty-one metric tonnes of barley.

SMD was not comfortable with the name so in 1980 Hillside Distillery became 'Glenesk Distillery and Maltings'. A spelling modification, to 'Glen Esk', occurred a few years later. The distillery became silent in December 1985 and the licence to distil was cancelled in 1992. However, the malting operation is still going strong. In 1996 the complete site was sold, including the silent Glen Esk and the malting operations, to Pauls Maltings. Pauls is one of the major players in Scottish malting, and is a subsidiary to the Irish Greencore Inc. Nowadays Glen Esk is renowned as an important malting plant, not as a distillery.

Water for the process and cooling was obtained from the River North Esk. When the distillery was converted back to a malt whisky distillery in November 1965, own-floor malting was performed until 1968. That year new drum maltings were installed, serving a number of distilleries in the area. Hence, Glen Esk, like Glen Ord, could claim it was either a 'malting on site' distillery, or a distillery bringing in malt from a 'central maltster'. Barley strain used was Golden Promise. The peating level was specified as 'lightly peated'. The malt was crushed to grist by a Porteus mill. Glen Esk's cast iron mash tun was fitted with a copper top and had a capacity of ten metric tones of grist. Around 190 metric tones of grist were put through nineteen mashes per week, at full production. The wort was transferred for fermentation to the eight wooden wash backs made of Oregon pine, with a capacity of 64,000 litres each. The yeast strain used for the fermentation was a Distiller's yeast version from Newton. The distillation occurred with two wash and two spirit stills, new in 1965. They were based on the Craigellachie Distillery's onion-shaped stills and were some of the first to be heated indirectly by steam coils. Cooling was by condensers placed inside the still house. The stills were made by Abercrombie of Alloa. The wash stills and spirit stills had a capacity of 39,000 litres each. The maximum annual output was 2,500,000 litres of alcohol.

The cask management regime was based on a twelve-year maturation period, using a mix of mainly ex-bourbon casks and some reused sherry casks. Maturation occurred in six warehouses located on the premises, capable of holding 28,000 casks. Today, all maturing stocks have been removed and are held at a central maturing facility. A large amount of the production went into William Sanderson's Vat 69 and was bottled at their facilities in South Queensferry, near Edinburgh.

The distillery is closed and all distillery equipment is removed. It may, however, be possible to arrange visits. Contact Pauls Malt Ltd. Worth a visit is the House of Dun, a Georgian mansion situated to the west of Montrose overlooking the Montrose Basin. It was designed and built by William Adam in 1730 for David Erskine, Lord Dun. Another castle to visit is Red Castle, situated on an elevated mound overlooking Lunan Bay. Red Castle lies just 6km south of Montrose and is built of red sandstone. The ruins of the castle date largely from the fifteenth century.

GLEN ESK (formerly HILLSIDE)

Structural elements and their respective weights

Structure	Observations
Colour	1
Peaty/Phenolic	
Sherried/Winey	
Fruity/Estery	2
Floral/Aldehydic	2
Cereal/Malty	2
Feinty	
Medicinal/Maritime	
Woody	2
Vanilla/Honey	2
Nutty/Creamy	
Spicy	
Sulphury	

Conclusive organoleptic sensations

	Observations
Colour	Pale yellow, like young chardonnay.
Nose	Hint of oaky vanilla. Resinous, pine. Hay barn. Sweet, fresh malt grist. Toffee and clover honey.
Palate	Minty. Tropical stone fruits. Dry maltiness.
Finish	Acidic apples. Pine resin. Herbal, minty.
Comment	Light bodied. A pre-dinner dram.

Issued versions

Distilled	Age	% abv	Size	Box	Version
1969	25	61.9	0.75		
1969	25	61.9	0.75	None	USA
1969	25	61.9	0.2	Box 1	
1970	25	61.1	0.75		
1970	25	60.1	0.7		
1971	25	62	0.7		

GLEN MHOR

Pronounced 'glen VHORE', it means 'the big valley'. 'Mhor' or 'Mór' is Gaelic for 'big'. The Great Glen of Albyn, also known as Glen Mhor, or simply the Great Glen, runs across Scotland from the northeast to the southwest. Glen Mhor was situated at the Great North Road beside the Caledonian Canal at the Muirtown basin, opposite the Glen Albyn distillery. A shopping centre with two supermarkets now occupies Glen Mhor's and adjacent Glen Albyn's sites. A hotel with a restaurant in the city centre pays homage to the old distillery, having adopted its name.

Glen Mhor was founded in 1892 and ready for production on 8 December 1894. These dates are, however, questioned by a note from the Inverness Dean of Guild Court dated January 1886 approving a 'new distillery', the Glen Mhor, and confirming its opening in October the same year. One of the reasons for establishing a new distillery in the area was a trivial conflict. John Birnie was the manager of Glen Albyn at the time but quit when he was denied a block of shares of the distillery. James Mackinlay (involved with Charles Mackinlay & Co. Ltd of Leith) and Birnie formed a partnership and engaged Charles Doig to build another distillery in the area. Doig had his recently designed signature pagoda-roof kiln installed at the new distillery. After a few productive years Glen Mhor was reconstructed in 1906 as a limited partnership, Mackinlay & Birnie Ltd. The investors Charles Mackinlay & Co. and John Walker & Sons Ltd were the major shareholders. William, son of the founder John Birnie, was involved in the operation of the distillery very early on and was active until his death in 1973. In 1920, Glen Albyn was purchased by Mackinlay and Birnie Ltd. The two distilleries ceased to compete, and for decades to come were run in parallel. Major

DISTILLERY DETAILS

REGION Highlands (Northern)

OWNER Last owner was DCL before it became part of the UD-Guinness group

ADDRESS Telford Street, Inverness, Inverness-shire, IV3 5LD

ROADS A9, north-west side of Inverness near the Caledonian Canal renovation and modernisation works were initiated. In 1925 a third still, a larger mash tun and two new wash backs were installed. A water turbine provided power for the malt mill, the malt elevator and the mash tun's rummager. It was replaced with electric engines in 1950, but remained as a power source for the switchers in the tun room. The water turbine was finally retired in 1960. In 1963 the stills were converted to indirect heating but were still fired by a coal-stoked furnace. DCL controlled 43.5% of Mackinlay and Birnie Ltd via its subsidiary John Walker & Sons Ltd. In 1972 DCL took full control by purchasing all the stocks of the company and transferred it to its subsidiary Scottish Malt Distillers Ltd (SMD). SMD kept production going for some years and then mothballed Glen Albyn and Glen Mhor in the early 1980s. Both distilleries were closed in 1983 and demolished in 1986. The noted Highland novelist and whisky writer Neil Gunn spent his younger years as an excise man established at the distillery from 1924.

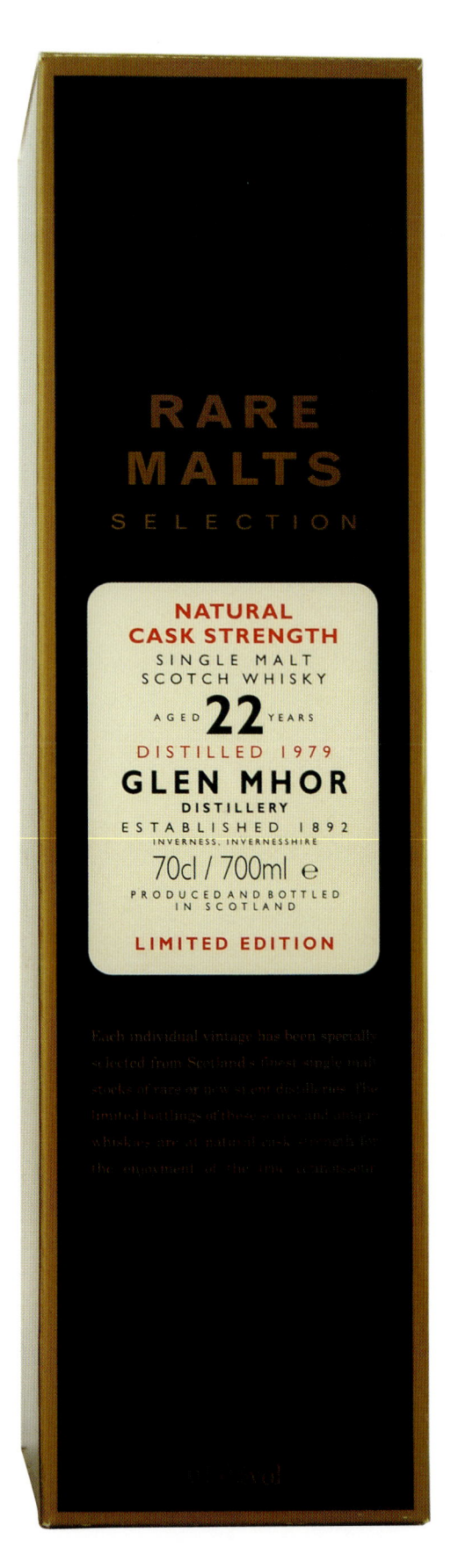

Water for the process and cooling was obtained from Loch Ness. One source claims that Glen Mhor abandoned floor malting on site in 1949 by installing a mechanical germination device, a Saladin box, which would have been the first in Scotland. Other sources claim that it was in 1954 and a few months after Glen Albyn installed their Saladin box, which would have been the first one in the whisky trade. Glen Mhor, like Glen Albyn, used its Saladin box until 1980, when it was replaced by malt brought in by lorry from the group's central maltsters. It is believed that the barley strains from the central maltsters where Golden Promise and Triumph versions peated to the preferred level. The barley used during the floor and Saladin box malting era was cultivated locally and the versions varied through the years. The kiln drying was made by heat and smoke generated by the same mix of peat , coke and coal used at Glen Albyn. Mixing coal, coke and peat was not an uncommon habit among the maltsters in those days. The peat used to be cut on the Dava Moor but was later replaced with peat from the Pitsligo in Aberdeenshire. The coal in the stoke mix added an oily/peaty character to the whisky, akin to Glen Albyn whisky but they were basically unrelated. The malt was crushed to grist by a Porteus mill. Around ten metric tonnes went into the mash tun. The number of mashes per week varied over time. The mash tun was made of Scottish larch. The wort was moved to wooden wash backs, also made from larch. Each had a capacity of about 21,000 litres. It is believed that the yeast strain used for fermentation was a Distiller's yeast, at least during the SMD days. The distillation occurred in three traditional onion-shaped stills. The two original wash and spirit pot stills were similar to Glen Albyn's and were built by the Glasgow producer Fleming, Bennet & McLaren. The wash still held a volume of 8,128 litres and the spirit still a volume of 6,919 litres. The volume of the third (a wash) still, bought in 1925, is not known by the author. Cooling was by traditional submerged worms and indirect heating by steam coils. The maximum annual output was 1,300,000 litres of alcohol per annum.

Cask management was in ex-bourbon casks only and is believed to have been based on a ten-year maturation period. The warehouses, on site and shared with Glen Albyn, had a capacity of 60,000 casks. In 1988 the warehouses held a mix of Glen Albyn, Glen Mhor and other distilleries amounting to around 40,000 casks. These casks were distributed to other warehouses within the United Distillers Ltd (UD) group at the time of demolition. Several of the few remaining Glen Mhor casks are now in the possession of independent bottlers.

All the distillery buildings have been demolished. For more information on what to see in the area, see the chapter on Glen Albyn.

GLEN MHOR

Structural elements and their respective weights

Structure	Observations
Colour	3
Peaty/Phenolic	1
Sherried/Winey	
Fruity/Estery	2
Floral/Aldehydic	2
Cereal/Malty	2
Feinty	
Medicinal/Maritime	
Woody	
Vanilla/Honey	2
Nutty/Creamy	1
Spicy	1
Sulphury	

Conclusive organoleptic sensations

	Observations
Colour	Gold with greenish tinge.
Nose	Grassy. Complex cereal notes, wholemeal. Fragrant smoke. Fresh citrus character up front. Hint of William pears in the background. A whiff of freshly ground black pepper.
Palate	Herbal. Rich fruit cake with a touch of lemon. Pronounced heather honey. Vanilla and creamy toffee.
Finish	Very long lingering finish. A bit dryish on the finale, which balances the biscuity and fruity orchestration.
Comment	Medium bodied. An after-dinner dram.

Issued versions

Distilled	Age	% ABV	Size	Box	Version
1976	28	51.9	0.7		
1979	22	61	0.7		

GLEN ORD

Pronounced 'glen ord', meaning 'the valley with the round hill' in Gaelic, it is located in the little village of Muir of Ord. The distillery has had several different names over time and named its products Ord, Glenordie, Muir of Ord, Glen Oran. Glen Ord is the last survivor of the dozen distilleries that used to operate in the area of the Eilan Dubh, or the Black Isle, on the east coast of the Northern Highlands. Its survival may be explained by its function not only as a distillery but also as a central maltster for a large part of the whisky distilling trade. Behind a rather dull, factory-like building hides the handsome classic distillery complex with its twin pagoda roofs. Glen Ord is one of a number of distilleries that have a glass wall on the still house, which allows the large copper stills to be viewed from the outside. The factory-like building beside is the central malting complex that serves not only Glen Ord's distillery but also a string of distilleries in the Diageo portfolio, among others. Glen Ord is one of Diageo's four largest malt whisky distilleries.

The 'legal' Glen Ord distillery was founded in 1838 and licensed to Robert Johnstone and Donald MacLennan as the Ord Distillery Co. An illegal operation had been ongoing on the site years before. The legal and the illegal distillery shared water resources, the Alt Fionnaidh Burn, with an adjacent oatmeal mill which was in operation from 1549 to 1958. The land was leased from the estate of Thomas Mackenzie of Ord. King Alexander III granted the land to the Mackenzie family in 1263 and Thomas Mackenzie inherited his estate in 1820. With a legal distillery on his estate he secured a market for the barley he cultivated and the by-products from the distillery served his piggery. Initially the distillery was powered by two large water wheels driven by water from Loch nam Bonnach and Loch nan Eun. They were

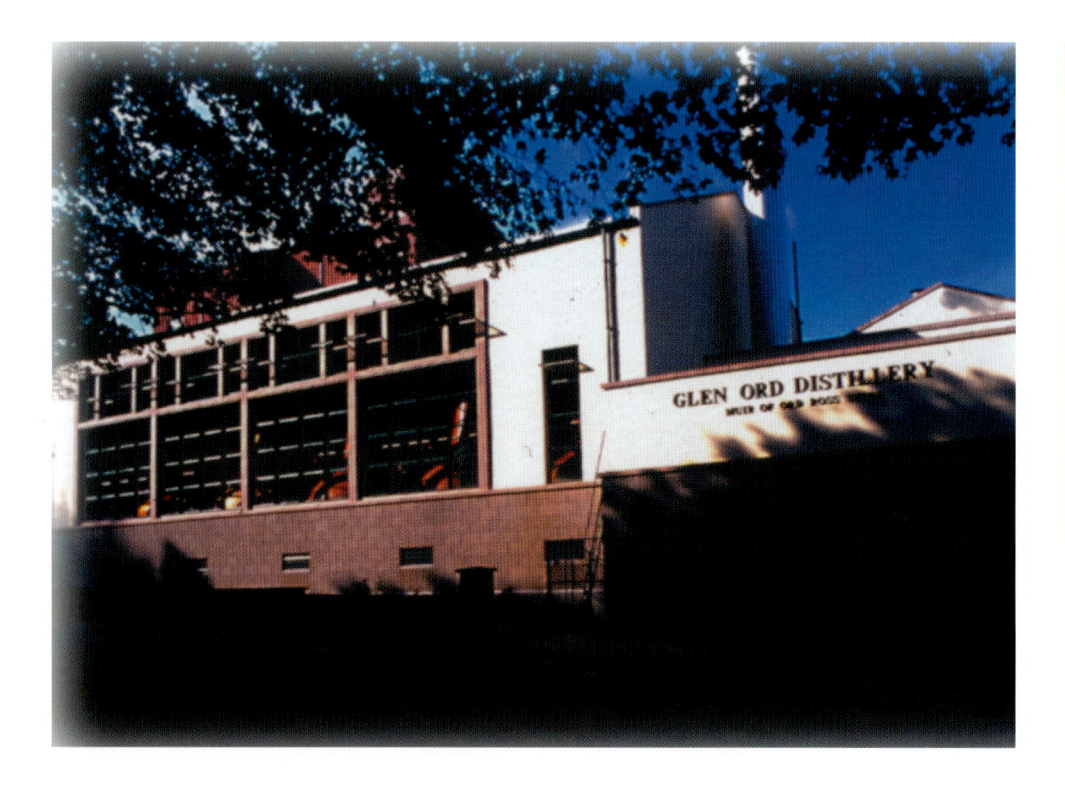

DISTILLERY DETAILS

REGION Highlands (Northern)

OWNER Diageo

ADDRESS Muir of Ord, Beauly, Ross-shire, IV6 7UJ

ROADS Junction of A832 and Altgowrie road, 29km north of Inverness

TEL 01463 872000, visitor centre 01463 872004

FAX 01463 872008

both replaced by electricity in 1949. Until then the distillery was lit by paraffin lamps, a risky business with highly flammable fumes around. One water wheel was kept until the early 1960s for some minor power assistance. Robert Johnstone went bankrupt in 1843, left the partnership the same year and sold his shares to Donald MacLennan.

Thomas MacGregor and Alexander MacLennan bought the distillery from David MacLennan in 1855. In 1867 Alexander MacLennan became the sole owner of the distillery. When he died, broke, in 1870, his widow remarried a bank clerk, Alexander Mackenzie, from the nearby town of Beauly. Mackenzie was put in charge of the distillery's operations and became a trailblazer for the whisky trade as he opened distant export markets such as Singapore, South Africa and other Commonwealth entities. Granted a lease in 1877 to operate the distillery for nineteen years, he expanded the facilities by erecting a new still house in 1878, only to see it going up in flames on 8 November the same year. A new still house was quickly erected. A few years later, in 1882, Mackenzie changed the distillery's trade name from Ord to Glen Oran, a name taken from the nearby Oran Burn. In 1896 Mackenzie died and the distillery was sold for £15,800 to the owner of Pulteney and Parkmore distilleries: the Dundee blending firm James Watson Co. Ltd. James Watson Co. refurbished and enlarged the distillery by adding new stills and considerably enhanced the malting floors. Due to restrictions at the end of World War I the distillery was silent from 1917 until 1919.

An eighteenth-century scene – horses carrying casks

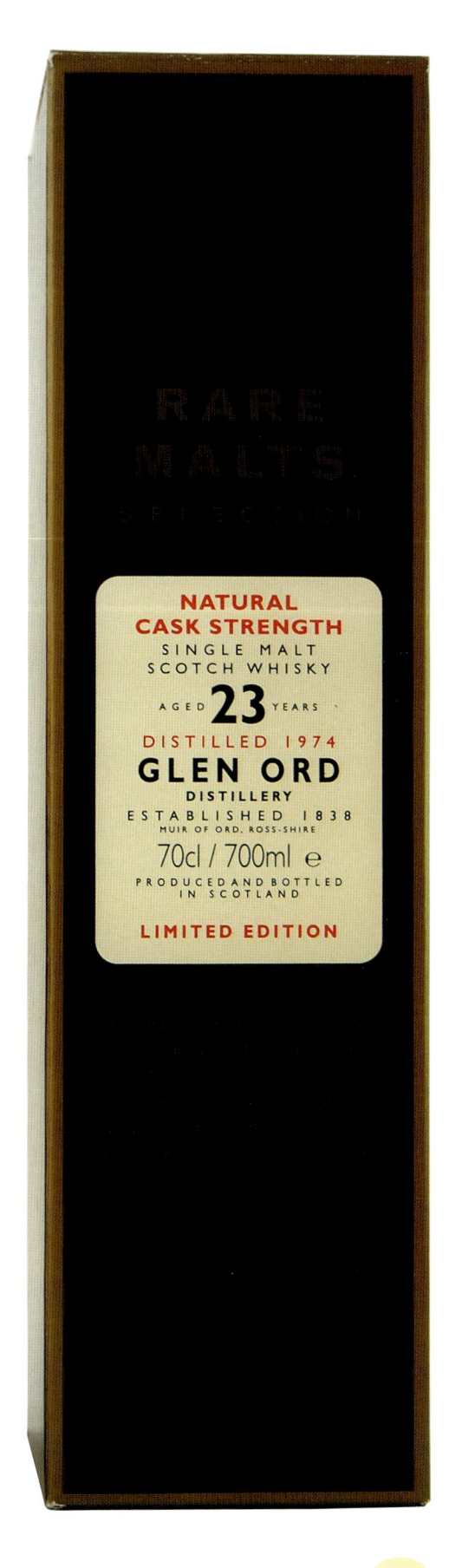

When Jabez Watson, James Watson's son and only heir, died in 1923 the James Watson Co. was bankrupt and went into voluntary liquidation. John Dewar & Sons of Perth purchased the distillery and changed the name of the company to Glen Ord Distillery Co. Ltd and the trademark from Glen Oran to Glen Ord. John Dewar & Sons, as did so many others, amalgamated with the Distillers Company Ltd (DCL) in 1925. DCL transferred the operations to its subsidiary Scottish Malt Distillers Ltd (SMD) in 1930. The lack of barley and government restrictions led to a new dormant period, which lasted from 1939 until 1945. In 1958 the distillery decided to launch a single malt; this time the whisky was simply trademarked as 'Ord'. The same year Glen Ord became the site of an eight-year experimental programme set up by DCL to compare coal, oil and steam as means of heating the stills. Batches of spirit were produced by each heat source and monitored to see if and how the different versions developed over time. To carry out the experiment two of the distillery's four direct coal-fired pot stills, heated by hand stoking of coal, were first converted to direct oil-firing. Later, in 1961, these two stills were again converted but to indirect heating by steam coils. The outcome of these three heating experiments was that indirect heating was not only economical but also feasible as no degrading of quality could be detected. A modernisation took place in 1961 when floor malting was abandoned and a Saladin malting box was installed. A larger renovation programme initiated in 1966 increased the number of pot stills from four to six. Both new pot stills were oil fired, indirectly heated by steam coils and two old pot stills, which were kept as direct coal fired, were converted to indirect heating. A new tun room and new mash and still houses were erected. In 1968 a new malting facility, a drum malting plant, was built beside the distillery to meet the needs of seven of SMD's distilleries. However, Glen Ord continued to use its own Saladin box until 1983 and Glen Ord drew nothing from its drum malting facility until 1983. In 1968 a dark grains plant was added, and later the single malt 'Glenordie' was released. A further modernisation and expansion of the drum malting plant occurred in 1996. In 2001, Glen Ord became the first company in the UK to use the new Biobed Modular Plant (MP) technology, a pioneering application of high-rate anaerobic granular treatment for waste water with low chemical oxygen.

Water for the process and cooling is obtained from the Alt Fionnadh, or the White Burn. Water from the burn flows over peat and granite on its way to the sea via the distillery. The burn is fed by overflow water from two small lochs, Loch nam Eun (Loch of the Birds) and Loch nam Bonnach (Loch of the Smoke). Eun is filled by melted snow every spring and Bonnach by rain water. Barley used is mostly cultivated locally (around 85%) and the strains used vary over time and seasons. Today mainly Optic and Decanter are processed. New strains are gradually introduced and trialled. Currently, the strain Troon is also used experimentally. Since 1983 barley is malted at Ord's large drum malting facility. Today, Ord Maltings is the common malt source for a string of Diageo-owned distilleries, but it also serves distilleries in other companies. Glen Ord used to be a distillery definitely 'malting on site', however, it may be disputed as to whether or not Glen Ord today is a distillery bringing in malt from a 'central maltster'. Glen Ord's drum malt facility consists of eighteen drums, each with a capacity of 30 metric tonnes of barley. The kilning segment of the pro-cess, performed in any of Ord's kilns, lasts for up to fifteen hours per malt batch, longer when the specification is medium to heavy peated. It uses around 1,250 metric tonnes of peat per annum but also uses oil as a heat source. The peat used as drying agent and phenol source is harvested from the Tomintoul Peat Moss. Harvest occurs during the spring season; it dries over the summer months and is brought in and stored on site in autumn. When burnt it is mixed with heather to create a signature flavour. The barley is peated to a very light specification, designed to be noted in the final, matured, whisky but difficult to detect in the new make spirit. The malt is crushed to grist by a four-roller Porteus mill. Glen Ord's green cast-iron mash tun has a volume of 46,000 litres and a capacity of 12.5 metric tones of grist under its copper canopy. Around 80 metric tonnes of grist are put through by seven mashes per week. The wort is transferred for fermentation to the eight old wooden wash backs, made from Oregon pine. They have a capacity of 60,000 litres each. The yeast strain used for fermentation is a Distiller's yeast version. The fermentation cycle is of the short type, lasting forty-four hours. The distillation occurs in three wash and three spirit stills, all traditionally onion-shaped, indirectly heated by steam coils and cooled by condensers.

The stills were built by Abercrombie of Alloa. The volume of the wash stills is 18,000 litres each and the spirit stills 15,500 each. The maximum annual output is 3,400,000 litres; however recent production has been as low as 1,200,000 litres of alcohol.

Cask management is based on a twelve-year maturation period, using a mix of ex-bourbon casks and twice reused sherry casks. Maturation occurs in five warehouses located on site but most of the Ord spirit is sent to central bond at Menstrie. The warehouses on site have a capacity of 12,000 casks. Bottling is performed in Leven in Fife. A large amount of the production goes into Johnnie Walker and Dewar's blends.

The distillery is open to visitors and has a visitor centre and shop. Worth a visit near Inverness is Cromarty, on the Black Isle peninsula (Eilan Dubh), the Highlands's best-preserved eighteenth century town. This is Mackenzie country and full of clan castles – such as Eilean Donan, Kintail and Brahan. Brahan, near Ord, was the home of the remarkable Coineach Odhar. He was known as the Brahan Seer and forecast important future events in detail – most of them properly documented – and for his trouble was boiled in oil on a headland near Ord for 'dabbling in witchcraft'.

GLEN ORD

Structural elements and their respective weights

Structure	Observations
Colour	4
Peaty/Phenolic	1
Sherried/Winey	1
Fruity/Estery	3
Floral/Aldehydic	2
Cereal/Malty	1
Feinty	
Medicinal/Maritime	
Woody	1
Vanilla/Honey	1
Nutty/Creamy	2
Spicy	2
Sulphury	

Conclusive organoleptic sensations

	Observations
Colour	Pale buttercup, unripe corn.
Nose	Heather. Gentle, fragrant peaty smoke. Malt grist. Faint, distant shimmering sherry notes.
Palate	Walnuts and almonds. Sultanas. Hint of fresh ginger and lemon peel.
Finish	Black pepper. Ginger and peat. Whiff of a rosy Gewürztraminer.
Comment	Medium bodied. Clean, smooth and silky in a self-confident way. An after-dinner dram.

Issued versions

Distilled	Age	% abv	Size	Box	Version
1972	23	62.43	0.75		
1973	23	59.8	0.75		
1974	23	60.8	0.7		

GLENDULLAN

Pronounced '*glen DULLan*', it means 'the valley of the standing stone'. The Gaelic 'Dullán' comes from 'Dallán', meaning 'plug' or 'stopper' or 'stone'. Glendullan is located on a pretty spot on the banks of the River Fiddich. When Glendullan was erected it was the last of the 1890s boom in building distilleries in and around Dufftown. When the town was bestowed with its seventh distillery it gave rise to the local saying: 'Rome was built on seven hills, Dufftown was built on seven stills'. Glendullan was, however, not the last to be built in the area; it was followed by Pittyvaich in 1975 and Kininvie in 1990. This distillery is exceptional in that for a period was two distilleries running in tandem. Glendullan was the only such operation, besides Linkwood and Teaninich, not questioned by the trade organisation Scotch Whisky Association (SWA). Other 'tandems' are Brora/Clynelish, Mannochmore/Glenlossie and Dufftown/Pitlyvaich. Glendullan was granted a Royal Appointment in 1902 and it is said that whisky

DISTILLERY DETAILS

REGION Highlands (Speyside)

OWNER Diageo

ADDRESS Dufftown, Banffshire, AB55 4DJ

ROADS A941/A920 junction in Dufftown

TEL 01340 822100

FAX 01340 822102

• GLENDULLAN •

from Glendullan became the favourite not only of King Edward VII but also of the Speaker of the House of Commons. It was chosen in 1992 by the first female Speaker, Betty Boothroyd, as the Speaker's whisky. The distillery is the second largest within the Diageo group.

Glendullan-Glenlivet, as it was called from the beginning, was the original distillery. It was built in 1896–97, received its first consignment of barley on 28 January 1898 and was in full production by 25 April 1898. Its founder was William Williams & Sons Ltd, a prominent blender from Aberdeen. Rumours have it that the distillery was built because an attempt by William Williams & Sons to buy Glenfiddich and Balvenie distilleries fell through. Hence, it was decided to erect a new distillery near these two in order to guarantee a whisky of the same quality. Glendullan's main purpose was to produce malt whisky at low cost for the firm's popular blends Three Star and Strathdon. Hence, Glendullan shared a private railway siding with Mortlach Distillery next door to save on transport and operated a large 4.3m water wheel driven by River Fiddich to save on the energy bill. The wheel, capable of delivering 16hp of power, was still producing energy for the distillery post World War II. William Williams & Sons merged in 1919 with the blending firm Greenlees Brothers Ltd, who had recently merged with the blenders Alexander & MacDonald Ltd to form Macdonald, Greenlees & Williams (Distillers) Ltd, under the management of John Calder. The Greenlees brothers, who had set up their firm in 1871, had become very successful with their blend, Old Parr, and needed distillery resources. Alexander & MacDonald brought their two distilleries Auchinblae (closed 1926) and Stronachie (closed 1928) into the new limited partnership. A reorganisation occurred in 1925 where the name was changed to MacDonald Greenlees Ltd. Shortly thereafter, in 1926, the company was absorbed by the Distillers Company Ltd (DCL), followed by a transfer in 1930 to DCL's subsidiary Scottish Malt Distillers Ltd (SMD).

Except for a period from 1940 to 1947, the old Glendullan distillery ran non-stop until it was mothballed in 1985. In 1962 a new still house, mash house, tun room and equipment were added. With this modernisation, it could have been reopened without too much effort, but it is now sadly declared as definitively closed. The old Glendullan is now in use as a central workshop for ongoing maintenance and repair work of distillery equipment. When in operation its equipment consisted of one wash still and one spirit still, both onion-shaped, but with a profile that differed from the six stills that

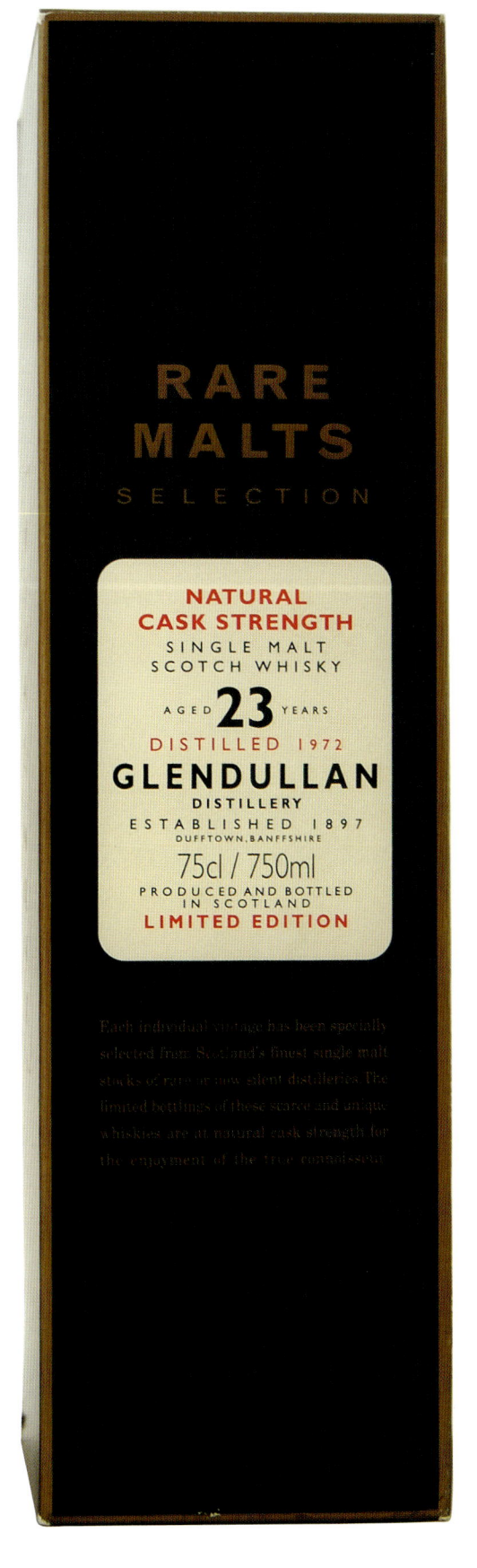

107

are installed at the 'new' Glendullan. The stills were equipped with the traditional cooling system, copper coils, or 'worms', submerged in wooden tubs. Its mash tun, like the five wooden wash backs, was rather small. At full operation the old distillery was capable of handling twelve mashes of 3.6 metric tonnes each per week, or producing 1,000,000 litres of alcohol per annum.

The new Glendullan, essentially a completely new distillery, was built in 1971–72 beside the old still house and was fully operational in 1972. Its task was to dramatically increase capacity without stopping production. It has its own set of onion-shaped stills, three wash and three spirit stills all fitted with condensers, not worm tubs. When the 'new' Glendullan was ready in 1972 it shared some resources and the mash bill with the old distillery, including water sources. Barley strains were brought in from the same central malsters, and peated to the same specification. The barley was milled to grist by the same mill. The grist was mashed in different mash tuns but fermented under the influence of identical yeast strains in different sets of wash backs. Another difference was the size and shape of the old Glendullan's two stills compared with the new Glendullan's six. The same maturation regime was applied. It is claimed that exactly identical whisky was produced from the two distilleries during their tandem years, 1972 to 1985. Whisky stemming from this period was always vatted (mixed together before bottling) and not bottled separately.

Water for the process is fetched from Goats well in the Conval Hills. The cooling water is obtained from the River Fiddich. Barley has varied over time and may vary over seasons. Today it is Decanter that is used, brought in from the central maltster Burghead. The malt is non-peated, crushed to grist by a Porteus mill and mashed in Glendullan's semi-Lauter cast-iron mash tun, with a capacity of 45,000 litres. Around 165 metric tonnes of grist are put through fifteen mashes per week. The wort is then transferred for fermentation to the eight wooden wash backs made from Scottish larch. They have a capacity of 85,000 litres each. The yeast strain used for the fermentation is a Distiller's yeast version from Mauri. The distillation occurs in three wash and three spirit stills, all traditionally onion shaped, indirectly heated by steam coils and cooled by condensers. The stills were built by Abercrombie of Alloa. The volume of the wash stills is 23,800 litres each and the spirit stills 33,700 each. The maximum annual output is 3,700,000 litres of alcohol; however, recent production has been lower.

Cask management is based on a twelve-year maturation period, using a mix of ex-bourbon casks and twice reused sherry casks. Maturation occurs in some of the warehouses located on site but most of the spirit is sent to central warehousing. The warehouses on site have a capacity of 8,000 casks. Bottling is performed in Leven in Fife. A large amount of the production goes into Greenlees' Old Parr blends.

The distillery is open to visitors, by appointment. Worth a visit is the nearby Balvenie Castle, founded during the thirteenth century. The Dufftown Highland Games, held during the summer months, is a highly popular activity to watch and participate in.

GLENDULLAN

Structural elements and their respective weights

STRUCTURE	OBSERVATIONS
Colour	11
Peaty/Phenolic	1
Sherried/Winey	1
Fruity/Estery	1
Floral/Aldehydic	3
Cereal/Malty	2
Feinty	1
Medicinal/Maritime	
Woody	
Vanilla/Honey	2
Nutty/Creamy	
Spicy	1
Sulphury	

GLENDULLAN

Conclusive organoleptic sensations

	OBSERVATIONS
Colour	Amontillado sherry.
Nose	A medley of assorted meadow flowers. Creamy fudge. Sweet malt. New leather. A delicate hint of smoke at the far end.
Palate	Heather honey, vanilla and oak. Malty. Creamy. Restrained sherry.
Finish	Peppery. Floral. Herbal like crushed mint sprigs during the phasing out.
Comment	Medium bodied. A pre-dinner dram.

Issued versions

DISTILLED	AGE	% ABV	SIZE	BOX	VERSION
1972	22	62.6	0.7	None	
1972	23	62.43	0.75		
1972	23	62.43	0.75	None	USA
1972	23	62.43	0.2	Box 2	
1973	23	58.6	0.75		
1974	23	63.1	0.7		
1978	26	56.6	0.7		

GLENLOCHY

Pronounced 'glen LOCHee', it means 'Valley of the Black Goddess'. The Gaelic 'lóchy' (not related to 'loch' – 'lake') is spelled 'lóchdae', meaning 'black goddess'. Glenlochy was situated in the Great Glen, close to the Loch Lochy ('the lake of the black goddess') at the southern end of the Caledonian Canal, in a pretty setting on the outskirts of Fort William. The distillery was closed in 1983 and all equipment was dismantled in 1986. Request for demolition permission was filed in April 1986. The permission, a conditional one, was not granted until six years later. It saved the pagoda-roofed kiln, which is now preserved as a historic building. However, there is nothing in the archives of Charles Doig linking him and his business either to the construction of the Glenlochy Distillery or to its pagoda-roofed kiln. It seems that the high-pitched pagoda roof is a modified copy of Doig's unique design. A lodging house, Distillery Guest House, was established on the premises by the new owners, West Coast Inns Ltd. Permission to convert the kiln to seven flats and the malt barn to sixteen flats has been granted, and construction started in 2005.

Until 1908 Glenlochy was one of three distilleries active in the area, with Ben Nevis and Nevis. Only Ben Nevis distillery, owned by Japanese Nikka Distillers, has survived. Founded in 1825 by

Distillery details

REGION Highlands (Western)

OWNER Last owner was Distillers Company Ltd (DCL) via its subsidiary Scottish Malt Distillers Ltd. Now West Coast Inns Ltd

ADDRESS North Road, Nevis Bridge, Fort William, Inverness-shire, PH33 6LR

ROADS A82 to Forth William

TEL Distillery Guest House, 01397 700103

FAX Distillery Guest House, 01397 702980

EMAIL Distillery Guest House, disthouse@aol.com

Glenlochy

Long John McDonald, it was the first distillery in the area. After his death, his son, Donald Peter McDonald, took over the operation. Donald became so successful with the sale of his whisky, Long John's Celebrated Dew of Ben Nevis, that he had to build a second distillery to keep up with the demand. Built in 1878 and partly integrated with Ben Nevis in 1908, it was named 'Nevis' or 'Lochaber' or, according to other sources, 'Glen Nevis' (not to be confused with a distillery of the same name located in Campbeltown). It was part of Nevis Distillery that later became known as the Lochaber Maltings and subsequently Lochaber Warehouses. When Train & McIntyre Ltd acquired the Ben Nevis complex from the McDonald family in 1941 the Lochaber premises, with its four warehouses and a floor malting site, were transferred to Glenlochy. The distillery had entered an expansive period, requiring additional malting facilities and storage space, and their growing production overflowed their single warehouse.

The company, Glenlochy-Fort William Distillery Co. Ltd, and the distillery were created in 1897 by David McAndie of Glen Cawdor distillery in Nairn. The foundation for the new distillery was laid in 1898, and the buildings were completed in April 1900. Glenlochy was up for business on 4 April 1901. The land chosen for the distillery belonged to Lord Abinger's Black Park and was purchased by the founders in 1897, with water rights for the River Nevis and peat cutting rights for nearby Dalvenie Moss. The water rights included power generating as well as process and cooling water. Glenlochy was partly driven by water power until the 1960s. McAndie also persuaded the North British Railway to build a siding to serve his distillery; the spur was lost in 1970. Quick to make a profit, McAndie sold his share of the distillery for £7,500, four times more than he had invested, less than one year after the distillery became fully operational. Unfortunately, it coincided with the Pattison crash, which forced production to a minimum. The distillery struggled to survive throughout World War I but had to close from 1917 to 1924, longer than other malt distilleries at the time. The financial difficulties that had mounted forced liquidation. During this dark period a group of risk takers emerged in 1920. A partnership of English brewers from Lancashire and Yorkshire put forward an offer that the owners could not resist. Ownership changed hands and the distillery went on stream again in 1924. This time the saga lasted for only two years. The group gave up its strive for profit, closed Glenlochy in 1926, and disposed of it for a give-away price in 1934. The recipient was T.L.

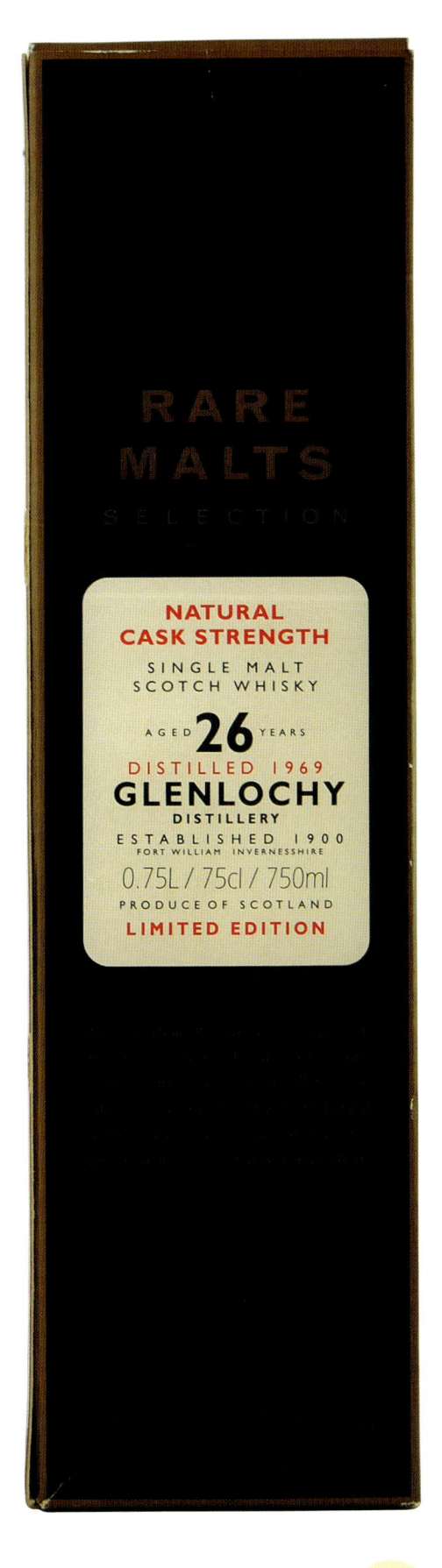

Rankin, a Lancashire car hirer. He did not restart the distillery but sold the premises for a nice profit in 1937 to Train & McIntyre Ltd, owned by the legendary Scottish-Canadian entrepreneur Joseph Hobbs, and the National Distillers of Americas Inc. (NDA). Hobbs is recognised for his creation of jobs and prosperity in the Fort William area. Train & McIntyre kick-started Glenlochy and in 1938 transferred the distillery to its subsidiary, the Associated Scottish Distilleries Ltd (ASD). Joseph Hobbs sold his interest in Train & McIntyre in 1940 to the NDA for capital to establish the Great Glen Cattle Ranch. The Distillers Company Ltd (DCL) took over the NDA in 1953, thereby acquiring Train & McIntyre and ASD. DCL transferred Glenlochy to their subsidiary, Scottish Malt Distillers Ltd (SMD), the same year. Under the SMD management Glenlochy was modernised in several steps. In 1960, the water wheel was replaced with electric equipment. The last major overhaul occurred in 1976 when, it is said, indirect heating of the post stills was introduced. It was the end of an era when DCL put Glenlochy to a final rest in 1983.

Glenlochy in the 1950s

Water for the process and cooling was obtained from the River Nevis, a river which is fed by numerous springs from the Ben Nevis mountainside. The distillery's own on-floor malting was abandoned in 1968. After that Glenlochy relied on malt from the DCL group's central maltster, Glen Ord's drum maltings. A supplementary old malt floor, which initially belonged to Nevis, later called Lochaber Maltings, was in use until the beginning of the 1960s. It was demolished in August 1984, a year after Glenlochy was closed. Barley strains used varied over time and may at the end have been mainly Golden Promise and Triumph. The peating level is said to have been specified as 'lightly peated'. The malt was crushed to grist by a mill of unknown type, probably a Porteus. Glenlochy's small cast-iron mash tun had a capacity of 5 metric tonnes of grist. Around 45 metric tonnes of grist were put through nine mashes per week. The wort was transferred for fermentation to four wooden wash backs, made of Oregon pine. They had a capacity of 29,000 litres each. It is believed that the yeast strain used for the fermentation was Distiller's yeast. The distillation occurred with one wash and one spirit still, traditionally onion shaped and indirectly heated. The wash still's volume was 14,580 litres, and the spirit still's was 14,380 litres. Cooling was performed by condensers, which were bought in 1962. The maximum annual output was 1,000,000 litres of alcohol.

It is believed that cask management was based on a twelve-year maturation period, using a mix of ex-bourbon casks and twice reused sherry casks. Maturation occurred in one warehouse on site and four located on the other side of the railroad tracks that divided the premises. These four warehouses were initially built for the Nevis or Lochaber Distillery. The warehouses had a capacity of 11,000 casks. Most of the casks held for maturation were not from Glenlochy but from a variety of distilleries managed by Scottish Malt Distillers (SMD). All of Glenlochy's production went to the blending trade and the whisky was never bottled as a single malt when Glenlochy was active.

Worth a visit are Ben Nevis, Britain's highest peak at 1,344m, and Neptune's stairs, a flight of eight locks designed by Thomas Telford that form the most spectacular part of the Caledonian Canal.

GLENLOCHY

Structural elements and their respective weights

Structure	Observations
Colour	6
Peaty/Phenolic	
Sherried/Winey	2
Fruity/Estery	2
Floral/Aldehydic	
Cereal/Malty	
Feinty	
Medicinal/Maritime	
Woody	1
Vanilla/Honey	1
Nutty/Creamy	1
Spicy	1
Sulphury	

Conclusive organoleptic sensations

	Observations
Colour	Old gold, reddish tinge.
Nose	Vanilla. Toasted oak wood. Oxidized winey notes, as from Madeira.
Palate	Coconut and citrus. Chestnut purée. Creamy-oily.
Finish	Citrus oil from rubbed lemon peel. Peppery, dusty white pepper. A bit tannic, bitter dryness.
Comment	Medium bodied. An uncomplicated all-around dram.

Issued versions

Distilled	Age	% abv	Size	Box	Version
1969	25	62.2	0.75		
1969	26	59	0.75		
1969	25	62.2	0.2	Box 1	
1969	25	62.08	0.75	None	USA
1969	26	58.8	0.75	None	B297

GLENURY ROYAL

Pronounced *'glen yoy-ree royal'*. 'Ury' (older form 'urie' or 'úire') is the name of the famous estate where the distillery was erected. Early Gaelic 'úire', Norse 'aurr', means 'loam', 'wet clay', 'mud'. Hence, the meaning may be 'the valley of fertile soil'. Another interpretation is 'Gleann ugeach' meaning 'Glen of the Ugie'. The suffix 'Royal' is said to have been added by the distillery's flamboyant founder, the athletic Captain Robert Barclay-Allardice. Along with serving as a Member of Parliament he was known as an extreme marathon walker, boxer and short-distance runner. Through political connections he secured King William IV's permission for the whisky made at his distillery to be designated as Glenury 'Royal'. It is said that John Windsor, a partner of the company, had a great influence with the King, who was known to be a keen patron of Scotch whisky. The now-demolished distillery was located on the north bank of Cowie Water, situated on the northern outskirts of Stonehaven. It is now replaced with a development of houses and flats. Building work started around the end of 2001. On the opposite side of the river lay the extensive Glenury playing fields with cricket and football pitches.

In the year 1648, David Barclay purchased Ury, an estate flanking the stream known as Cowie Water, which flowed a short distance down to the North Sea near the small seaport town of

DISTILLERY DETAILS

REGION Highlands (Eastern)

OWNER Last owner was United Distillers (UD)

ADDRESS Stonehaven, Kincardineshire, AB39 2PY

ROADS Where A92 joins A90, 25km south of Aberdeen (B979)

GLENURY ROYAL

Stonehaven. Throughout the centuries, the ownership of the Ury estate passed by inheritance through a succession of Robert Barclays, all direct descendants of David and, like him, defender of the religious Quaker movement. It is said that the Glenury Distillery was originally established by initiative of the fourth Duke of Gordon, with a view to reducing smuggling, alarmingly prevalent then, and to encourage agriculture. It is clear that the Barclay's Ury estate included a still for making whisky in 1825, as these excerpts from *The Aberdeen Journal* show:

20 April 1825. We are sorry to learn, that between two and three o'clock in the afternoon of Saturday last, 16th current, a fire broke out in the malting premises of Messrs Barclay, Macdonald, and Co., Distillers at Glenury, near Stonehaven, which spread with the utmost rapidity, and in the course of little more than an hour, burnt down the kiln, the greater part of the grain lofts and malting barn, and also the stock of barley and malt belonging to the company, notwithstanding the great exertions made by the people connected with the work, assisted by a large body of men from Stonehaven. The distillery is separated from these buildings by the mill-lade, but communicated with them at upper storey, by means of a covered passage or platform. The flames laid hold of this passage, and extended to part of the roof of the distillery, when a few intrepid individuals, at the hazard of their own lives, dashed into the passage, and by quickly demolishing it, removed the communication between the two buildings and thereby saved the distillery, spirit cellar, and whole brewing and distilling machinery. The flames in the meantime raged with the greatest fury in the malting premises, and although by four o'clock of the afternoon, it was so far got under as to prevent any further risk, the ruins continued smoking all night and the greater part of the following day. It was purely accidental.

And again from *The Aberdeen Journal*, dated 11 May 1825 shows:

On Saturday last, about one o'clock, Andrew Clark, one of the workmen employed at Glenury Distillery, being sent to examine the state of the great boiler, by some unfortunate accident fell backwards into it and was so dreadfully burned, that he died in extreme agony at 7 o'clock in the evening. The water was nearly at burning point, and he was entirely immersed in it. No one was at hand but

Mr. Buchanan, the distiller, who rushed to his assistance and had his hands and arms dreadfully scalded in pulling him out; indeed the heat of the liquor and the weight of the unfortunate man had nearly overcome him, so that it was with difficulty he escaped being drawn into the boiler himself, by his humane exertion; on behalf of the sufferer, who, we understand, was but recently married.

Captain Barclay's motivation for operating a commercial whisky still lay in his push for a market for locally cultivated barley, following the post Napoleonic war slump in agriculture. A partnership was formed in 1825, the Barclay & McDonald Co., which applied for and received a licence to operate a still under the name Glenury Distillery. After the fire a new facility was rebuilt and in production by 5 January 1833. On 24 March 1838 *The Aberdeen Herald* proudly announced:

> The propriety of this well-known Distillery have much pleasure in announcing that one of the partners, John Windsor, Esq., has been appointed "Distiller of Whisky to Her Majesty." The present excellent arrangements and very superior Spirits produced at this establishment are facts extensively and well known. The Distillery has been lately greatly enlarged, and machinery has been added to it to such an extent as to make it the first Distillery in the north. The Distillery is situated near Stonehaven upon the Cowie, a small stream which takes its rise a short distance above in a mossy district, which renders its waters so peculiarly desirable for the purposes of Distillation. Note – The Glenury Distillery was originally established by the late Duke of Gordon, with a view to put down smuggling, then alarmingly prevalent, and to encourage agriculture. Captain Barclay of Ury is now the head of the firm, and though that celebrated sportsman has of late years retired to the 'halls of his fathers' he continues to devote his best exertions to the advancement of the general interest of agriculture. We wish the proprietors of this establishment ample success in their spirited undertaking.

Captain Barclay died in 1854 and the distillery licence and lease was sold at auction in 1858 to William Ritchie of Glasgow. The Ritchie family owned the property until July 1936, when they had to give up their long-term lease. The Ritchies carried out several extensions and modernisations during their ownership, despite having to close the distillery on several occasions: first between 1911 and 1913 because of the depression, then for the war years from February 1917 until March 1919, and finally from May 1925 until the sale in July 1936. The new owners, John Hobbs and Hattam Atari, bought the licence and lease from the legal owner, Lord Stonehaven, for the sum of £7,500. The duo quickly brought Glenury back into production and sold it in 1938 for £18,500 to the Associated Scottish Distillers Ltd (ASD), a subsidiary of the National Distillers of America, Inc. (NDA). As a key shareholder of NDA, Hobbs was closely involved in its operations. Under his supervision Glenury became the centre for quality control and development of all the distilleries that belonged to ASD. In 1953 the ASD assets were purchased by Distillers Company Ltd (DCL). They took over NDA, the formal owner of ASD. DCL passed Glenury to their subsidiary the Scottish Malt Distillers Ltd (SMD) the same year. During the SMD era on-site floor malting was abandoned in 1968 and Glenury was modernised in several steps. In 1965 the water wheel was replaced with electric equipment. A new mash house and a new mill and tun room were also added. The last, major renovation occurred in 1966 with an expansion of the still house and addition of two new stills, totalling four. At this time, it is said, indirect heating of the pot stills was introduced and probably the old worm coolers replaced by condensers. United Distillers Ltd (UD), formerly DCL, closed Glenury in March 1985, like several of their distilleries. Glenury's operating licence was cancelled in February 1992 and the site was sold for residential development. Building work started around the end of 2001.

Water for the process and cooling was obtained from the Cowie Water, a small river that for a time was also the water supply for the town of Stonehaven. Own-floor malting was abandoned in 1968, whereafter Glenlochy had to rely on malted barley from the DCL group's central maltsters, such as Glen Esk and Montrose maltings. Barley strains used varied over time, and may at the end have been mainly the Golden Promise and Triumph varieties. The peating level seems to have been specified as 'lightly peated'. The malt was crushed to grist by a mill of unknown type, probably a Porteus. Glenlochy's medium-sized cast-iron mash tun had a capacity of 8.6 metric tonnes of grist. Around 132 metric tonnes of grist were put through sixteen mashes per week, at full production. The wort was transferred for fermentation to the eight wooden wash backs made of Oregon pine. They had a capacity of 45,000 litres each. It is believed that the yeast strain used for the fermentation was Distiller's yeast. The distillation was performed by two wash and one spirit stills, all traditionally onion-shaped, indirectly heated by steam coils and cooled by condensers. It is believed that the wash stills' volume was around 18,000 litres each, and the spirit still's was around 13,600 litres each. The maximum annual output was 2,500,000 litres of alcohol; however, for the last years the production was halved.

Cask management seems to have been based on a twelve-year maturation period, using a mix of mainly ex-bourbon casks and some reused sherry casks. Maturation occurred in warehouses located on the premises, capable of holding 1,900 casks. The lion's share of production went to central warehousing and bottling. Bottling was performed in Leven in Fife. A large amount of the production went into John Gillon & Co. Ltd blends such as King William IV and Auld Toun, and to Long John.

The distillery is closed and has been replaced with a development of houses and flats. Worth a visit is Dunnottar Castle, an impressive cliff-top ruin, only about a mile south of Stonehaven. It may be reached by a dramatic cliff-top footpath. Its recorded history goes back to the year 681.

GLENURY ROYAL

Structural elements and their respective weights

Structure	Observations
Colour	5
Peaty/Phenolic	1
Sherried/Winey	3
Fruity/Estery	1
Floral/Aldehydic	2
Cereal/Malty	1
Feinty	
Medicinal/Maritime	
Woody	
Vanilla/Honey	2
Nutty/Creamy	1
Spicy	
Sulphury	

Conclusive organoleptic sensations

	Observations
Colour	Bright, polished gold.
Nose	Aromatic, a gallery of aromas. Mature Oloroso cream sherry. Nutty, almondy. Whiff of burning heather peat. Sweet citrus.
Palate	Flowery, flaunted in a stylish manner. Sweet notes as from orange blossom honey. Sherry marks its presence in a light way and so do the peat and malt.
Finish	Long and silky. Honey sweetness developing into light peppery notes with hints of cinnamon trotting in same pace.
Comment	Medium bodied. Perfect as a dram with the sweets for a dinner finale.

Issued versions

Distilled	Age	% abv	Size	Box	Version
1970	28	58.4	0.75		
1970	29	57	0.7		
1971	23	61.3	0.7	None	Bottle size
1971	23	61.3	0.75	None	Bottle size

INCHGOWER

PRONOUNCED '*inch gavver*', it means 'island in the stream'. 'Inch' is a corrupt form of 'innis' (Scottish-Gaelic for 'island') and 'gower' is a word that has been anglicised from different Gaelic words meaning 'stream' or 'well' such as: ghabha, gabhar, gabhair, gobhair. The distillery is situated near Cullen some 15km away from the Victorian town of Buckie, a small fishing town on the northeast coast of Scotland. It is here that the show ponies 'Rathburn Hackneys' were originally raised. Inchgower distillery was founded to replace the old cramped and outdated Tochineal Distillery. Tochineal was built by John Wilson in 1825 and closed around 1860 due to lack of proper water resources. The new distillery, situated a few miles down the road, got two kilns topped with classic Charles Doig pagoda roofs.

Inchgower was built in 1871, on land owned by the Countess of Seafield, by Alexander Wilson and the Alexander Wilson Co. Wilson was a nephew to John Wilson, the owner of Tochineal Distillery. The countess did not like the idea of another distillery on her land but was willing to compromise by doubling the rent. As the company celebrated its fiftieth anniversary on 12 July 1922, July 1872 ought to have been when the distillery began operation.

DISTILLERY DETAILS

REGION Highlands (Speyside)

OWNER Diageo

ADDRESS Fochabers, Buckie, Banffshire, AB56 5AB

ROADS A98 to Buckie, close to A942

TEL 01542 836700

FAX None

INCHGOWER

Wilson's plan was to build 'the great distillery of Inchgower', a grand scale distillery with its own cooperage, carpenter shop, smithy and a vast warehouse complex. The main buildings were situated in the form of a quadrant that covered nearly 16,000 square metres. One side of the maltings, for instance, was 120m long and had forty-five windows. The distillery workers' buildings were grouped in a long row leading out to the main road. Much of the inventories for the new distillery were bought by Alexander Wilson Co. from John Wilson's Tochineal estate. The initial workforce was recruited from the Tochineal distillery. The company was incorporated as a limited partnership in 1913. Inchgower remained in the hands of the Wilson family until economic hardship in 1929 led to liquidation. It is not clear if the distillery became dormant then. However, in 1933 or 1936 (records are not precise) the Buckie Town Council bought the distillery and the Wilson family home, Arradoul House. The sum paid was £1,000, and Buckie Town Council continued operations. In 1938, the Council sold the distillery to Arthur Bell & Sons Ltd for £3,000. Inchgower became an important element of the successful Bell blends, and it still is.

Major renovations occurred in 1966 when capacity was doubled by the installation of two new pot stills. Own-floor malting was abandoned the same year and a dark grain plant was added together with five new modern warehouses. Not much in terms of layout has changed since the days of the distillery's inauguration.

Water for the process is obtained from the springs in the Menduff Hills, about 5km south of the distillery. The springs flow over red sandstone to the distillery's own reservoir. Water for cooling comes from the Buckie Burn, which flows over vast peat mosses, past the distillery, on its way to the sea. The same burn is the source for Buckie's town water. The malted barley, the Optic variety, is brought in from the group's central maltster, Burghead Maltings in Elgin. It is specified to be lightly peated, defined as four ppm. The malt is crushed to grist by a Porteus mill and mashed in the stainless steel, full Lauter, mash tun which has a capacity of 8 metric tonnes of grist. Full capacity is twenty, nine-hour mashes per week. Fermentation occurs in six wooden wash backs, made from Scottish larch. Their capacity is 40,000 litres each. The yeast strain has varied from Distiller's and Brewer's, depending on the character obtained by the choice of a slow (approximately eighty-five to ninety hours) or a quick (forty hours) fermentation. Today, fermentation is usually for seventy-two hours, by which time the wash contains around 8% alcohol by

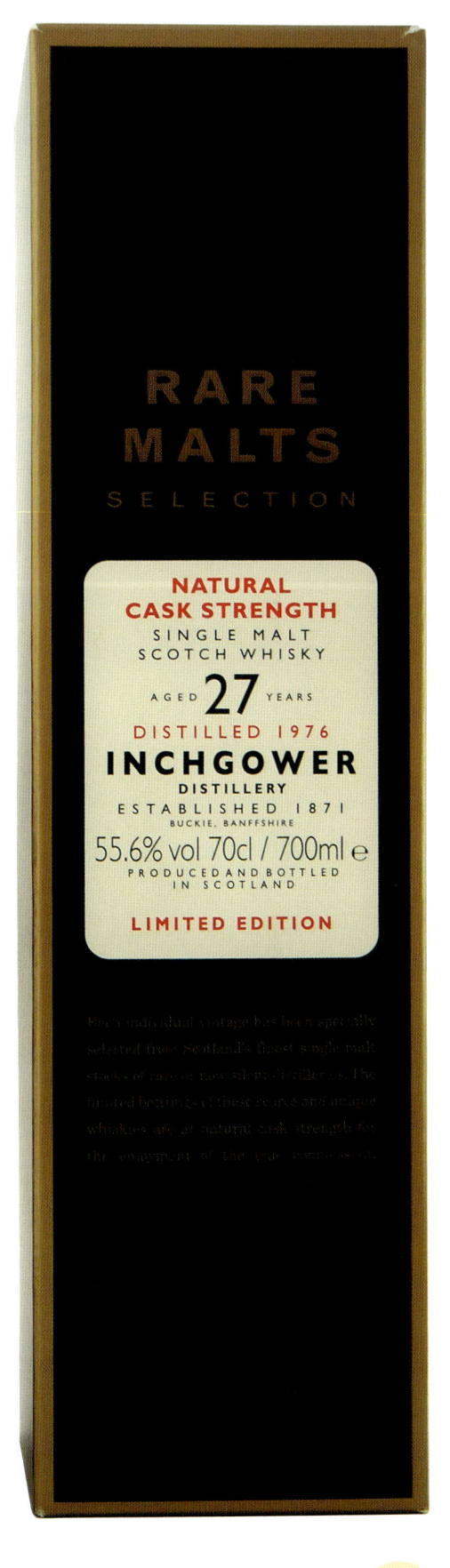

THE INCHGOWER DISTILLERY.

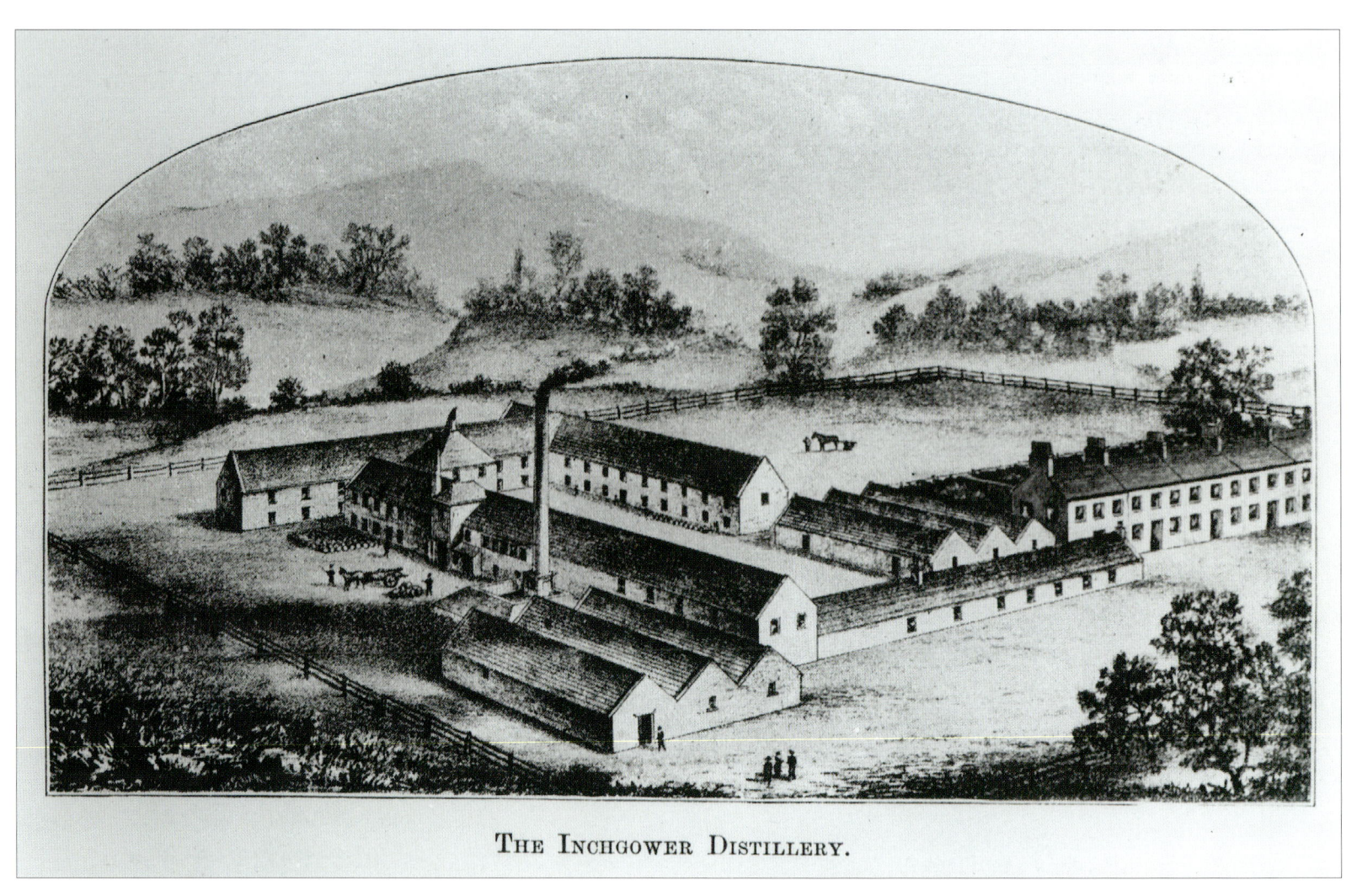

Nineteenth-century engraving of Inchgower

volume. The distillation is performed by two wash and two spirit stills, all traditionally onion-shaped, and indirectly heated by steam coils. The wash stills' volume is about 13,500 litres, and the spirit stills' is about 10,000 litres. Cooling is performed via conventional vertical copper tube condensers. The maximum annual output is 2,300,000 litres of alcohol.

Cask management is based on a twelve-year maturation period, using a mix of new and refilled ex-bourbon casks and sherry butts. Clients may specify a cask regime of their own preference. Maturation occurs in five new as well as old dunnage types of warehouses. They are located on the premises and capable of holding 70,000 casks all together, making it the third largest warehousing facility within the Diageo group. Casks from other distilleries are also held for maturation at Inchgower. A large amount of the production goes into Johnnie Walker, White Horse and Bell's various blends. Bottling occurs in Leven and Glasgow.

The distillery is open to visitors, by appointment. Worth a visit is Cullen, a very attractive town originally built around the mouth of the Burn of Deskford (Cullen Skink originated here) and the fifteenth-century village of Findochty, crowded around the natural harbour known as Crooked Haven.

INCHGOWER

Structural elements and their respective weights

Structure	Observations
Colour	3
Peaty/Phenolic	1
Sherried/Winey	
Fruity/Estery	2
Floral/Aldehydic	2
Cereal/Malty	1
Feinty	
Medicinal/Maritime	2
Woody	
Vanilla/Honey	1
Nutty/Creamy	1
Spicy	2
Sulphury	

Conclusive organoleptic sensations

	Observations
Colour	Pale gold.
Nose	An aromatic, flowery, sweetness. Oatmeal biscuit with honey spread. A whiff of salt water and camphor oil.
Palate	Seville oranges. Oak, vanilla and brazil nuts. Malted cereal. Mild chilli peppery.
Finish	A vague hint of peat smoke and iodized table salt. Complex and dry.
Comment	Light bodied, a pre-dinner dram.

Issued versions

Distilled	Age	% ABV	Size	Box	Version
1974	22	55.7	0.75		
1976	27	55.6	0.7		

LINKWOOD

Pronounced 'linkwood', it takes its name indirectly from the surrounding woodlands. The woodlands, in turn, gave their name to Linkwood House, which belonged to the Brown family. When Peter Brown built the distillery in 1821 he called it Linkwood after the family estate. The Brown family was well established in the area. Peter's father was one of Telford's surveyors for the roads he built throughout the Highlands, and his brother was a Commander of the Light Brigade in the Crimean War. Linkwood distillery, with its classic Doig pagoda-roofed kiln has a very picturesque setting in a wooded landscape. An adjoining pond acts as a reflecting pool; swans and other migrating birds use the pond as a temporary home in the well-kept grounds of the distillery. The dam is, de facto, the distillery's cooling water reservoir. The nearby Burn of Linkwood, which backs up floodwaters from the River Lossie, has an insufficient flow capacity, hence, the reservoir. The Linkwood distillery bridge, crossing the burn, is rather narrow and was the main cause of severe flooding in 1997 and 2002. Linkwood used to be a 'twin' distillery in the sense that it operated two different production lines on its premises from 1971 to 1985.

Peter Brown was a man of local importance. Serving as a factor at the Seafield estates in Moray and Banffshire, he had a large influence on the agricultural development of the area. In this capacity he decided to build a distillery to process the abundance of barley cultivated here. Building activities started in 1821, a licence was given in 1824 and the distillery came on stream 1825. Linkwood pioneered by processing the distillery's waste for cattle feed, an extra feature unique for its time. Brown was in charge of the operations until 1842, when James Walker was employed to run the distillery. Walker had previously managed the Aberlour

DISTILLERY DETAILS

REGION Highlands (Speyside)

OWNER Diageo

ADDRESS Elgin, Morayshire, IV30 8RD

ROADS On A941, 2km south of Elgin

TEL 01343 553800

FAX None

Linkwood c.1910

distillery together with his brother and John and James Grant. James Walker was in charge of the Linkwood production until 1868, the year Peter Brown died. Upon his death Walker left and formed the famous James Walker & Co. Peter's son, William Brown, took charge and ran the distillery for several years, from 1868 to 1893. The genuine and solid reputation Linkwood had achieved under Peter Brown was retained and further elevated by William. He razed the old Linkwood to the ground and, from 1872 to 1874, with the assistance of the Elgin architect J. Methven, erected a new distillery. The new Linkwood was inaugurated in April 1874. In 1897 a further expansion occurred, and a limited partnership was formed – the Linkwood-Glenlivet Distillery Ltd. The board of directors that formed the new partnership was Gilbert R. Brown, J.T. Townsend of Scapa Distillery and R.C. Cameron of Elgin. In 1902, Innes Cameron, a whisky broker and partner in the Teaninich Distillery, joined the board. Later, he became the managing director and principal shareholder of the company. Cameron concentrated on the role as a supplier for the blend trade and was one of the consistent contributors to the White Horse blend. When he died in 1932 the company was wound up and sold for £80,000 to Scottish Malt Distillers Ltd (SMD). Linkwood had two silent periods, 1941 to 1945 and 1985 to 1990, and underwent two comprehensive modernisations after World War II.

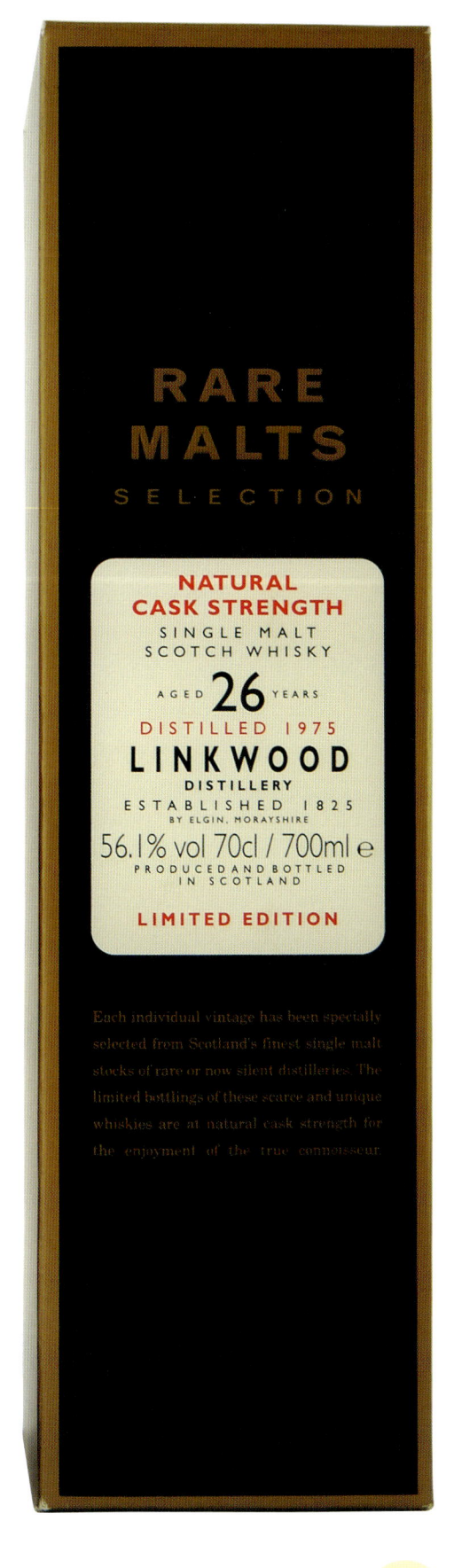

Staff members at Linkwood in the 1950s

When Linkwood reopened in 1945, former employee Roderick Mackenzie was at the helm. Like many distillery managers before him he wasn't certain what exactly caused the unique flavour of Linkwood, or other whiskies, so he insisted that absolutely nothing could be changed at the distillery. He went so far as to forbid the removal of cobwebs in the still house and warehouses. Mackenzie was the manager until he retired in 1963. Comprehensive modernisation started during the end of his era. In spite of his vigilance bordering on fanaticism, he was put in charge of overseeing and directing the expansion. The renovation work, which began in 1962 and finished the year after, changed the format of the distillery completely. On this occasion the traditional power source, the water wheel, and the floor malting were abandoned. In 1971, the number of pot stills was increased from two to six, with indirect heating. Four new stills were added and installed in a separate building. These were identical, down to the last seam and bolt, to the old ones and paired in the same manner. This tripled the distillery's capacity. The 'new Linkwood' also got its own mash tun and a set of five wash backs. The mash tun and the six wash backs at the 'old Linkwood' became a shared resource. This made Linkwood a 'double distillery' with one old and one new distillery on the same premises. The two distilleries were run in parallel from 1971 until 1985 when the old Linkwood closed; however, it is said that experimental production occurred until 1995. The units were internally called Linkwood A (the old) and Linkwood B (the new). The spirit that flowed from the old complex was vatted with spirit from the new complex. The official standpoint was that there was no recognisable difference between the two spirits and, hence, they could be vatted in any combination without jeopardising the flavour profile inherited from past days or the 'blend' deprived of its right to be characterised as a single malt.

Water for the process is obtained from the springs near Milbuies Loch, located in the Black Hills about 5km south of Elgin. Water for cooling purposes comes from the nearby Burn of Linkwood and is held in the distillery's own reservoir, the pond, situated between the old maltings and the new still house. Additional cooling water is piped from the Burn of Bogs. The malted barley, Decanter, is brought in from the group's central maltster, Burghead Maltings. It is specified to be unpeated. The malt is crushed to grist by a Porteus mill. Mash tun for Linkwood A is a traditional one (with rakes) made of cast iron and with a copper top. It is a non-Lauter and its capacity is 24,000 litres. This tun is still in place but was taken out of service and will not function again. Fermentation for Linkwood A occurs in six wooden wash backs, made from Oregon pine. Their capacity is 30,000 litres each. The mash tun for Linkwood B is a modern type made of cast iron and with a copper top, and is a semi-Lauter. Its capacity is 48,500 litres. Fermentation at Linkwood B occurs in five wooden wash backs, made from Oregon pine. Their capacity is 87,000 litres each; however, the working capacity is usually 58,000 litres. Full capacity is twenty mashes per week, each lasting nine hours.

The yeast strain is Distiller's from Kerry Bioscience. The distillation used to be performed either by one wash still holding 14,275 litres and one spirit still holding 15,500, both situated in the Linkwood A complex, or by two wash and two spirit stills, all four situated in the Linkwood B complex. The two wash stills have a volume of 14,275 litres each, and the two spirit stills 15,500 litres each. All six stills are built by Abercrombie of Alloa. They are the traditional onion shape and are indirectly heated by steam coils. Since 1995 Linkwood A has been taken out of production, but all the equipment remains in the complex. Cooling for Linkwood B is performed via conventional vertical copper tube condensers and for Linkwood A by a traditional cast-iron tank with a submerged copper coil, the worm. As the surface area of copper available to the vapours in a worm tub is a fraction of that in a condenser, the whisky made in a distillery with worm tubs is typically much more meaty and sulphury in character. The only distillery which utilises both types of cooling is the Linkwood distillery. The maximum annual output for Linkwood A was 1,300,000 litres and for Linkwood B it is 2,500,000 litres of alcohol.

Cask management is based on a twelve-year maturation period, using a mix of new and refilled ex-bourbon casks and sherry butts. Maturation on site no longer occurs. The new make spirit is taken by road tankers for cask filling and maturing at central warehouses. Bottling occurs in Leven and Glasgow. A large amount of the production goes into White Horse, Haig, Dimple, Abbott's Choice and Bell's various blends.

The distillery is open to visitors, by appointment. Worth a visit is Pluscarden Abbey, located 10km from Elgin town centre, one of Scotland's most unusual attractions. It was founded in 1230 by Alexander II for Valliscaulian monks. It is the only medieval monastery in Britain still inhabited by monks and being used for its original purpose. It is situated in a sheltered, south-facing glen against a background of forested hillside; this adds to the beauty of its architecture and the restful atmosphere.

LINKWOOD

Structural elements and their respective weights

STRUCTURE	OBSERVATIONS
Colour	6
Peaty/Phenolic	1
Sherried/Winey	2
Fruity/Estery	3
Floral/Aldehydic	1
Cereal/Malty	1
Feinty	
Medicinal/Maritime	
Woody	
Vanilla/Honey	1
Nutty/Creamy	
Spicy	1
Sulphury	

Conclusive organoleptic sensations

OBSERVATIONS	
Colour	Old gold.
Nose	Rich in estery aromas from lemon sherbet, to bananas and fruit-gum. Tea-roses. Faint peat. A whiff of dry sherry.
Palate	Floral tones with a hint of Gewürztraminer. Malty sweetness. Creamy with a slight touch of cocoa.
Finish	Slightly dry. Light bitter orange-lemony zest. Traces of almonds and oak vanilla.
Comment	Light to medium bodied, an after-dinner dram.

Issued versions

DISTILLED	AGE	% ABV	SIZE	BOX	VERSION
1972	22	59.3	0.7	None	
1972	23	58.4	0.75	None	(RSA)
1974	22	61.2	0.75		
1974	23	61.2	0.75		
1974	30	54.9	0.7		
1975	26	56.1	0.7		

Mannochmore

Pronounced *'man NOCHmore'*, 'the big place of the monks' takes its name from the Gaelic 'mannoch' and 'mór'. 'Mohr' or 'Mór' is Gaelic for 'big', 'manach' is 'monk'. The distillery, nestling under the cover of a fir-clad hill, is a rather modern facility. It is situated in the Lossie valley in the vicinity of Elgin, just a few kilometres south of the town. The distillery is similar in design to the other UDV/Diageo distilleries units which were new, rebuilt or added to existing ones in the late 1960s and early 1970s. For a comparison study, see Teaninich and Linkwood with their 'old A' and 'new B' sites, and also the new Clynelish. Mannochmore is placed directly behind Glenlossie Distillery and stands as a separate distillery on the common premises. From the road it is difficult to spot the distillery as it lies in the heart of the site and has no indication on the building that it is the Mannochmore. The distillery was quickly erected in 1971, on a 10 hectare tract, to create a much-needed backup resource for Glenlossie, the main provider of malt whisky for their subsidiary, John Haig & Co. and Haig's various blends. Another reason was to create an additional supplier for the unexpected growth in demand for whisky in the early seventies. Mannochmore/Glenlossie could be classified as a tandem distillery such as Brora/Clynelish and Duffton/Pityvaich.

Two distilleries in close proximity may contribute to a synergy effect by having them working in tandem. Hence, Glenlossie and Mannochmore share personnel and administrative functions but also fundamental things like water resources and warehouses.

Distillery details

Region Highlands (Speyside)

Owner Diageo

Address Birnie, Elgin, Morayshire, IV30 8SS

Roads West of A941 on the B9014 junction, 3km south of Elgin, near Thomshill

Tel 01343 862000 (same as Glenlossie)

Fax 01343 862007 (same as Glenlossie)

• Mannochmore •

After a few years the prosperous days faded and Mannochmore became dormant from 1985 until 1989, and again from 1995 to 1997. A sudden surge in demand for single malt whiskies motivated a resurrection of the distillery in 1989. The first attempt surfaced in 1996 when the ill-fated Loch Dhu whisky (Gaelic for 'Black Lake') was released. It is said its colour, pitch black, was derived from heavily charred casks pre-treated under pressure with sherry syrup (pajarete) and a high volume of spirit caramel (colour E150a). Spirit caramel is the only permitted additive to Scotch whisky, besides water. E150a adds an unmistakably wormwood-like bitterness when mixed un-proportionally as in this case. Needless to say the success was not there. However, the two distilleries are no longer running in parallel, instead they alternate their production in twelve-month intervals. A short break in production occurred from 1991 to 1992 for updates and maintenance.

In spite of similar water, barley, yeast and nearly identical pot stills there is a major difference in the weight of flavours found in Mannochmore, compared to Glenlossie. It is said to be explained by the lack of purifiers on the Mannochmore spirit stills. Purifiers, which are mounted between the lyne arms and the condensers, modify the distilling process. The purifier, or rather mini-condenser, returns (reflux) a proportion of the alcohol vapours back to the pot still to be re-distilled. The action of a mini-condenser increases the amount of returns (reflux) within the stills, which theoretically should result in a lighter and more delicate whisky. On site is a dark grains plant, shared not only with Glenlossie but also with twenty-one other distilleries. On a weekly basis, it can process 2,600 tonnes of draff and eight million litres of pot ale to produce 1,000 tonnes of dark grains for cattle feed.

Mannochmore was designed to obtain water from regular mains and has done so at times but relies in principal on the same water resources as Glenlossie. Hence, process water is drawn from the Bardon Burn and cooling water from Gedloch Burn and Nurn of Foths. The waters run from the Mannoch Hills to be collected in a reservoir just south of the distillery. The malted barley, Optic and Chariot, is brought in daily from the group's central maltster, Burghead Maltings. It is specified to be unpeated. The malt is crushed to grist by a Porteus mill. Glenlossie have a Boby Mill that was acquired from the Teaninich Distillery. The mash tun is a cast-iron type with a copper dome – full Lauter. Its capacity is 11.5 metric tonnes of grist. Glenlossie's mash tun is made of stainless steel, also full-Lauter and has a

127

capacity of 8 metric tonnes. Fermentation, which lasts for around sixty-five hours, occurs in eight wooden wash backs, made from Scottish larch. Their capacity is 55,000 litres each. Glenlossie's eight wash backs are also made from larch and hold 45,000 litres each. Both distilleries use a strain of Distiller's yeast. It has varied over time from Distiller's to Brewer's. The distillation is performed by three wash and three spirit stills. Glenlossie has kept the shape and size of their stills identical since 1876. The stills at Mannochmore are all traditionally onion shaped and indirectly heated; the wash stills by steam kettles and the spirit stills by steam coils. The wash stills' volumes are 15,500 litres (Glenlossie 16,000) and the spirit stills' volumes are 17,500 litres (Glenlossie, the same). Cooling is performed via conventional vertical copper shell and tube condensers. Annual maximum production is 2,500,000 (Glenlossie 2,200,000 litres) litres of alcohol.

Cask management is based on a twelve-year maturation period, using a mix of new and refilled ex-bourbon casks and sherry butts. Maturation occurs on the premises in modern shelf storage buildings, shared with Glenlossie. A small volume is matured in traditional warehouses, altogether with a combined capacity of 19,000 casks. A large amount of the production goes into Haig's various blends. Bottling occurs in Leven and Glasgow.

The distillery is open to visitors, by appointment. For more information on what to see in the area, see the chapter on Linkwood.

MANNOCHMORE

Structural elements and their respective weights

Structure	Observations
Colour	3
Peaty/Phenolic	1
Sherried/Winey	1
Fruity/Estery	1
Floral/Aldehydic	1
Cereal/Malty	
Feinty	
Medicinal/Maritime	
Woody	
Vanilla/Honey	1
Nutty/Creamy	1
Spicy	1
Sulphury	

Conclusive organoleptic sensations

	Observations
Colour	Pale gold with greenish tinge.
Nose	Fragrant and aromatic as freshly cut mint. A slight shade of peat. Roses.
Palate	Light, tropical fruity flavours, lime, pineapple and cocoa. Buttery and creamy. Heather honey sweetness. Some pepper fruit acting as counterweight.
Finish	Malty notes. Faint oak, vanilla and hazelnut hints. Trace of peat.
Comment	Light bodied, a pre-dinner dram in the summer garden.

Issued versions

Distilled	Age	% ABV	Size	Box	Version
1974	22	60.1	0.7		No versions

Millburn

Pronounced '*MILL burn*', 'the stream of the mill', it takes its name from the Gaelic 'a'Mhullin' meaning 'mill' and 'burn' meaning 'stream'. The distillery was situated at the end of Millburn Road, near old Perth Road in Inverness. It was the oldest distillery in the area and was nearly completely demolished in 1988. It was closed in 1985 due to outdated equipment, no room for expansion and a growing Inverness not wanting a distillery in a populated area of the town. The site was purchased by the Beefeater restaurant chain in 1990 and converted to a steak house named The Auld Distillery. Chimneys and a few of the buildings still stand but the kiln and kiln pagoda are gone. The

Distillery details

REGION Highlands (Northern)

OWNER Last distillery owner was United Distillers Ltd

ADDRESS Millburn Road, Inverness, Inverness-shire, IV2 3QX

ROADS A96 near Moray Firth, B865 (Raigmore interchange)

TEL None (The Auld Distillery 01463 712010)

FAX None

• RARE MALTS •

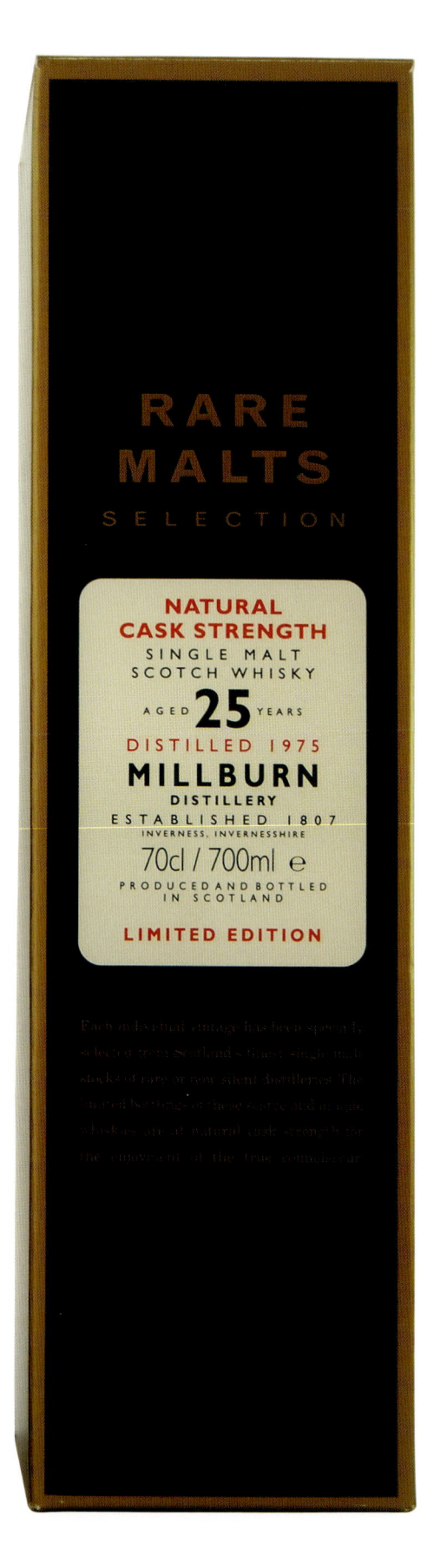

remaining structures are not from the founding days but stem from the modernisation in 1876.

The distillery is believed to have been founded on this site, but this is not proven. It may initially have been erected elsewhere and later moved to the actual site. The site is located about 2km from the town beside the Mill Burn and was initially called Inverness Distillery. This was the name given by the distillery's first owner and operator, a Mr Welsh. According to licence files the distillery started production in 1807 but the construction may have started in 1805. However, local contemporary Inverness chronicles on the subject of local distilling and distilleries don't mention the proprietor or the distillery before 1817. Alexander McCallum & Co. was registered as the owner from 1817 to 1821. The next registered ownership was for Rose & McDonald Co., who became the legal owner on 21 December 1825. This company was dissolved in 1829. There is evidence that a licence was taken in 1829 to operate the distillery under the name of the Millburn Distillery Co. but production is believed to have ceased in 1837 and the name reverted back to Inverness Distillery. During this era the distillery shifted hand several times. From 1829 to 1832 it was run by McDonald, Leslie & Co., from 1832 to 1837 by McDonald & Co., and during 1837 for a short period by Colin Chisholm. The distillery was dormant until 1853. That year the premises were leased by a local cereal merchant, David Rose, to be used as a flour mill. The mill operation went on for several years until a need for diversification surfaced. Rose decided to update the premises with a state-of-the-art distillery. He applied for a licence to distil but also to tap needed water from Inverness water supplies. Both licences were granted. Ross, a local architect and builder, was commissioned and the distillery was erected under his supervision.

The updated Millburn began production on 28 September 1876. It quickly became a reputed producer and in 1878 won a large contract to supply whisky for the British garrison in Cyprus. In 1881 David Rose handed over management to his son George, who decided to sell out in 1892. The new owners were the Haig brothers and A. Haig & Co. The Haigs increased the capacity in 1898 and changed the name to the Millburn Distillery Co. in 1904. In 1921 they sold the distillery to the famous gin rectifiers Booth Distillery Ltd and some of Millburn's production showed up in Booth's own whisky blend, the Cabinet. During the Booth era the distillery was not continuously in production. A fire broke out on 26 April 1922 and the local fire brigade, assisted by the Cameron Highlanders, saved the still house and storage warehouses; however, a comprehensive renovation was necessary. The rebuilding was entrusted to Charles Doig who carried out a considerable upgrading and enhancement of the plant. Booth Distillery was taken over by the Distillers Company Ltd (DCL) in 1937 and transferred to their subsidiary Scottish Malt Distillers Ltd (SMD) in 1943. In 1958 Millburn was converted to electrical power and the old steam engine, which delivered power to the malt mill and the equipment in the mash and tun room, was removed. The pot stills were still externally heated but automatic coal stokers were installed. When the still house was rebuilt in 1966 the stills were changed to indirect heating. The heating method was converted from coal to oil firing in 1970. The traditional floor malting was abandoned in 1964 and a Saladin box system was installed. The Saladin box system was closed down in 1984 and malt was brought in from the group's central maltsters in Ord. When malting was performed on site the malt was dried by peat fire at a rather high peating level. Milburn came to a final rest 1985.

The cooling water was drawn from the Mill Burn, on whose banks the distillery stands, and in competition with a chain of various water-dependent industries in the neighbourhood. Process water was piped from the Loch Duntelchaig, situated about 12km from the distillery, a loch on which the city of Inverness water supply also depends. Initially the Mill Burn water was used for processing too but had to be changed due to insufficient access. The malted barley was, during the last years, brought in from the central maltster Ord maltings. It was specified to be peated in line with the house style when malting was performed on site. Several barley strains have been used over the years; at the end of production it was Golden Promise and Triumph. The malt was crushed to grist by a Porteus mill. The cast-iron mash tun had a capacity of ten mashes per week, at full production. Fermentation occurred in four wooden wash backs, believed to be made from Scottish larch. Capacity was 18,000 litres each. The yeast strain used is not known by the author. The distillation was performed by one wash and one spirit still. The stills were both a traditional onion shape and indirectly heated by steam coils. The wash and spirit stills each had a volume of 13,500 litres. It is believed that the cooling was performed via worms submerged in tubs. Annual maximum production was 2,000,000 litres; at the time of closing the production was down to about 600,000 litres of alcohol per annum.

Cask management is believed to have been based on a ten-year maturation period, using a mix of new and refilled ex-bourbon casks and sherry butts. Maturation occurred partly on the premises in traditional warehouses with a combined capacity of 13,000 casks. The lion's share of the production was in later days sent to central warehouses in Menstrie. Some of the whisky went into the blend Macleay Duff and vatted malt The Mill Burn.

The distillery is closed. For more information on what to see in the area, see the chapter on Glenlochy.

MILLBURN

Structural elements and their respective weights

Structure	Observations
Colour	6
Peaty/Phenolic	2
Sherried/Winey	2
Fruity/Estery	2
Floral/Aldehydic	1
Cereal/Malty	2
Feinty	
Medicinal/Maritime	1
Woody	
Vanilla/Honey	
Nutty/Creamy	1
Spicy	1
Sulphury	1

Conclusive organoleptic sensations

	Observations
Colour	Old gold.
Nose	A bit perfumed. Lots of fruity flavours like citrus and orchards. Handsomely seaweed-peat-smoky with a slightly acidic medicinal edge. A whiff of sulphur.
Palate	Robust and rich with a sweet barley-sugar taste. Another layer of sweetness as the concentrated aromas of smoky, dried fruits found in cream sherry. Hints of almond and citrus. Traces of dark chocolate in the background.
Finish	Luscious and smooth, rich, complex and very long on the palate, with a balance of clean citric acidity at the finish. Some (black) peppery notes at the very end.
Comment	Medium to full bodied. Night-cap dram.

Issued versions

Distilled	Age	% abv	Size	Box	Version
1969	35	51.2	0.7		
1975	18	58.5	0.7		
1975	18	58.9	0.7	None	
1975	25	61.9	0.7		

MORTLACH

Pronounced 'mort LACH', it takes its name from the Gaelic 'morlay' meaning 'the great hollow'. An alternative translation is 'the bowl-shaped valley'. A battle was fought here in 1010 at which King Malcolm II, the second king of Scotland, defeated the ruling Danish Vikings by breaking a dam holding the River Dullan, which flooded the Danish camp. A Viking gravestone from these formative days was used by the builders of the Balvenie Castle. It became known as the Aqua Vitae Stone as it served as a 'bar' counter. A forerunner to the legal Mortlach is believed to have been constructed on the site. This still, it is said, was fed by water from the well called John's or Jock's Well and became a well-reputed but illicit still. This well still exists and is the water source for the Dufftown distillery; however, Mortlach draws its water from other sources today. The distillery is the first and oldest licenced one in Dufftown, dating back to 1823. The second oldest, Glenfiddich, was built sixty years later. Mortlach is scenically situated near a public road between the wooded banks of the Dullan Water and the River Fiddich. It was granted one of the first licences based on the Excise Act of 1823, almost before the ink had dried on the Act. For some aficionados this is the site where the mightiest Speyside malts of the classic type still are produced.

Mortlach was founded in 1823 by James Findlater and his Dufftown friends, Donald McIntosh and John Alexander Gordon.

Distillery Details

Region Highlands (Speyside)

Owner Diageo

Address Dufftown, Banffshire, AB55 4AQ

Roads A941/A920 junction towards the east of Dufftown

Tel 01340 820318

Fax None

• RARE MALTS •

The old archway at Mortlach

They hired the grounds on which the distillery resides from the Earl of Macduff. In 1831 Findlater sold the distillery for the sum of £279 to John Robertson, who operated the distillery for a short period and sold it in 1833 to Arthur Thomas Gregory of Buschromb. He closed the distillery in 1837 and later sold it. For a few years, from 1837 to 1842, it was owned by the Grant brothers, James and John, who were involved in the Aberlour Distillery founded in 1826. Sometime before 1842, the Grant brothers left Mortlach, leaving an empty shell behind. They had simply removed all distillery equipment to be used at their newly founded (in 1840) Glen Grant distillery. There are no records showing that the brothers ever distilled at Mortlach. The barley granary came to serve as a place of worship for the Free Church of Scotland during the Disruption, until a Free Church building in Dufftown could be erected. Mortlach was bought back in 1842 by one of its founders, John Alexander Gordon. He used the premises initially as a brewery but returned to distilling after a short time. After renovating, enlarging and modernis-ing, the distillery's flagship was launched: The Real John Gordon. In 1854 Gordon went into partnership with George Cowie. They formed John Gordon & Co., to which the ownership of Mortlach was transferred. Cowie was a surveyor for railroad com-panies and later became the provost of Dufftown. When Gordon died in 1867 Cowie became the sole owner.

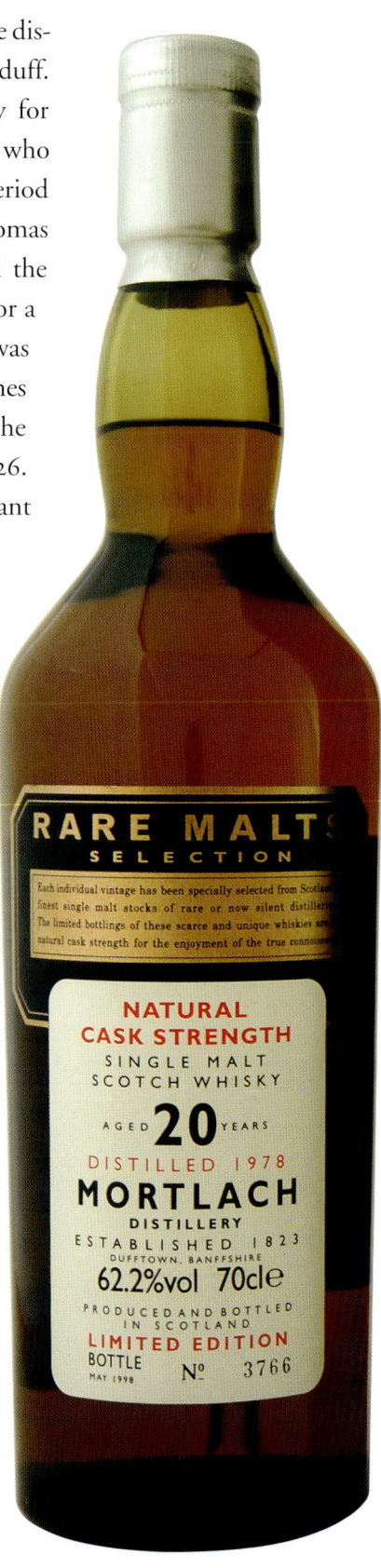

At that time a William Grant worked for the Mortlach Distillery. He stayed at Mortlach for twenty years and left in 1886 to start his own enterprise, the legendary Glenfiddich distillery. Cowie had two sons, George and Alexander. Alexander became a doctor of medicine practising in Hong Kong. George remained in Dufftown to help his father and became a partner in 1895. George died tragically at the age of thirty-four, in February 1896. Alexander was called home from Hong Kong but his father died in November the same year. Alexander then took control of the business and participated in the modernisation that had started before his arrival and was finalised in 1897. The still house was ex-panded from three to six stills with two spirit safes. A railway siding connecting Mortlach with the Great North of Scotland Railway's Dufftown station was installed. Electric light was brought in and a hydraulic lift system, still in use, was installed in the warehouses. At the same time the firm was restructured as George Cowie & Sons Ltd. Further upgrades were carried out in 1903 and 1923. Alexander Cowie's only son George was killed in 1917 at the age of eighteen. Having no male heirs, combined with the post-war depression, the family decided to sell out. The business was sold to John Walker & Sons Ltd in 1923. At the time Mortlach was sold it was the largest distillery in the area. Walker & Sons merged with Distillers Company Ltd (DCL) in 1925, which transferred the distillery to its subsidiary Scottish Malt Distillers Ltd (SMD) in 1930. During World War II Mortlach, together with Macallan, was one of the few distilleries that had a licence to produce whisky, and did so except for the year of 1944. An extensive rebuilding was carried out in 1964 designed to keep the classic 'turn-of-the-century look' intact. The six old, un-paired stills were not replaced but modified to automatic coal stoking in 1964. This was replaced by indirect heating fired by oil burners in 1971. At the 1971 refurbishing the equipment was moved to a new still house accommodating all six stills. When the on-site floor maltings were abandoned in 1968 the two pagoda kiln tops were kept for decorative purposes. Full computer control was introduced and a new Lauter mash tun was installed in 1996. For the investment of £1.5 million Mortlach now became fully automated, needing only one man to run the entire plant.

The cooling water is drawn from the River Dullan and the process water from the Priest's Well in the Conval Hills and no longer from Jock's Well. The malted barley is brought in from the group's central maltsters, Roseisle Maltings and Burghead Maltings. The malt is specified to be peated to 5ppm, in line with the house style when malting was performed on site. Several barley strains have been used over the years, but Decanter seems now to be the predominant. The malt is crushed to grist by a rather new Porteus mill, installed in the early 1960s. The mash tun is a modern semi-Lauter made of stainless steel. Its capacity is 12 metric tonnes of grist. At full production, twelve to thirteen mashes are made per week. Fermentation occurs in six tall wooden wash backs, made from Scottish larch, each with a capacity of 60,000 litres. The yeast strains used are Distiller's as well as Brewer's and the fermentation is of the short type: sixty hours. The distillation is performed in a rather unique still house, due to configuration, sizes of the wash and spirit stills and their operations. The stills are nearly similar and onion-shaped but their sizes and shapes are unusually varying. They are equipped with boiling balls. The heating is indirect by steam coils and firing is by oil burners. None of the stills are paired. Two of the wash stills have a volume of 7,500 litres and the third 15,000 litres. The three spirit stills accommodate 7,900, 8,200 and 8,800 litres. The smallest one is known as the 'Wee Witchie'.

Regarding the operation of the stills, Mortlach is one of the few distilleries that practise the two-and-half distillation regime; Springbank, Benrinnes and Rosebank (closed) are others. Two-and-half distillation has been practised at Mortlach since 1896. More information regarding this practice is found in the section 'Nomenclature and Definitions'. The cooling is of the classic type, performed via worms submerged in tubs. The tubs are wooden and made from Scottish larch, instead of the usual cast iron. They are situated on a platform outside the rear end of the still house. Mortlach is one of the few remaining distilleries that still practise this traditional way of cooling. Annual maximum production is 3,000,000 litres of alcohol.

Lyne pipes at Mortlach

Cask management is based on a sixteen-year maturation period, using a mix of new and refilled ex-bourbon casks and sherry butts. On the premises are five traditional dunnage warehouses, with a combined capacity of 21,000 casks. Maturation occurs partly on site but the lion's share of the production is sent to central warehouses in Menstrie and others. Some of the whisky goes into the various Johnnie Walker blends. However, an EU regulation in 1977 lead to the withdrawal of Red Label from the UK market; hence, a new brand based upon Mortlach was introduced: the successful John Barr.

The distillery is open to visitors, by appointment. Worth a visit is the Mortlach Parish Church, one of the oldest churches in Scotland. It claims to have been in regular use as a place of Christian worship since Moluag of Bangor in Ireland (a contemporary of St Columba) came to Mortlach about AD566. The site may have been of significance to the Picts – in the graveyard there is a weathered Pictish cross.

MORTLACH

Structural elements and their respective weights

STRUCTURE	OBSERVATIONS
Colour	5
Peaty/Phenolic	1
Sherried/Winey	2
Fruity/Estery	1
Floral/Aldehydic	1
Cereal/Malty	1
Feinty	
Medicinal/Maritime	
Woody	
Vanilla/Honey	1
Nutty/Creamy	2
Spicy	3
Sulphury	0.1

Conclusive organoleptic sensations

	OBSERVATIONS
Colour	Deep yellow, like maturing Sauternes.
Nose	Redolent of ripe autumn fruits. A touch of Pedro Ximénez sherry sweetness and crème brûlée. Leathery notes. Peaty smoke. Spices, black pepper. Hint of sulphur.
Palate	Gentle fruitiness, Golden Delicious apples. Pecan nuts, toffee and vanilla. Malted barley sweetness.
Finish	The long and complex finish reveals almond, nuts and bitter chocolate notes but also oscillates between slight acidic citrus and immense flavours of raisins and candied orange peel. A whiff of peaty smokiness.
Comment	Full bodied, an after-dinner dram.

Issued versions

DISTILLED	AGE	% ABV	SIZE	BOX	VERSION
1972	22	65.3	0.75		
1972	22	65.3	0.2	Box 1	
1972	22	65.3	0.75	None	USA
1972	23	59.4	0.75		
1972	23	59.4	0.75	None	B297
1978	20	62.2	0.7		

NORTH PORT

PRONOUNCED '*north port*', it derived its name from its positioning at the north gates of the once-walled Royal Burgh of Brechin. These gates are long gone. Brechin stands on the South Esk River in Strathmore. North Port was closed in 1983 and completely demolished in 1993. A Safeway supermarket is now erected on its site. Of the two distilleries established in Brechin only Glencadam has survived.

North Port was built in 1820 by the Townhead Distillery Co. and it operated under this name until 1823. The founder of the company and the distillery was David Guthrie. His three sons

DISTILLERY DETAILS

REGION Highlands (Eastern)

OWNER Diageo

ADDRESS Trinity Road, Brechin, Angus, DD9 6BE

ROADS A90 to A935 towards Brechin

TEL No

FAX No

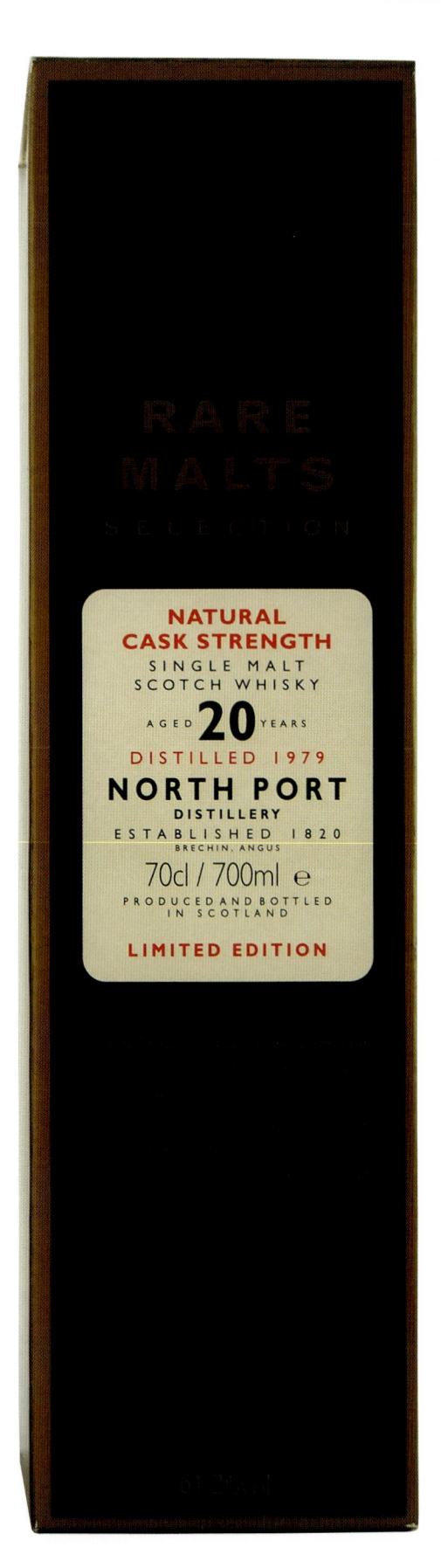

John, David and Alexander took over the company in 1823. The Guthrie family included a cousin, the famous Thomas Guthrie. He was a theologian, devoted teetotaller and social reformist. One of his initiatives was the so-called 'Ragged Schools' offering free schooling to the poor. During the Guthrie brothers' management the name changed to Brechin Distillery Co., after the town. In 1825 the name was changed to Guthrie, Martin & Co. and the premises were expanded: a new kiln and malt barns were added. Another restructure was carried out in 1893 when the company was converted into a limited partnership. North Port was closed from 1917 until 1919. The distillery stayed within the family until 1922, when control was passed to W.H. Holt & Co. and the Distillers Company Ltd (DCL). DCL transferred North Port to its subsidiary the Scottish Malt Distillers Ltd (SMD) the same year. SMD closed North Port in 1926 and kept it dormant until 1937. From that year until it closed, it was licenced to the Glasgow wine merchant Mitchell Bros Ltd. In 1939 it was time for another and final name change. Brechin Distillery became the North Port Distillery. Production was halted for the war years and until 1947. During the war a part of the Polish infantry was billeted here. This contingent later distinguished itself in the fighting at Monte Cassino in Italy. When North Port reopened it produced continuously until it was mothballed in March 1983. Its last major structural improvements occurred in 1905. However, equipment had been replaced at updates performed in 1926 and 1978. The water wheel, driven by the flow from Doctor's Dam, submerged in a tunnel 6 metres below ground, delivered power to the distillery until it was put to rest. Conversion to indirect heating by oil-fired burners occurred in 1964 and a part of the mash house was replaced in 1970. North Port was demolished in 1993.

The process water was drawn from the city mains fed by Loch Lee at the head of Glenesk. The cooling water was drawn from the Den Burn, arriving via a collecting dam (nicknamed 'Doctor's Dam' after Dr. Alexander Guthrie) emptying its flow at the South Esk River. The malted barley was brought in from local farmers and floor malted on site. Peat was cut from the nearby slopes of the Grampian Mountains. However, the floor malting was abandoned in 1972 and the kiln was converted to a malt deposit. The malt was then brought from the group's central maltsters. The malt was specified to be peated, in line with the house style when malting was performed on site. Several barley strains have been used over the years but Golden Promise and Triumph seem now to have been the predominant ones at the end of production. It is believed that the malt was crushed to grist by a Porteus mill. The mash tun was a traditional cast-iron type and had a capacity of 5 metric tonnes. At full production ten mashes were made per week. Fermentation occurred in five wooden wash backs. It is believed that the yeast strains used were Distiller's. The distillation was performed in a rather unique still house as it was constructed half a storey below ground level. North Port's two onion-shaped stills had been converted to oil-fired indirect heating by steam coils in 1964. The capacities of the paired wash and the spirit still are not known to the author. The cooling was of the classic type, performed via worms submerged in tubs. Annual maximum production was 750,000 litres of alcohol.

Cask management is believed to have been based on a twelve-year maturation period, using a mix of new and reused ex-bourbon casks and sherry butts. Maturation occurred partly on the premises in a warehouse with a capacity of 2,500 casks. The lion's share of the production was sent to central warehouses. The whisky went into various blends such as the vatted malt Glen Dew for the Italian market and the blend Heather Dew for other markets.

The distillery is closed and demolished. Worth visits are the Round Tower and the Brechin Bridge. The tower was established around AD990 and pre-dates the cathedral, founded by David I, in the mid-twelfth century. The tower is a striking example of Celtic architecture and there is only one other in Scotland. Both were strongholds and served as a refuge from raiding Vikings. Another historic relic is Brechin Bridge, known locally as the Auld Brig, and one of the oldest stone bridges in Scotland.

North Port as it was in 1927

NORTH PORT

Structural elements and their respective weights

Structure	Observations
Colour	5
Peaty/Phenolic	
Sherried/Winey	
Fruity/Estery	3
Floral/Aldehydic	1
Cereal/Malty	2
Feinty	
Medicinal/Maritime	
Woody	3
Vanilla/Honey	
Nutty/Creamy	
Spicy	
Sulphury	

Conclusive organoleptic sensations

Observations	
Colour	Bright gold.
Nose	Newly sawn cedar wood. Resin. Apple cider and acidic lime aroma. Grassy. Some aniseed. Slightly musty and acidic, like over-ripe purple plums.
Palate	Dark, minty chocolate. Candied apricots and pineapple. Maltiness. Pronounced woody oakiness.
Finish	Astringent tannic. Dryish. Spirity.
Comment	Medium bodied, a brunch dram.

Issued versions

Distilled	Age	% ABV	Size	Box	Version
1971	23	54.7	0.75	None	USA
1971	23	54.7	0.2	Box 1	
1971	23	54.7	0.75		
1979	19	61	0.75		
1979	20	61.2	0.7		

PORT ELLEN

PRONOUNCED '*port ellen*', it derived its name from the town with the same name. The town got its name from Lady Ellenor, the wife of founder Walter Frederick Campbell, Laird of Islay. The little town of Port Ellen was founded in 1821 and is the island's second largest settlement. Built around Loch Leodamais, Port Ellen has Islay's main deep water harbour and one of two ferry terminals on the island. The other one is Port Askaig. Port Ellen was built as a resettlement for 4,000 people living on the Oa peninsula – a forced resettlement or contemporary 'clearing' of the type that occurred on the northern part of the Scottish mainland. Port Ellen distillery was closed in 1983 but was converted to a malting site. Port Ellen is now a central malting facility for several distilleries, on and off Islay. The Port Ellen Single Malt is considered 'the rarest of Islay Malts' by whisky enthusiasts.

Port Ellen distillery was established in 1825 by the conversion of a malt mill to a distillery. The conversion work was performed by A.G. Mackay & Co., a partnership of which John Morrison and Walter Campbell were members. Soon after Alexander Mackay was involved in bankruptcy proceedings and his stake in Port Ellen was taken over by some of his relatives, Hugh and Thomas Mackay, consecutively. It is said that Port Ellen changed hands five times until 1836, when John Ramsey, cousin to John Morrison, became the sixth proprietor. Ramsey was a sherry importer, a Liberal MP for Stirling and chairman of Glasgow Chamber of Commerce. Not only did he start scheduled ferry transports to Islay, Ramsey was also one of the great whisky trade promoters at the time. He built a large blending and bottling plant in Glasgow and pioneered whisky exports to United States. He made Port

DISTILLERY DETAILS

REGION Island

OWNER Diageo

ADDRESS Port Ellen, Isle of Islay, Argyll, PA42 7AJ

ROADS Ferry to Port Ellen Ferry terminus from Kennacraig near Tarbert. Port Ellen is on A846

TEL 01496 302700

FAX None

• RARE MALTS •

Sunset – Port Ellen

Ellen the centre of innovation for the industry. Here, the spirit safe was first introduced and the system of bonding whisky free of duty experimented. The spirit safe construction invented by Septimus Fox in the 1820s was improved with the assistance of John Stein (inventor of the Stein still) at the Ardenistiel Distillery. It was Ramsey who encouraged Robert Stein (owner of the Irish Kilbagie Distillery) and Aeneas Coffey to continue and carry out their research work with 'continuous stills' on Port Ellen's premises. They influenced each other, but it was Coffey's construction, the 'patent still', that was singled out as the most efficient. Coffey's solution became the foundation for the modern distilling apparatus.

Continuous stills, or patent stills, are used in the production of grain whisky, gin, vodka, etc. The batch-oriented system, with pot stills, are used for the production of malt whisky and artisan armagrac, calvados, cognac, and rum. In 1855, before Ramsey went into public service he purchased the land of Laphroaig, Lagavulin and Ardbeg for £70,000. Ramsey made a long-lasting impression on the life and economy of the island and was much mourned when he died in 1892. His widow, Lucy, together with her assistant Mr Osborne, took charge and managed the Port Ellen distillery until 1906. She was not alone in her role as a female manager for a distillery on Islay or the mainland; there were other contemporaries.

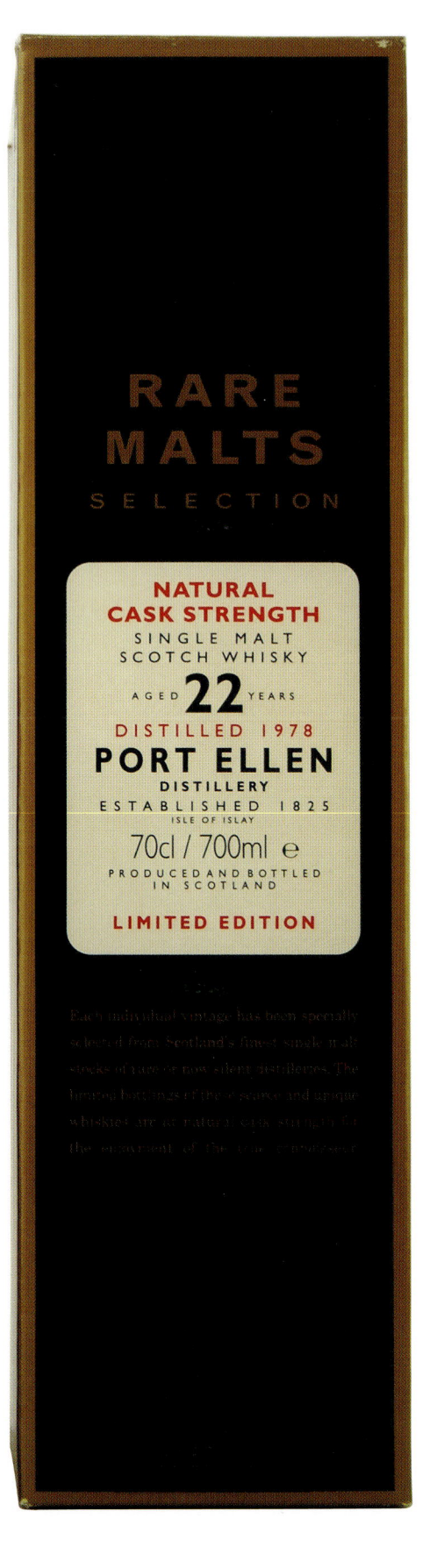

142

Lucy Ramsey died in 1906 and her son, Captain Iain Ramsey of Kildalton, took over responsibilities. The Pattison crash, the World War I years and the general depression led to hardship for Iain Ramsey and he was forced to dispose of his holdings in 1920. A newly formed limited partnership, the Port Ellen Distillery Co. Ltd, jointly owned by James Buchanan Co. and John Dewar & Sons Ltd, bought the assets the same year. In 1925, the partnership merged with the Distillers Company Ltd (DCL). DCL closed the distillery in 1929 and transferred it, in 1930, to their subsidiary the Scottish Malt Distillers Ltd (SMD). SMD used the warehouses and maltings for the following thirty-six years. The distillery operation stayed dormant until 1966, when DCL began reviving Port Ellen by an extensive modernisation programme. Two new stills were installed and Port Ellen resumed production in April 1967. In 1973 new buildings were constructed and a comprehensive 30m high drum malting facility was installed. In May 1983 Port Ellen was finally closed as a distillery and its still house and bonded warehouses were demolished. In 1987 a 'proclamation' was issued and signed by the active distilleries on Islay and Jura to acquire part of the malt needed for their operations from Port Ellen maltings; this was to save job opportunities on the island. The distillery equipment was removed piece by piece during the 1990s, and it is said that the pot stills were shipped to India. The destruction process continues and in 2004 one of the three Doig pagoda-roof kilns was removed. The distilling licence was cancelled in 1992.

The process water was drawn from one of the nearby Leorin Lochs, where the distillery had water rights. The cooling water was also drawn from one of the Leorin Lochs. Port Ellen Distillery used mainly the Golden Promise and Triumph barley varieties at the end of its era. Much of the barley used in the old days was locally cultivated. Since the installation of the drum malting facility the barley has mainly been brought in from the mainland. The seven drums, each with a capacity of 48.5 metric tonnes of germinating barley, may handle up to 400 metric tonnes per week. Germination takes five days and the drying, which is performed in the Doig pagoda kilns, takes thirty to thirty-six hours depending on peating level. The barley arrives in specially designed vehicles, 900 metric tonnes per load. Sucked into silos on the pier, it is transferred by road transport to the silos at the maltings. The barley used by the distillery was, since 1973, malted at the large drum malting facility on site. This is now the common malt source for several local distilleries, not only Diageo group members. Before 1973, on site floor malting was performed. Hence, it may be claimed that Port Ellen for a period was either malting on site, or the Port Ellen Distillery was bringing in malt from central maltsters. The degree of peating was not consistent at the Distillery but varied according to its own and various customers' specification.

Port Ellen water supply

The band of peating level recorded oscillated between forty to sixty ppm (parts per million of phenol) for Port Ellen's own usage. Contrary to common belief the ppm level, referred to for the barley used, is the input value at the distilling process and not a value reflected in the casked version of a whisky sent to maturation. Barley peated from forty to sixty ppm would yield about eight to ten ppm in the cask; the remainder is lost in the distillation process.

The peat used at the floor maltings and later the drum maltings for Port Ellen was cut at the Macrie and the Old Lagavulin moss close to the main Port Ellen to Bowmore Road, but also from Lagan moss near Bowmore. In the mid-eighties Port Ellen Maltings established new peat sources: the Duich peat moss and Castlehill. The malt used at the Port Ellen Distillery was crushed to grist by a Porteus mill. The mash tun was a traditional cast-iron type with a copper top. It had a capacity of about 5 metric tonnes. At full production ten mashes were made per week. Fermentation occurred in eight Oregon pine wash backs. It is believed that the yeast strains used were Distiller's. The distillation was performed by onion-shaped stills converted to indirect heating by oil firing via steam coils in 1970. The capacity of the two wash stills was 28,700 litres each and the two spirit stills 27,500 litres each. The cooling was of the classic type, performed via worms submerged in tubs. Annual maximum production was 2,500,000 litres of alcohol.

Cask management was based on a twelve-year maturation

period, using a mix of new and reused ex-bourbon casks and sherry butts. Maturation occurred on the premises in thirteen dunnage warehouses with a combined capacity of 10,000 casks. During the heydays every cask was tapped on a rotating scheme by a workforce of three to trace spillage and leaks. It is said it took two working days for these three men to check all the 10,000 casks. Surviving Port Ellen casks are held at dunnage warehouses at the premises of the defunct Lochindaal distillery, managed by Caol Ila.

The distillery is closed and demolished but the malting operations are up and running. The malting site is open to visitors, by appointment. Worth visits are all the distilleries when on a whisky pilgrimage to Islay, and the nearby Isle of Jura (ferry from Port Askaig). Other highlights are the ruined remains of Dunyvaig Castle, a fortress of the MacDonald 'Lords of the Isles' before James IV asserted his authority in 1493 and the 'Big Strand', the superb seven mile stretch of beach along west-facing Laggan Bay.

PORT ELLEN

Structural elements and their respective weights

Structure	Observations
Colour	8
Peaty/Phenolic	4
Sherried/Winey	1
Fruity/Estery	1
Floral/Aldehydic	1
Cereal/Malty	1
Feinty	
Medicinal/Maritime	3
Woody	1
Vanilla/Honey	
Nutty/Creamy	2
Spicy	2
Sulphury	

Conclusive organoleptic sensations

	Observations
Colour	Polished copper with a shimmer of old gold.
Nose	Aromas from peat reek and bonfires carried by a salty wind from the sea. Briny as from brackish water. Medicinal in a distinct iodine way. Hints of crustaceans. Gristy as fresh ground barley malt. Acidity from green apple. Whiff of oaky vanilla, leather and linseed oil.
Palate	The clear peat and smoke flavours are perfectly balanced and in total harmony with other aromas spanning from subtle Oloroso sherry to citrus and black peppercorn via fresh grist, heather and vanilla.
Finish	Smoky. Sea salty. Oaky. Peppery. Hint of dark chocolate with a touch of fruity acidity. The sea is present all the time.
Comment	Full bodied, a dram for any occasion and not only for the Islayophiles.

Issued versions

Distilled	Age	% abv	Size	Box	Version
1978	20	60.9	0.7		
1978	22	60.5	0.7		

Rosebank

Pronounced '*rosebank*', it derived its name from the wild rose-clad bank of the River Carron. The distillery was founded on the grounds of Rosebank House, which covered five acres of ground. Three acres were devoted to the distillery and the remainder formed the grounds and gardens of Rosebank House. The Royal Burgh of Falkirk with its sloping land above the River Carron is where the Romans built a great fort during their occupation in the first and second centuries AD. It is believed that the river was navigable as far as Camelon, where the distillery was erected. The area has been of strategic importance since Roman times, when the Antoine Wall was built

Distillery details

REGION Lowlands

OWNER Last distillery owner was United Distillers Ltd, now British Waterways Board

ADDRESS Main Street, Camelon, Falkirk, Stirlingshire, FK1 5BW

ROADS A9 through Falkirk to intersection with A803

TEL (The Beefeater Pub, 01324 611842)

FAX (The Beefeater Pub, 01324 617154)

• RARE MALTS •

between the Firths of Forth and Clyde to form the northern frontier of the Roman Empire. The Rosebank distillery, often called the Queen of the Lowlands, is settled on the banks of the Forth and Clyde canal near Falkirk. It has been mothballed since 1993. A Beefeater pub and restaurant is using the bonded warehouses across the road. In 2002 the premises were sold to the British Waterways Board, a public corporation maintaining the network of canals and navigable rivers in the UK. There are firm plans for converting the distillery premises into seventy-two residential flats and office spaces with bar and restaurant facilities nearby. Permission for demolition has been granted. Work was expected to begin in late 2004–05 and run through to early 2007, however the structures are still standing.

Rosebank was founded in 1840 by James Rankine and situated on the east bank of the Forth and Clyde canal. A James Robertson also held a licence for a distillery named Rosebank. It was active between 1817 and 1819. Robertson's operation was short-lived and had no connection to Rankine's Rosebank. Rosebank proper straddled the canal by using the maltings from the old Camelon Distillery, which was situated opposite on the west side of the canal. Camelon, initially licenced to the two Stark brothers in 1798, had been taken over by Rankine by 1840. Rankine introduced a new business model: prepaid maturing! He launched this idea with some success in 1845; however, some decades later he suffered economic problems and had to close the distillery from 1862 to 1864. His son R.W. Rankine took over in late 1864.

R.W. Rankine's first task was to completely remodel the distillery by bringing all units except the maltings together, improving logistics and making the best use of available space. In 1865 he had all the old Camelon buildings demolished and built a new maltings and a swing bridge to facilitate the transportation of malted barley to the distillery. Literally, he converted a maltings to a distillery and a distillery to a maltings. One of the novelties brought in was the second Morton's refrigerator used by the trade. There is only one of this type left in the trade and it is used by the Edradour Distillery.

Rosebank was reconstructed in 1894 to become a limited partnership the Rosebank Distillery Ltd. On 7 July 1914 Rosebank became one of the five Lowland distilleries that jointly founded the umbrella organisation Scottish Malt Distillers Ltd (SMD) to pull together their common resources. The other four were Clydesdale, Glenkinchie, Grange and St Magdalene, all suffering from the Pattison crash and expecting further hardship from the winds of war. Like so many other distilleries Rosebank had to be closed during World War I due to wartime restrictions but managed to keep the production up during World War II. SMD, in 1925, merged and became the operative and administrative arm of the Distillers Company Ltd (DCL) with responsibility for the daily management of all malt whisky distilleries owned by the group. Rosebank's old malting facilities were demolished and replaced in 1968. No major renovation work seems to have been performed since then. Rosebank was mothballed in June 1993. The distilling licence is now cancelled.

The process water was drawn from a public water supply, the Carron Valley reservoir. The reservoir is constantly filled with water flowing from the Bantaskine tract. The cooling water was drawn from the Clyde canal, beside the distillery. Rosebank Distillery used different barley strains over time, much of it locally cultivated in the old days. Several varieties have been used over the years but Triumph and Chariot seem to have been the predominant ones at the end of the era. The peat used at the floor maltings was cut at a moss about 6km away from the distillery. The malt used was crushed to grist by an old Robert Boby Mill, overhauled in 1983. It was installed in 1932 and had earlier served at the Port Ellen distillery. The mash tun was a traditional cast-iron type with a copper top. It had a capacity of about 8.8 metric tonnes. At full production eight mashes were made per week. Each mashing lasted nine hours. Fermentation occurred in eight wooden wash backs made from Scottish larch, each with a volume of 16,000 litres. It is believed that the yeast used was Distiller's. Regarding operation of the stills, Rosebank was one of the few distilleries that practised the two-and-half distillation regime, also used at Benrinnes, Mortlach and Springbank distilleries. More regarding this practice can be found in the section 'Nomenclature and Definitions'. The distillation was performed by three onion-shaped stills converted to indirect heating by oil firing via steam coils in 1970. The capacity of the wash still was 13,500 litres, the intermediate still's capacity was 6,800 litres and the spirit still was 13,500 litres. The cooling was of the classic type, performed via worms submerged in tubs. The tubs were made from Scottish larch, instead of the usual cast iron, and were situated on a platform outside the still house. Annual maximum production was 1,000,000 litres of alcohol.

Cask management was based earlier on an eight-year and later on a twelve-year maturation period, using a mix of new and reused ex-bourbon casks and sherry butts. Maturation occurred on the premises in warehouses with a combined capacity of 5,000 casks. The production overflow was transported to the group's central warehouses in Menstrie and others. Bottling was performed in Leven and Glasgow. Rosebank contributed to the blends King George IV and Swing.

The distillery is closed and stripped of its equipment but not demolished as of 2005. Worth a visit is the 'Falkirk Wheel' boat lift. It was designed to reconnect the Forth and Clyde and Union Canals and sited in a natural open amphitheatre at Rough Castle near Falkirk. This is the only rotating boat lift in the world. It is an exceptional achievement of modern engineering, which is already being recognised as an inspirational sculpture for the twenty-first century. Another point of interest is the Callendar House, home from the fourteenth to the eighteenth centuries of the Livingston family, who were often centre-stage in Scottish history.

ROSEBANK

Structural elements and their respective weights

Structure	Observations
Colour	2
Peaty/Phenolic	1
Sherried/Winey	1
Fruity/Estery	3
Floral/Aldehydic	3
Cereal/Malty	1
Feinty	
Medicinal/Maritime	
Woody	
Vanilla/Honey	1
Nutty/Creamy	1
Spicy	1
Sulphury	

Conclusive organoleptic sensations

	Observations
Color	Pale straw like a white wine.
Nose	Perfumed and floral, scent of violets. Fruity, preserved pears with custard sauce. Hint of smoke and toasted oatmeal cookies. A veil of cut grass. Aromatic spices. Oak wood.
Palate	Lavender flowery and honey sweet, initially. Pear fruity. Creamy. Chocolate toffee. Citrus sourness balances the sweetness.
Finish	Dry. Slightly tannic and astringent. Walnuts and a hint of fino sherry.
Comment	Medium bodied, a pre-dinner dram.

Issued versions

Distilled	Age	% abv	Size	Box	Version
1979	19	60.2	0.75		
1979	20	60.3	0.7		
1981	20	62.3	0.7		
1981	22	61.1	0.7		

ROYAL BRACKLA

Pronounced '*royal BRACKlach*', 'Brackla' is Gaelic for 'speckled hill slope'. The prefix 'Royal', which the distillery shares with two other distilleries, was given as a Royal Warrant in 1835 by King William IV and renewed by Queen Victoria in November of 1838, one year after William's death. The other two are Royal Lochnagar and Glenury Royal Distilleries, but the honour was first given to Brackla. The distillery is situated in the little village of Cawdor, built around the famous Cawdor Castle – Shakespeare's setting for Macbeth. The village lies just to the west of the castle, across the steep-sided valley of the Allt Dearg as it flows north to join the River Nairn. Cawdor grew largely as an estate village serving the castle, and much of the village is comprised of stone cottages and beautifully tended gardens. The distillery overlooks a large pond, the Old Mill pond, which with the surrounding landscape was transformed to a home for wildlife in 1997 by a grant of £5,000 from the Water of Life fund.

DISTILLERY DETAILS

REGION Highlands (Northern)

OWNER Bacardi (from 1998, former owner UDV/Diageo)

ADDRESS Cawdor, Nairn, Morayshire, IV12 5QY

ROADS Off B9090, between Nairn and Cawdor

TEL 01667 402002

FAX 01667 402004

Royal Brackla was erected on the Cawdor Castle estate on the site of a former brewery which was founded in 1773. The distillery was founded in 1812 by Captain William Fraser and it stayed in the Fraser family until 1898. Captain Fraser's timing and site selection was poor because of the area's abundance of illicit stills. Among the local distillers was the notorious and fabled smuggler Tarrick. The competitors, who used the same water resources, had more or less monopolised the local market. Captain Fraser, with a distilling licence, lamented that he was surrounded by people who drank nothing but whisky but he could not sell a small amount such as a hundred gallons a year on the local market. Hence, he was forced to find other outlets for his legal Highland distillery so he turned to the distant Lowlands. Here, he succeeded at last, perhaps by uprooting competition with the help of the administration. The outcome of this was the Excise Act of 1823, which laid the foundation of the modern whisky industry. In 1844, the Edinburgh whisky merchant Andrew Usher & Co. was appointed sales agent for Royal Brackla and became a partner during the 1860s. Usher & Co. was first to commercially practise the mixing of grain and malt whiskies, and de facto one (William Sanderson was the other) of the inventors of the blend whisky concept. It is said that the first malt whisky used in its concoctions was the Royal Brackla. A blend whisky is sold under the blender's trademark, guaranteeing a normalised and consistent quality (e.g. Usher's Green Stripe). A relative to Captain Fraser, Robert Fraser, took over the helm in 1852 via his Robert Fraser & Co.

The distillery was substantially rebuilt in 1890, and again in 1898 the year Andrew Usher died. The same year a reconstruction occurred and a limited partnership was formed, the Brackla Distillery Co. Ltd. The partnership was later that year sold to two Aberdeen merchants: John Mitchell and James Leict. They continued operations and carried on even during the difficult times stemming from the Pattison crash and World War I. In 1926, Royal Brackla was taken over by the blending firm John Bisset & Co. Ltd., which with its holdings was absorbed by the Distillers Company Ltd (DCL) and transferred to their subsidiary Scottish Malt Distillers Ltd (SMD) in 1943. During World War II the distillery was closed, renamed RAF Brackla and converted into the No. 2 Air Gunnery School. It was also assigned to be a relief landing site for the nearby RAF Dalcross base. At the end of the war the RAF used Brackla as a disposal site for many of the surplus warplanes to be broken up for scrap. Brackla as a distillery was reopened in 1946. SMD doubled the production by rebuilding the distillery in 1965–66. At this time the malt floor was abandoned and two new stills were brought in. Conversion to indirect heating was also applied. Further upgrades were performed in 1970. A dormant period occurred between 1985 and 1991 due to the decreased demand for whisky and other brown alcohols. When the distillery resumed production in 1991 further modernisation took place. In 1997 Royal Brackla became fully automated, at a cost of £2.2 million. The same year the distillery had to be sold. DCL by acquisition and mergers via the United Distillers Ltd (UD), a subsidiary of Guinness, became a part of United Distillers & Vintners Ltd (UDV), a subsidiary of Diageo, in 1997. However, antitrust laws forced it to dispose of some of its holdings. Hence, Bacardi International stepped in and took over control of Royal Brackla.

The process water is drawn over a distance, from the famous Cawdor Burn located near Cawdor Castle. The cooling water comes from a spring near the distillery. This spring water is of great purity but has never been used for production as it is said it may ruin Brackla's character. The peat used when floor malting was performed on site was cut at the nearby Cawdor moss. Several barley strains have been used over time, mostly locally cultivated. Lately it has been Optic, Chariot and Prisma, all peated to the preferred level of about 5ppm. However, Chalice, the latest version brought in, is unpeated. Since the on-site floor malting was abandoned in 1966, malt was brought in from central maltsters in Ord and Burghead but is now from Baird's of Inverness. The malted barley is crushed to grist by a traditional Porteus mill. The mash tun is a modern semi-Lauter tun made of stainless steel and has a capacity of about 12 metric tonnes. Twelve mashes are performed per week. Fermentation occurs in six wooden wash backs, all made from Oregon pine, each with a volume of 36,000 litres. Both short and long fermentation, allowing malolactic conversion, is practised. The yeast used is Distiller's and Brewer's produced by Quest. The distillation is performed by four onion-shaped stills. Two new stills, built by Abercrombie of Alloa, were brought in during the rebuilding in 1965–66. They were built for indirect heating via steam coils by oil firing. They have boiling balls between the body and the neck. The two older stills had been directly fired by coal, first manually and later by an automatic coal stoker. They were converted to indirect heat via steam coils by oil firing during the rebuilding in 1965–66. Gas firing is planned to replace oil firing. The capacity of all four stills is 22,000 litres each. Cooling is of the modern copper condenser type. Annual maximum production is 2,850,000 litres of alcohol.

Cask management is based on a ten-year maturation period, using a mix of new and reused ex-bourbon casks and sherry butts. When Bacardi took over they made a fifteen-year agreement with Diageo to have its production matured at Diageo's central warehouses in Coatbridge and Glasgow and bottled in Leven and Glasgow. The warehouses on site used to have a combined capacity of 47,000 casks and maturation occurred on the premises. Today the total production is sent by road tanker for cask filling, off site. Most of the production goes into Bisset's Finest Old, Dewar's and Johnnie Walker's different blends.

The distillery is open to visitors, by appointment. Worth visits are Brodie Castle and Cawdor Castle. The link between Macbeth, Cawdor and Shakespeare is a 'poetic licence'. The truth is that Cawdor Castle was not built until the late fourteenth century and it is therefore impossible for King Duncan in Shakespeare's play to have lost any blood here or that Lady Macbeth slept in this particular house.

ROYAL BRACKLA

Structural elements and their respective weights

Structure	Observations
Colour	3
Peaty/Phenolic	1
Sherried/Winey	
Fruity/Estery	3
Floral/Aldehydic	2
Cereal/Malty	2
Feinty	
Medicinal/Maritime	
Woody	1
Vanilla/Honey	2
Nutty/Creamy	1
Spicy	2
Sulphury	

Conclusive organoleptic sensations

Observations	
Colour	Pale gold.
Nose	Malty and sweet. Fruity with traces of melon, bananas and ginger. Slightly grassy and a fading hint of smoke.
Palate	Fruity as a mixed fruit cake. Vanilla and ginger peppery. A hint of lemon zest. Creamy.
Finish	Dry and ginger spicy with a hint of red garden berries. Oaky vanilla.
Comment	Medium bodied, a pre-dinner dram.

Issued versions

Distilled	Age	% ABV	Size	Box	Version
1978	20	59.8	0.7		No versions

ROYAL LOCHNAGAR

Pronounced '*royal LOCHnáger*', it got its name from the Lochnagar (1155m), which oddly is the name of a mountain range and not a loch. It is believed that 'Lochnagar' stands for 'loch of the laughter' or 'little noisy loch', derived from Gaelic 'loch' meaning 'lake' and the corrupt version of 'gaire' meaning 'laughter' or 'noise', a name initially given to a mountain lake in the area. The prefix 'Royal' was awarded as a Royal Warrant following a visit by Queen Victoria and Prince Albert in 1848. Royal Lochnagar Distillery is located at Easter Balmoral, to the south of Crathie, and set in the natural outstanding beauty of Royal Deeside. The Balmoral Estate is owned personally by the Queen. The distillery has a visitors' centre where a special exhibition of Queen Victoria's visit is on display (also how an illicit still could be hidden away in a cave). To commemorate the Queen's visit a special bottling is issued on 12 September each year. It is said Queen Victoria preferred to dilute Lochnagar with claret (red Bordeaux). Royal Lochnagar is the smallest malt whisky distillery within Diageo.

The first Lochnagar distillery was founded in 1825 in Glen Feardon, located on the north side of the banks of River Dee, by a reformed smuggler, James Robertson of Crathie. That operation was burned down in 1827 by fellow 'colleagues' upset that one of their number had decided to go legal. The distillery was rebuilt, but on 12 May 1841 it was again engulfed in flames. A new licence holder, Alexander Farquharson & Reid, rebuilt the distillery but it closed for good in 1860. John Begg and his partnership Begg & Buyers Co. built a second distillery in the area in 1845. It was called New Lochnagar and was erected on the south side of the River Dee,

DISTILLERY DETAILS

REGION Highlands (Eastern)

OWNER Diageo

ADDRESS Crathie, Ballater, Deeside, Aberdeenshire, AB3 5TB

ROADS A93 Deeside road, take the B976 for Balmoral

TEL 01339 742700

FAX 01339 742702

Press report of Queen Victoria's visit to Lochnagar in 1842

Royal Lochnagar and the Lochnagar hills

on grounds rented from the Abergeldie Estate. The Estate owners consistently refused to sell the distillery the grounds it occupied, preferring to see value being added to their land through the extensions and erection of new buildings necessary for the development of the new Lochnagar. Three years later, in 1848, the Royal family acquired Balmoral. John Begg recorded in journals of the distillery that he wrote a note inviting Prince Albert and was rewarded with a visit the very next day by Queen Victoria, Prince Albert and their two sons. Prince Albert tasted the malt whisky, which found a very royal approval. Begg also wrote 'I asked whether he would like to taste the spirit in its matured state as we had cleared some that day from bond, which I thought was very fine.' The Prince swallowed the cask-strength whisky in a single gulp and found it to be excellent. Soon afterwards the distillery was awarded a Royal Warrant of Appointment as a supplier to the Queen's household and became known as 'Royal Lochnagar'.

Another royal visit occurred on 15 September 1863 when the Prince and Princess of Wales paid a visit. The Begg & Buyers Co. partnership was dissolved in 1851 and John Begg became the sole owner. When he died in 1880 his only son Henry Farquharson Begg succeeded him. Henry died in 1896 and the Begg property, including the distillery, was put in trust for Henry's children. The trust was converted to a limited partnership, John Begg Ltd in 1902. When Henry's son Albert died in World War I in 1916 the distillery was put up for sale. John Dewar & Sons Ltd acquired all shares of John Begg Ltd the same year and became the owner of Royal Lochnagar. Dewar's merged with the Distillers Company Ltd (DCL) in 1925. DCL transferred the distillery to its operating subsidiary the Scottish Malt Distillers Ltd (SMD) in 1930. When Dewar's took over in 1916 they dropped the prefix 'Royal' but it was reinstated by United Distilleries Ltd (UD).

In 1906 a refurbishing of the distillery occurred and it stayed in that shape until other comprehensive modernisations occurred in 1963 and in 1967. At the 1963 rebuilding most of the old structures were demolished but the tun room was enlarged and the roof of the still house raised. Further, the two hand-stoked stills were updated with mechanical stokers. Only the malt barn and the kiln survived but they have not been in use since 1966. In 1967 the mash house was rebuilt and in 1969 the stills were converted to internal heating. As late as 1949 the distillery was lit by paraffin lamps and not electricity. Power for operation was generated by a water wheel into the early 1960s.

There are two dams on the premises. Both are filled with rain and melted snow from burns on the foothills of Lochnagar hills, and filtered through a peat base. Water from the top dam is used for the processes and water from the bottom dam, alongside the distillery, is used for cooling. Several barley strains, often locally grown, have been used over time. Lately, Decanter has been the preferred variety. Since on-site floor malting was abandoned in 1966 malt has been brought in from the central maltsters Roseisle in Roseisle near Elgin. It is specified to be lightly peated. The malt is crushed to grist by a Boby two-roller mill installed in 1919. The top-less mash tun, manufactured by Abercrombie of Alloa, is cast iron with a stainless steel bottom equipped with an old-fashioned agitator. Its capacity is about 5.2 metric tonnes and seven mashes per week are possible. Fermentation occurs in three wooden wash backs, made from Scottish larch. Two hold 28,000 litres each and one odd-shaped one holds 14,000 litres. The yeast strain used is Distiller's. A short fermentation cycle, seventy hours, is practised. The distillation is performed by two stubby onion-shaped stills, both with broad, straight necks and manufactured by Abercrombie of Alloa. Their lyne-arms (the tapering conical top sections) are unusual as they dip downwards with a steep angle. The stills are indirectly heated and were converted to oil firing in 1969. The wash still, which holds 7,410 litres, is heated by steam pan. The spirit still, which holds 5,450 litres, is heated by steam coils. The cooling is the traditional method, with each worm submerged in a rectangular tub made of cast iron. This equipment is also manufactured by Abercrombie of Alloa. Annual maximum production is 425,000 litres of alcohol.

Cask management is based on a twelve-year maturation period, using a mix of hogshead, ex-sherry butts and puncheons. Ex-bourbon casks are scarcely used. Maturation occurs partly on the premises. The three-storey warehouse, on site, is rather small as it accommodates only 2,000 casks. The production overflow is matured at the group's central warehouses in Alloa. Bottling is performed in Leven, Fife. A large portion of the production is sold as single malt whisky but some goes into the blended whisky Vat 69 and Johnnie Walker's various blends.

The distillery has a visitors' centre and shop. Worth a visit is Balmoral Castle, a working estate that provides for and is closely integrated with the local community. Its management objectives include providing employment, housing, and generating economic activity in the local area, as well as the conservation and regeneration of the natural environment. Nearby Braemar and its annual Highland Games is a must, too.

ROYAL LOCHNAGAR

Structural elements and their respective weights

STRUCTURE	OBSERVATIONS
Colour	5
Peaty/Phenolic	2
Sherried/Winey	2
Fruity/Estery	3
Floral/Aldehydic	
Cereal/Malty	2
Feinty	
Medicinal/Maritime	
Woody	
Vanilla/Honey	2
Nutty/Creamy	2
Spicy	2
Sulphury	

Conclusive organoleptic sensations

	OBSERVATIONS
Colour	Golden.
Nose	Aromatic nose with a fabric of hazelnut, honey, fudge and tropical fruits but also malted barley and yeasts. Slight smoky. Oloroso sherry.
Palate	Cane sugar and malt sweetness. Ginger spicy with a hint of liquorice. Oloroso sherry nuttiness.
Finish	A clean and dry finish with some bitterness as from Old English marmalade.
Comment	Full bodied, an after-dinner dram.

Issued versions

DISTILLED	AGE	% ABV	SIZE	BOX	VERSION
1972/1974	24	55.7	0.75	Box	Misprint
1973	23	59.7	0.7		
1974	30	56.2	0.7		

ST. MAGDALENE

Pronounced '*saint MÁGdelain*', St. Magdalene is also known as Linlithgow Distillery. The distillery got its name from a site set aside for a leper colony, going back to the twelfth century. The colony later became a convent and a hospital called St. Magdalene's Cross. The site for the hospital and later the distillery was once owned by the Knights Templar of Saint John of Torpichen. St. Magdalene Distillery is now closed, with parts of the site converted to luxury flats. The last conversion occurred in 2002, when thirty flats were added at a cost of £3,000,000. The distillery's external character has been preserved as the structures are registered as historic buildings. The two Charles Doig pagoda roofs, for instance, are still present. The distillery was situated in the royal burgh of Linlithgow, the county town of West Lothian and the birthplace of Mary Queen of Scots. The south shore of Linlithgow Loch enhances this, one of Scotland's most historic towns.

Linlithgow township has a long, meandering history of illicit and legal distilleries. At one time there were five operating in parallel. The first licenced, legal distillery in the Royal Burg of Linlithgow was Bulzion Distillery, which was granted a licence in the early 1750s. It was followed in the early 1790s by Bonnytoun Distillery, founded by Adam Dawson, owner of a distillery in the Carse near Falkirk. Bonnytoun was situated 2km away from the site of the present St. Magdalene Distillery. A few years later, after Bonnytoun opened, Sebastian Henderson leased some land from the Countess of Dalhousie at St. Magdalene adjacent to Bonnytoun Distillery. The distillery he founded on this site was called St. Magdalene as well as Linlithgow Distillery. As the distillery was situated along the Union Canal, fronting 200m towards the main road, and was later equipped with its own railroad siding, transport logistics were excellent. Dawson wanted to get rid of

DISTILLERY DETAILS

REGION Lowlands

OWNER Last distillery owner was United Distillers Ltd (UD). UD sold it for residential developments

ADDRESS Edinburgh Road, Linlithgow, West Lothian, EH49 6AQ

ROADS M9 the A803 to Linlithgow, follow B9080 for 2km

• RARE MALTS •

competition so he bought St. Magdalene in 1800, merged it with his two other distilleries, and formed one giant distillery by moving all operations to the St. Magdalene site. The Dawson family ran the distillery for more than one hundred years. When the family head Colonel Ramage Dawson died in 1892 the business was reorganised as a limited partnership, A. & J. Dawson Ltd, and was registered on 6 November 1894. A. & J. Dawson Ltd, like many other distillery companies, did not survive the Pattison crash and the following depression. Insolvent and liquidated in 1912, A. & J. Dawson Ltd was purchased by the Distillers Company Ltd (DCL) the same year. DCL decided to perform a comprehensive restructuring of the malt whisky distilling industry by placing malt distilleries under one common umbrella. With St. Magdalene at hand they quickly acquired four other Lowland distilleries in 1914 and laid the foundation for its successful subsidiary, Scottish Malt Distillers Ltd (SMD). The other four were Clydesdale, Glenkinchie, Grange and Rosebank. SMD became DCL's administrative and operating arm for its malt whisky distilleries. SMD closed St. Magdalene from 1920 until the end of World War II, but the two malting operations on site – one floor and one drum – were kept in operation during this period. Some renovation works were performed during this semi-silent period. Electrical power was installed in 1927, replacing the steam engine, a 20hp beam engine, and a water wheel that had delivered power for the operations since 1824. In 1945 St. Magdalene was on stream again and ran uninterrupted until its final closing in 1983. Updating and maintenance work was performed on several occasions. In 1961 the coal stoking was mechanised, in 1968 on-site maltings were abandoned and in 1971 the stills were converted to indirect heating.

Water for the process used to be drawn first from a spring on a nearby hilltop and from a 100m deep artesian well, but was later drawn from the city mains, which were fed with water from Loch Lomond. In the early 1970s there was a switch from this source to the distillery's own reservoir on the other side of the canal. It is said that this switch drastically improved the quality of the whisky. Water for cooling purposes was drawn directly from the Union Canal, alongside the distillery. The Canal was also driving the distillery's power source, its water wheel. Since the floor malting was abandoned in 1968 malt was brought in from the central maltster Glen Esk in Montrose. Several barley strains, often locally grown, were used over time. The last varieties to be used are believed to have been Golden Promise and

158

Triumph. When floor malting occurred on site the peat used was cut from moors near Falkirk and Slamannan. The malt brought in was specified to be lightly peated according to the distillery's preferred peat profile and is believed to have been crushed to grist by a traditional Porteus mill. The mash tun was made of cast iron, and its capacity was 7.75 metric tonnes. Fourteen washes per week were possible. Fermentation occurred in six wooden wash backs. They held 29,000 litres each. The yeast strain is believed to have been Distiller's. The distillation was performed by two wash and two spirit stills, all onion shaped. They had been converted from manual coal stoking to mechanical in 1961, and to indirect heating by oil firing, by the means of steam coils, in 1971. The wash and the spirit stills' volumes are not known to the author. The distillation process deviated from the Lowlands standard as not being triple distilled. Instead the Highland double distilling protocol was followed. The cooling was by copper condensers, which had replaced the traditional method of each worm submerged in tubs made by cast iron or wood. Annual maximum output was 1,300,000 litres of alcohol.

Cask management was based on a ten-year maturation period, using a mix of new and reused ex-bourbon casks and sherry butts. Maturation occurred on the premises. The warehouses on site, all of traditional type, accommodated 40,000 casks. Most of the production went into the blended whiskies.

The distillery has been closed since 1983 and has been converted to luxury flats. Worth a visit is Linlithgow Palace, an important royal residence. It is now in ruins, but enough of it still stands.

ST. MAGDALENE

Structural elements and their respective weights

STRUCTURE	OBSERVATIONS
Colour	7
Peaty/Phenolic	1
Sherried/Winey	
Fruity/Estery	3
Floral/Aldehydic	3
Cereal/Malty	1
Feinty	1
Medicinal/Maritime	
Woody	1
Vanilla/Honey	2
Nutty/Creamy	
Spicy	1
Sulphury	

Conclusive organoleptic sensations

	OBSERVATIONS
Colour	Baltic amber.
Nose	Pronounced floral with a flow of fresh-cut grass and meadow flowers, especially violets. Liquorice and Hessian cloth. Smokiness as from burnt hay. A whiff of bourbon.
Palate	Refreshing lemony-orangey citrus. But also some tannic bitterness. Dusty maltiness. Linseed oil.
Finish	Dry. Bourbon, vanilla and the grassy notes lingers.
Comment	Medium bodied, a pre-dinner dram.

Issued versions

DISTILLED	AGE	% ABV	SIZE	BOX	VERSION
1970	23	58.1	0.7	None	
1970	23	58.43	0.7		
1971	23	59	0.7		
1979	19	63.8	0.7		

TEANINICH

Pronounced *'tee-an-inich'*, it means 'the house on the moor' from Gaelic 'taigh' or 'house' and 'aonaich' or 'moor land'. Alness, a thirty-minute drive from Inverness, is where Teaninich Distillery is situated, almost hidden on the edge of the town. The little town of Alness is located on the Cromarty Firth with the River Averon dividing it in two parts. The town has won acclaim with its Scotland In Bloom Awards and is known for its summer floral displays, which are well worth viewing. Behind the distillery a glimpse may be caught of the summit of the towering Ben Wyvis. Other distilleries in the neighbourhood are Dalmore and Glenmorangie. Teaninich, like a few other distilleries in the Diageo group, has operated or is operating with two

DISTILLERY DETAILS

REGION Highlands (Northern)

OWNER Diageo

ADDRESS Alness, Ross-shire, IV17 0XB

ROADS A9 north of Inverness, at Dalmore turn of on B817 towards Alness

TEL 01349 885001

FAX 01349 883864

TEANINICH

sides, an A and B side, or a copy of the main distillery within or beside an existing distillery. The other ones fitting this format are Linkwood/Glendullan, Brora/Clynelish, Dufftown/Pityvaich and Mannochmore/Glenlossie.

The Teaninich distillery was founded in 1817 by Captain Hugh Munro, owner of the Teaninich Estate. The location of choice for his project was Alness and the left bank of the river that divides the village. Here, a blooming cottage industry had been at work for decades: homemade whisky. The production of 'illegal' whisky had propagated a skilful, artisan, workforce. But also, due to its product quality and success, absorbed most of the barley grown for bread production in the area. A famine was near, and an upheaval as well. To ease the pressure the administrators convinced the landowners to control the trade by establishing legal distilleries and by doing that, control the access of fermentable cereals. The scheme turned out to be successful; most of the illegal operators were forced out of business. An explanation for the positive outcome was probably the tax relief granted for distillery licence takers. Teaninich became an instant success; within fifteen years its production multiplied. In 1837 when Hugh Munro died, his son Lt. General John Munro took the helm. Later, John was posted for service in India for several years. Hence, he had to find someone who could carry out the responsibilities. John was duped into leasing the distillery to the (later) infamous con artist Robert Pattison, the root of the industry collapse that occurred at the turn of the century. The lease lasted from 1852 until 1867.

The next lessee, from 1867 to 1895, was John McGilchrist, who pioneered electric power, electric light and the telephone system. Teaninich became one of the first distilleries with these technologies installed and working. In 1895 the Munro & Cameron Co. of Elgin obtained the lease and in 1898 purchased the assets. One of Munro & Cameron's shareholders, Robert Ian Cameron, a whisky broker with interests in Benrinnes, Linkwood and Tamdhu, became the company's sole proprietor in 1904. During his career he also did a sojourn as a board member at the Scottish Malt Distillers Ltd (SMD). Cameron died at the age of 72 in 1932 and a year later his trustees disposed of the distillery to the Distiller Company Ltd (DCL). As a result of wartime restrictions the distillery was closed from 1939 until 1946. When Teaninich resumed production in 1946, only two of its four pot stills were revived for production, the others, the smaller paired set, were removed, and the operation churned on with no other changes. The two water wheels and the steam engine continued to deliver power until the next modernisation. In 1962 the still-house was refitted and the number of stills was brought back to four. The coal firing was removed and the stills were all converted to indirect heating. The old power systems were replaced with electric motors. The old milling, mashing and fermentation facilities were rebuilt in 1973–74 and integrated with the old facility as 'a distillery within a distillery', a feature that became known as 'Teaninich Side B'. At this time the architectural link to the past was lost. A new complex had been added 1969, the 'Teaninich Side A'. This complex contains six paired and indirectly heated pot stills. The on-site floor malting was abandoned in 1973. A dark grains plant was added in 1975. Teaninich Side B became dormant at the end of June 1984, closing officially on 1 October the same year, whilst Teaninich Side A continued until 31 March 1985, when it too officially closed. Teaninich Side A was revived in 1991 and the original Side B buildings were demolished in 1999.

Teaninich has water rights to the Dairywell Spring, on the nearby Novar Estate, where it draws its water for the process as well as for cooling purposes. The old floor malting was made on a clay floor and not on a traditional concrete floor. Since the floor malting was abandoned in 1973 malt has been brought in from the central maltster, Glen Ord. Several barley strains, often locally grown, have been used over time. At the time of writing the one being used was Optic. When floor malting occurred on site the peat used was cut from nearby moors. The malt brought in today is specified to be unpeated. The malt is crushed to grist by an Asnong Hammer mill. It is a type of mill that creates more powdery grist than the traditional Porteus and Boby mills, which Teaninich used before. This type of mill is unique for the trade.

Another oddity is the Teaninich mashing process, which was introduced in 2000 and is unique for the whisky distillery trade but common in the brewing industry. No traditional mash tun is used, instead the grist is mixed with the first water in the 'Mash Conversion Vessel', then a vortex stirs the mash to the consistency of a watery porridge. The 'porridge' is then transferred to a Meura filter press where the mash is squeezed between twenty-four cloth plates and the wort is collected. A second water is then added through the filter. The remaining liquid in the press is known as 'weak worts' and is returned as 'water' for the next mash. The filter plates are then separated to allow the draff to be collected. This process takes place three times to fill one wash back, with each 'pressing' taking two hours to complete. The 'Mash Conversion Vessel' is made of cast iron and has a capacity of 12 metric tonnes but is only utilised to a third, which is equal to 20,000 litres. Twenty-four mashes per week are possible.

Fermentation occurs in eight wooden wash backs, made from Scottish larch. They hold 60,000 litres each. The yeast strain used is Distiller's. A short fermentation cycle, sixty hours, is practised. The distillation is performed by three wash and three spirit stills, all onion shaped, equipped with a boiling ball and short, broad necks. The six new stills were bought in 1969–70, with heating by oil firing with steam pans in the wash and steam coils in the spirit stills installed from the beginning. The wash stills' volumes are 17,500 litres each and the spirit stills' volumes are 15,600 each. Cooling is performed by shell and tube condensers. Teaninich B had a primary set of two stills of the same type and size as Teaninich A, but also a secondary pair. This pair was drum shaped, with straight sides, and had volumes a bit larger than the primary pair. They were converted from manual coal stoking to mechanical and in 1962 to indirect heating by oil firing. Annual maximum production is 3,000,000 litres of alcohol, but was

Highland scenery – water supply at Teaninich

6,000,000 at the time when sides A and B were in full swing. At this time Teaninich was one of the largest Scottish malt whisky distilleries ever.

Cask management was based on a ten-year maturation period, using a mix of new and reused ex-bourbon casks and sherry butts. Maturation occurred partly on the premises. The warehouses, on site, accommodated 7,000 casks. Today all of the new make spirit is sent away for maturation at warehouses in Menstrie. Bottling is performed in Leven, Fife and Glasgow. Most of the production goes into blended whiskies such as Johnnie Walker, Haig, Vat 69 and Robert Burns and also into the famous whisky liqueur Drambuie.

The distillery is open to visitors, by appointment. Worth a visit is Culloden Moor, located 8km east of Inverness off the A9 Inverness to Perth Road. Here, on 16 April 1746, the last battle to be fought on British soil took place.

TEANINICH

Structural elements and their respective weights

Structure	Observations
Colour	5
Peaty/Phenolic	1
Sherried/Winey	
Fruity/Estery	3
Floral/Aldehydic	3
Cereal/Malty	2
Feinty	1
Medicinal/Maritime	1
Woody	2
Vanilla/Honey	2
Nutty/Creamy	
Spicy	3
Sulphury	

Conclusive organoleptic sensations

	Observations
Colour	Bright, polished gold.
Nose	Enduring estery fragrance dominated by citrus and ripe autumn apples. A faint, leathery note.
Palate	Malty. Rich, oak woody vanilla. Brown sugar and a tang of briny saltiness. Lemongrass. Bergamot, like Earl Grey tea.
Finish	Dry and clean. Spicy as pepper vodka. A whiff of peat reek and a lingering streak of vanilla.
Comment	Medium bodied, an after-dinner dram.

Issued versions

Distilled	Age	% ABV	Size	Box	Version
1972	23	64.8	0.2	Box 2	
1972	23	64.95	0.75	None	USA
1972	23	64.95	0.75		
1972	27	64.2	0.7		
1973	23	57.1	0.7		

Special Items and Releases

Ten of the Rare Malts Selection series have been bottled as 200ml bottles. Seven of these are identical with the reciprocal 750ml versions bottled at the same time. They were packaged five by five in handy collection boxes and released on two occasions, 1995 and 1996. These ten versions, illustrated below, are all listed in the related version tables.

To assist learning about the tastes, culture and history of the whiskies in the RMS series, the Collection boxes may offer a heady and educational journey through Scotland's whisky producing regions, to be taken at your own pace.

Box 1

Distilled	Age	% ABV	Size	Version
1972	22	58.95	0.2	Clynelish
1969	25	61.9	0.2	Glen Esk (former Hillside)
1969	25	62.2	0.2	Glenlochy
1972	22	65.3	0.2	Mortlach
1971	23	54.7	0.2	North Port

All exist in larger bottles (0.75).

• SPECIAL ITEMS AND RELEASES •

Box 2

Distilled	Age	% ABV	Size	Version
1975	20	60.75	0.2	Brora
1975	20	61.12	0.2	Caol Ila
1973	22	61.8	0.2	Dailuaine
1972	23	62.43	0.2	Glendullan
1972	23	64.8	0.2	Teaninich

Only Caol Ila and Glendullan exists in larger bottles (0.75). The other three have a unique % ABV.

Plinth

A handy wood plinth for displaying four 700ml versions of the RMS series was manufactured, sadly, in a very limited amount and distributed mainly in the UK and France.

165

BIBLIOGRAPHY

Arthur, Helen, *Whisky – The Water of Life*, London, Firefly Books, 2000

Barnard, Alfred, *The Whisky Distilleries of UK*, Edinburgh, Lochar Publishing, 1987

Broom, Dave, *Whisky, a Connoisseur's Guide*, London, Carlton Books, 1998

Broom, Dave, *Handbook of Whisky*, London, Hamlyn Publishing, 2000

Brown, Gordon, *The Whisky Trails*, London, Multimedia Books, 1993

Cooper, Derek (F. Godwin co-author), *The Whisky Roads of Scotland*, London, Jill Norman Publishing, 1982

Craig, C, *The Scotch Whisky Industry Record*, Dumbarton, Index Publishing, 1994

Cribb Stephen & Julie, *Whisky on the Rocks*, Nottingham, British Geological Survey, 1998

Daiches, David, *Scotch Whisky its Past and Present*, London, André Deutsch, 1969

Darwen, J., *The Illustrated History of Whisky*, London, Harold Starke Publishing, 1993

Goldammer, Ted, *The Brewer's Handbook,* Essex, Apex Publisher, 2000

Graham, Duncan & Wendy, *Visiting Distilleries*, Glasgow, Neil Wilson Publishing, 2003

Hills, Philip, *Appreciating Whisky*, Glasgow, Harper Collins, 2000

Hughes, John. Scotland's *Malt Whiskey Distilleries*, survival of the fittest, Gloucestershire, Tempus, 2002

Greenwood, Malcolm & Green, Martin, *Collecting Malt Whisky*, Elgin, Greenwood Publishing, 2002

Jackson, Michael, *Malt Whisky Companion*, London, Dorling Kindersley Books, 1986

Jackson, Michael, *Scotland and its Whiskies*, London, Duncan Baird, 2001

Lamond, John (R. Tucec co-author), *The Malt File*, Edinburgh, Canongate, 1996

MacLean, Charles, *Scotch Whisky*, London, Mitchel Beazley, 1997

MacLean, Charles, *Whisky – A Liquid History*, London, Octopus Publishing, 2003

McIvor, Dough, *Scotch Whisky Top Single Malts*, London, PRC Publishing, 1998

Moore, Graham, *Malt Whisky: A Contemporary Guide*, Shrewsbury, Swan Hill Press, 1998

Morrice, Philip, *The Whisky Distilleries of Scotland, In Alfred Barnard's Footsteps 100 Years Later*, London, Harper Publishing, 1987

Moss, Michael, (J. Hume co-author), *The Making of Scotch Whisky*, Edinburgh, James & James, 1981

Murray, Jim, *The Complete Guide to Whisky*, London, Carlton Books, 1997

Nown, Graham, *Malt Whisky*, London, Salamander Books, 1997

Piggot, J.R. et al., *The Science and Technology of Whisky*, Harlow, Longman Scientific & Technical Publishing, 1989

Russel, Inge, *Whisky – Technology, Production and Marketing*, London, Academic Press, 2003

Saintsbury, George, *Notes on a Cellarbook*, London, Macmillan, 1920

Skipworth, Mark, *The Scotch Whisky Book*, Twickenham, Hamlyn Publishing, 1987

Stirk, David, *The Malt Whisky Guide*, Hants, GW Publishing, 2003

Townsend, B., *Scotch Missed*, Glasgow, Neil Wilson Publisher, 1993

Weir, R., *The History of the Distillers Company (DCL) 1877–1939*, Oxford, Clarendon Press, 1995

Wilson, R., *Scotch, the Formative Years*, London, Constable, 1970

Wishart, David, *Whisky Classified*, London, Pavillion, 2002

Wisniewski, Ian, *Classic Malt Whisky*, London, Prion Books, 2001

The Whisky Magazine/UK

Malt Advocate Magazine/USA

The Archives of Diageo

The Archives of Scotch Whisky Association

Index

Abercrombie of Alloa, 44, 105
Age, 7
Ainslie & Co, 55
Alcohol By Volume, 2, 7
Alexander Wilson Co, 118
Armstrong, Raymond, 48
Arthur Bell & Sons, 26, 47, 51, 89, 119, 120
Associated Scottish Distillers Ltd, 43, 96, 112, 116
Athol Highlanders, 51
Awards, 8

Bacardi-Martini group, 33
Balmoral estate, 153
Barclay family, 114–116
Barley, 17
Barrels, 22–23
Begg, John, 153–154
Benmore Distillers Ltd, 85
Ben Nevis distillery, 110
Bioped Modular Plant technology, 104
Blair Castle, 50
Bonnytoun distillery, 157
Booth distillery Ltd, 130–131
Bottle sizes, 7
Bottling, 3, 93
Brechin distillery, 138
Brickhmann, F.W., 43
Brown family, 122, 123
Buchanan, James, 26, 74
Bulloch, Lade & Co., 59
Burghead Maltings, 30, 40, 82, 119, 124
Buxrud, Ulf, viii

Caille Heddle, John F., 96
Calder, R.J., 43, 107
Cameron, Robert Ian, 161
Casks, 22–24
Cawdor Castle, 149, 151
Clynelish distillery (old), 54–56
Connachar family, 51
Copper, 21
Condensers, 20
Colour bar, 12

Cowie family, 88, 134, 135
Cumming family, 63

Dawson family, 158
David Robertson spider web diagram, 14
De Ripley, William, 84-85
Dewar, John, 26, 34
Diageo,
    Contact information, 18
    The rise of, 15
    Global duty free, 2
Distillation, 20
Distiller's Co. Ltd, 25–26
Doig, Charles, 24, 71, 77, 88, 99, 110, 131, 157
Driver, Jonathan,
Drum Malting, 18
Duff, James, 88
Dufftown, 73, 106
Dukes of Atholl, 50

Edward, Alexander, 33, 39, 43, 77, 85
Excise Act, 24–25, 150

Fermentation, 18–19
Fires, 36, 37, 39, 74, 81, 85, 115, 131
Flavours, 14–16
Flavour Wheel, 13
Flemming, Bennet & MacLaren, 93, 101
Flemming, James, 81
Forres, 43
Forsyths, 44
Fraser family, 150

George Lawson & Sons Co., 55
Glenlivet, 88
Glenlossie distillery, 127, 128
Glen Mhor distillery, 92
Glen Ord, 112, 162
Glen Spey distillery, 30
Gordon & McPhail, 42, 44
Gregory & Co., 92
Grand Metropolitan Ltd, 26, 29, 51
Grant brothers, 134

Grant, William, 134
Greenlees brothers, 107
Guinness, 26
Guthrie family, 137–138
Gunn, Neil, 100

Haig brothers, 130
Henderson, Hector, 59
Highland Clearances, 54–55
Hillside distillery, 97
Hobbs, Joseph, 43, 96, 112

International Distillers and Vintners Ltd, 26, 28, 29, 30
International Wine and Spirit Competition Awards, 8–9

James Buchanan & Co., 81, 143
James Watson Co. Ltd, 103-104
J&G Stewart Ltd, 71
John Gordon & Co., 134
John Dewar & Sons, 33, 39, 59, 81, 104, 143, 154
Johnnie Walker, 34, 64, 120
Johnstone, Robert, 103
John Walker & Sons Ltd, 55, 71, 81, 93, 100, 135
J.P. O'Brien, 85
Justerini & Brooks, 28, 30

Keepers of the Quaich, 50

Labels, 7–8
    Misprints and inconsistencies, 10
Licence laws, 24–25
Lochabar maltings, 111
Louis Vuitton Moet Hennessy, 26
Lyne of Ruthrie distillery, 39

MacCallum, Duncan, 43
MacDonald, Greenlees & Williams, 43, 107
Mackenzie, Alexander, 103
Mackenzie & Co. Ltd, 89
Mackenzie family, 80–81
Mackenzie, Peter, 39, 88, 89

Mackenzie, Roderick, 124
Mackie, Peter, 77
Mackinlay & Birnie Ltd, 92, 93, 99, 100
MacLellan family, 103
McAndie, David, 111
McDonald family, 111
McLean, Charles, viii, 12
McLelland family, 47
Mash tuns: Lauter and traditional, 19–20
Maturation, 22
Medals, 8–9
Mike Collings, 2
Mile End Distillery Co., 36
Montrose Distillery, 96
Morgan, Dr. Nicholas, 2
Munro family, 161

National Distillers of America, 43, 112, 116
Nevis Distillery, 111
Nickerson, 17
North Esk Distillery, 96
Numbering systems, 7

Oak, 23
Ord Distillery Co., 102

Packaging, 3, 7
Pagoda-roofed kilns, 24
Patisson's Ltd, 25, 33, 59, 96, 111
Paul's Maltings, 97
Pentland wheel, 11–12
Philip Hill's bar chart, 14
Pittyvaich, 89, 106
P. Mackenzie & Co., 51

Ramsey, John, 141
Rankine family, 146
Rare Malts Selection series, 2, 164
Release policy and listings, 3–6
Risk, James, 55
Risk, John, 71
Ritchie family, 116
Robertson, John, 51
Robinson, Maureen, viii, 2
Rose, David, 130
Roseisle Maltings, 40, 82
Ross & Coulter, 47

Saladin box malting, 17–18
Scotch Distiller's Association, 25
Scotch Whisky Association, 67, 106
Scotch Whisky Research Institute, 11, 12
Scottish Malt Distilleries Ltd, 26
Septimus, Parsonage & Co. Ltd, 96
Simpson family, 36–37
'Skeppet' blend, 47
Spirit caramel, 127
Stills, 21
Sutherland, James, 92
Symon, John, 88, 89

Tasting,
    Methods, 11–12
    Conditions, 12–13
    Terms and explanations, 14–16
Taylor, Walker & Co. Ltd, 36
Thomas Bernard & Co., 96
Tochineal Distillery, 118, 119
Train & McIntyre Ltd, 111, 112
Two-and-a-half distillation, 20

United Distillers Ltd, 33, 48, 51, 60, 75, 78, 84, 116, 151
United Distillers & Vintners Ltd, 1, 2, 55, 151
Usher, Andrew, 73–74
Usher & Co., 150

Versions, 3

Walker, John, 26
Wash Act of 1784, 24
White Horse blend, 77, 78, 120
White Label blend, 34, 78
William Dunville & Co. Ltd, 47
William Grant & Sons, 63–64, 73, 75
William Smith & Co., 39
William Williams and Sons, 107
Winchester brothers, 71
Wishart Profile Table, 11
W.P. Lowrie & Co., 73–74
Wright & Grey Co., 85

Yeast, 18–19

Distilleries

Distillery map, 27
Auchroisk, 28
Aultmore, 32
Banff, 35
Benrinnes, 39
Benromach, 42
Bladnoch, 46
Blair Athol, 50
Brora, 54
Caol Ila, 58
Cardow (formerly Cardhu), 62
Clynelish, 66
Coleburn, 70
Convelmore, 73
Craigellachie, 76
Dailuaine, 80
Dallas Dhu, 84
Dufftown-Glenlivet, 88
Glen Albyn, 91
Glen Esk (formerly Hillside), 95
Glen Mhor, 99
Glen Ord, 102
Glendullan, 106
Glenlochy, 110
Glenury Royal, 114
Inchgower, 118
Linkwood, 122
Mannochmore, 126
Millburn, 129
Mortlach, 133
North Port, 137
Port Ellen, 141
Rosebank, 145
Royal Brackla, 149
Royal Lochnager, 153
St. Magdalene, 157
Teaninich, 160